ELSEVIER'S
BANKING
DICTIONARY

ELSEVIER'S BANKING DICTIONARY

IN SIX LANGUAGES
ENGLISH/AMERICAN - FRENCH - ITALIAN - SPANISH
DUTCH AND GERMAN

COMPILED AND ARRANGED ON
AN ENGLISH ALPHABETICAL BASE BY

JULIO RICCI
Montevideo (Uruguay)

Second, completely revised edition

ELSEVIER SCIENTIFIC PUBLISHING COMPANY
AMSTERDAM — OXFORD — NEW YORK
1980

ELSEVIER SCIENTIFIC PUBLISHING COMPANY
335 Jan van Galenstraat
P.O. Box 211, 1000 AE Amsterdam, The Netherlands

Distributors for the United States and Canada:

ELSEVIER/NORTH-HOLLAND INC.
52, Vanderbilt Avenue
New York, N.Y. 10017

Library of Congress Cataloging in Publication Data
Main entry under title:

Elsevier's banking dictionary in six languages.

   1. Banks and banking--Dictionaries--Polyglot.
2. English language--Dictionaries--Polyglot. I. Ricci,
Julio. II. Title: Banking dictionary in six languages.
HG151.E45 1980   332.1'03   79-26023
ISBN 0-444-41834-2

ISBN 0-444-41834-2

Electronic data processing:
Büro für Satztechnik W. Meyer KG
Hanau, W. Germany

Printed in The Netherlands

CIHd

PREFACE TO THE FIRST EDITION

This multilingual banking dictionary has resulted from an investigation, conducted during the last five years, into banking terminology currently in use.

The author is responsible for selecting the material included and also the manner in which it is presented. However, he wishes to emphasize that completion of the dictionary would not have been possible without the valued assistance of many cooperative and efficient collaborators. In particular, the author wishes to express his appreciation of the invaluable help received from the late Mr. Chr. van Balen Jr. Mr. Van Balen proved to be not only extremely capable and helpful, but was also always readily willing to discuss any difficult problems. The author will always remember the tenacity, conscientiousness and jovial spirit which contributed so fully to his magnificent personality.

A sincere debt of gratitude is also owed to Mr. Henri Leneutre, Paris, France; Mr. Klaus H. Roedler, Hamburg, Germany; Mr. and Mrs. Hugo Lundquist, Montevideo, Uruguay; Dr. Giorgio Lena, Stockholm, Sweden; and Prof. Fausto Rossetti, Montevideo, Uruguay.

A final word must be said in recognition of the enormous help which the author received from his Waldensian wife, Iris Malan de Ricci, without whose help this task could not have been accomplished.

August, 1965   *Julio Ricci*

PREFACE TO THE SECOND EDITION

The last twenty years have witnessed a revolution in the field of economics. The technological developments, the oil crisis and the inflationary pressures have deeply shaken the basis of the traditional economic system and have brought about substantial changes in the financial order of the world.

The structural changes which have taken place have given rise to new institutions and this situation has reflected upon banking activities.

The revision of this dictionary is an effort to update a work which was beginning to fall into misuse owing to its unforeseen shortcomings. The last fifteen years have buried a number of bank customs and institutions which did not fulfil any real function and as a result, a considerable number of terms have been dropped. The deletion of almost 50 entries from the original version proves this.

The new developments, on the other hand, have given rise to the coining of more than 600 new terms, which gives a definite idea of what has happened in the field of banking. A good dictionary must perforce be like a good barometer. It must capture the language phenomena just as they are at a given moment. As Wilhelm von Humboldt observed, languages and new institutions go hand in hand. New institutions become new concepts and these inevitably manifest themselves in new terms.

I would like to make known again my gratitude to those who assisted me in preparing the first version of this dictionary and wish to express a word in memory of those who passed away. I am indebted to Mr. Rolando Pet, Mr. Fausto Rossetti, Banca di Roma and to my friends and colleagues of the Central Bank of Uruguay. I am also grateful to my wife for her patient assistance during the preparation of the manuscript.

I alone am to be held responsible for any shortcoming, inadequacy or error in this work.

December, 1979   *Julio Ricci*

ABBREVIATIONS

f	feminine
m	masculine
n	neuter
pl	plural
US	English, American usage
SA	Spanish, South-American usage
pop.	popular
Sc.	Scottish

LANGUAGE INDICATIONS

f	Français
i	Italiano
e	Español
nl	Nederlands
d	Deutsch

Basic table

A

1 abate v
f rabaisser; rabattre; diminuer; réduire
i ribassare; diminuire; ridurre
e rebajar; disminuir; reducir
n korten; korting geven; verminderen
d verbilligen; vermindern; verringern

2 abatement
f rabais m; diminution f; réduction f
i ribasso m; diminuzione f
e rebaja f; disminución f
n korting f; vermindering f
d Verbilligung f; Erlass m; Rabatt m; Verminderung f

3 in abeyance
f en souffrance; en suspens
i in sospeso; pendente; giacente
e pendiente; en suspenso
n opgeschort; hangende; in afwachting; in behandeling; onbeslist
d in der Schwebe; unentschlossen

4 absolute endorsement
f endossement m absolu; endossement m inconditionnel
i girata f assoluta
e endoso m absoluto
n onvoorwaardelijk endossement n
d unbeschränktes Indossament n; unbeschränktes Giro n

5 absorptive capacity
f capacité f d'absorption
i capacità f di assorbimento
e capacidad f de absorción
n absorptievermogen n
d Absorptionsvermögen n; Aufnahmefähigkeit f

6 abstract *(US)*
f document m cadastral d'un immeuble
i documento m catastale dei beni immobili
e documento m catastral de un inmueble
n kadastraal uittreksel n
d Katasterauszug m für Immobilien

7 abstract of account; extract of account
f extrait m de compte
i estratto m di conto
e resumen m de cuentas; extracto m de cuentas
n uittreksel n uit een rekening
d Kontoauszug m; Rechnungsauszug m

8 accept v
f accepter
i accettare
e aceptar
n accepteren; aannemen
d akzeptieren; annehmen

9 acceptance
f acceptation f
i accettazione f
e aceptación f; letra f aceptada
n accept n; acceptatie f
d Akzept n

10 acceptance credit
f crédit m par acceptation
i credito m di accettazione
e crédito m de aceptación
n acceptkrediet n
d Akzeptkredit m

11 acceptance house; merchant bank
f banque f d'acceptation
i istituto m di accettazione
e banco m de aceptaciones
n acceptbank f
d Akzeptbank f

12 acceptance ledger
f livre m d'acceptations
i libro m delle accettazioni
e libro m de letras aceptadas
n acceptenboek n; acceptatieboek n
d Akzeptenbuch n

13 acceptance register
f registre m d'acceptations
i registro m delle accettazioni
e registro m de letras aceptadas
n acceptenregister n
d Akzeptenregister n

14 acceptor
f acceptant m; accepteur m
i accettante m
e aceptante m
n acceptant m
d Akzeptant m

15 accident insurance
f assurance-accidents f; assurance f contre les accidents
i assicurazione f infortuni
e seguro m contra accidentes
n ongevallenverzekering f
d Unfallversicherung f

16 accommodate v
f prêter de l'argent

i prestare
e prestar dinero
n geld lenen; uitlenen
d Geld leihen

17 accommodate *v*
f rendre service
i agevolare; favorire
e servir; ayudar
n ter wille zijn
d gefällig sein

18 accommodation
f prêt *m*
i prestito *m*
e préstamo *m*
n lening *f*
d Anleihe *f*

19 accommodation
f complaisance *f*
i favore *m*; agevolazione *f*
e favor *m*
n gunst *f*; minnelijke schikking *f*
d Gefälligkeit *f*

20 accommodation bill; kite; windbill
f effet *m* de complaisance
i cambiale *f* di favore; cambiale *f* di comodo
e pagaré *m* de favor; letra *f* de favor
n schoorsteenwissel *m*
d Gefälligkeitswechsel *m*; Kellerwechsel *m*

21 accommodation draft
f traite *f* de complaisance
i tratta *f* di comodo
e giro *m* de favor
n complaisancewissel *m*
d Gefälligkeitstratte *f*

22 accommodation endorsement
f endossement *m* de complaisance
i girata *f* di favore
e endoso *m* de favor
n schoorsteenendossement *n*
d Gefälligkeitsgiro *n*

23 accommodation note
f billet *m* de complaisance
i nota *f* di favore
e nota *f* de favor
n complaisancepapier *n*
d Gefälligkeitspapier *n*; Gefälligkeits-schein *m*

24 account
f compte *m*
i conto *m*

e cuenta *f*
n rekening *f*
d Konto *n*; Rechnung *f*

25 account analysis *(US)*
f analyse *f* des comptes
i analisi *f* dei conti
e análisis *m* de cuentas
n rekeningoverzicht *n*; rekeninganalyse *f*
d Kontoanalyse *f*; Kontountersuchung *f*

26 accountant
f comptable *m*; officier *m* comptable
i contabile *m*; ragioniere *m*
e contador *m*
n hoofdboekhouder *m*
d Buchführer *m*; Buchhalter *m*

27 account book
f livre *m* de comptes
i libro *m* di conti; registro *m* di conti
e libro *m* de cuentas
n rekeningenboek *n*
d Rechnungsbuch *n*; Kontobuch *n*

* **account current** → 820

28 accounting
f comptabilité *f*
i contabilità *f*; computisteria *f*
e contabilidad *f*
n boekhouden *n*; boekhouding *f*
d Buchführung *f*

29 accounting rate
f taux *m* comptable
i tasso *m* contabile
e tipo *m* para fines contables
n comptabiliteitswaarde *f*; comptabiliteitsvoet *m*
d Buchführungssatz *m*

30 account of charges; expense account
f compte *m* des frais
i conto *m* di spese
e cuenta *f* de gastos
n onkostenrekening *f*
d Unkostenkonto *n*; Spesenkonto *n*

31 account settled
f compte *m* payé
i conto *m* saldato
e cuenta *f* saldada; cuenta *f* pagada
n betaalde rekening *f*
d bezahlte Rechnung *f*

32 accounts payable
f comptes *mpl* à payer
i conti *mpl* da pagare

  e cuentas *fpl* a pagar
  n crediteuren *mpl*; te betalen rekeningen
     fpl; rekeningen *fpl* te voldoen
  d Kreditoren *mpl*; Buchschulden *fpl*

33 accounts receivable
  f comptes *mpl* à recevoir; créances *fpl*
     comptables
  i conti *mpl* da riscuotere; conti *mpl* da
     incassare
  e cuentas *fpl* a cobrar
  n debiteuren *mpl*; vorderingen *fpl*
  d Debitoren *mpl*; Buchforderungen *fpl*

34 accredit *v*
  f accréditer
  i accreditare
  e acreditar
  n accrediteren; crediteren
  d beglaubigen; gutschreiben

35 accrue *v*; **accumulate** *v*
  f accumuler; s'accumuler; s'ajouter
  i maturare; accumulare; accumularsi
  e redituar; producir; devengar; acumular;
     acumularse; agregarse
  n aangroeien; vermeerderen; toenemen;
     accumuleren; oplopen
  d auflaufen; ansammeln; anhäufen

36 accrued interest
  f intérêts *mpl* cumulés; intérêts *mpl*
     courus
  i interessi *mpl* accumulati; interessi *mpl*
     decorsi
  e intereses *mpl* acumulados
  n gekweekte interest *m*; opgelopen rente *f*
  d aufgelaufene Zinsen *mpl*

37 accrued liabilities
  f effets *mpl* à payer
  i ratei *mpl* passivi
  e pasivo *m* acumulado
  n geaccumuleerde schulden *fpl*
  d entstandene Verpflichtungen *fpl*; Rück-
     stellungen *fpl*

38 accrued loan commissions
  f commissions *fpl* courues sur prêts
  i commissioni *fpl* maturate su prestiti
  e comisiones *fpl* acumuladas sobre
     préstamos
  n geaccumuleerde commissies *fpl* op
     leningen
  d über Darlehen angehäufte Kommissionen
     fpl

  * **accumulate** *v* → **35**

39 accumulation
  f accumulation *f*
  i accumulazione *f*
  e acumulación *f*
  n accumulatie *f*
  d Akkumulierung *f*; Sammlung *f*

**40 acid-test ratio; liquidity ratio; quick
     ratio**
  f ratio *m* de trésorerie réduite
  i rapporti *mpl* fra l'ammontare di cassa e
     l'ammontare delle passività correnti in
     bilancio
  e relación *f* entre el activo disponible y el
     pasivo corriente
  n liquiditeitspositie *f*
  d Liquiditätsgrad *m*; Verhältnis *n* der
     Barmittel

41 acknowledgement of receipt
  f accusé *m* de réception
  i conferma *f* di ricevuta; accusa *f* di
     ricevuta
  e acuse *m* de recibo
  n ontvangstbevestiging *f*; bericht *n* van
     ontvangst
  d Empfangsbestätigung *f*

42 acknowledge *v* **receipt of**
  f accuser réception de
  i accusare ricevuta di
  e acusar recibo de
  n de ontvangst bevestigen van
  d den Empfang bestätigen

43 acquire *v*
  f acquérir
  i acquistare
  e adquirir
  n verwerven; aanschaffen
  d erwerben; beschaffen

44 acquirer
  f acquéreur *m*
  i acquisitore *m*; compratore *m*
  e adquirente *m*; adquiridor *m*
  n verwerver *m*
  d Erwerber *m*

45 acquisition
  f acquisition *f*
  i acquisizione *f*
  e adquisición *f*
  n verwerving *f*
  d Erwerbung *f*

46 acquit *v*
  f décharger
  i sollevare (dal pagamento); esonerare

e exonerar; descargar
n ontheffen; ontslaan
d entlasten; abschreiben

47 acquit *v*
f acquitter; payer
i pagare; abbonare
e pagar
n betalen
d bezahlen

* **acquitment** → 49

48 acquittal; acquitment
f décharge *f*
i esonero *m*
e descargo *m*
n ontheffing *f*
d Entlastung *f*; Abschreibung *f*

49 acquittal; acquitment
f payement *m*
i pagamento *m*; abbono *m*
e pago *m*
n betaling *f*
d Zahlung *f*; Bezahlung *f*

50 acquittance
f quittance *f*; décharge *f*
i quietanza *f*; scarico *m*
e quitanza *f*; carta *f* de pago; finiquito *m*
n kwitantie *f*; kwijting *f*; kwijtbrief *m*
d Quittung *f*; Schulderlass *m*

51 act *v*
f agir; procéder
i agire; attuare
e actuar; proceder
n handelen; optreden; te werk gaan
d handeln; auftreten; dienen

52 act
f action *f*
i azione *f*
e acción *f*
n handeling *f*
d Handlung *f*

53 act
f loi *f*
i legge *f*
e ley *f*; decreto *m*
n wet *f*
d Gesetz *n*

* **act** → 893

54 acting
f intérinaire; provisoire

i interino
e interino
n waarnemend
d stellvertretend

55 action
f action *f*; procès *m*
i azione *f*; ricorso *m*; causa *f*
e acción *f*; proceso *m*
n actie *f*; proces *n*
d Rechtshandlung *f*; Prozess *m*

56 active
f actif
i attivo
e activo
n actief; werkzaam
d aktiv

57 active account *(US)*
f compte *m* actif
i conto *m* attivo
e cuenta *f* bancaria en movimiento
n actieve rekening *f*
d Konto *n* mit Bewegung

58 active bond
f obligation *f* à revenu fixe
i titolo *m* a interesse fisso; obbligazione *f*
e título *m* a interés fijo; obligación *f*
n vastrentende obligatie *f*
d festverzinsliche Obligation *f*

59 active capital
f capital *m* productif
i capitale *m* attivo
e capital *m* productivo; capital *m* activo
n werkend kapitaal *n*
d arbeitendes Kapital *n*

60 active debt
f dette *f* active; dette *f* portant intérêt
i debito *m* attivo
e deuda *f* efectiva
n actieve schuld *f*
d effektive Schuld *f*

61 activity charge *(US)*
f frais *mpl* de banque
i spese *fpl* bancarie
e gastos *mpl* bancarios
n administratiekosten *mpl*
d Bankspesen *fpl*; Bankgebühren *fpl*

62 act of bankruptcy
f cessation *f* de paiements
i dichiarazione *f* di interruzione dei pagamenti
e declaración *f* de cese de pago

n verklaring *f* van staking van betaling;
faillissementsverklaring *f*
d Zahlungsunfähigkeitserklärung *f*;
Bank(e)rotterklärung *f*

63 act of honour
f acte *m* d'intervention; intervention *f*
i atto *m* d'intervento
e acto *m* de intervención; intervención *f*
n interventie *f*
d Intervention *f*

64 actuary
f actuaire *m*
i attuario *m*
e actuario *m*; perito *m* en estadísticas de
seguros
n actuaris *m*; wiskundig adviseur *m*
d Aktuar *m*; Versicherungsstatistiker *m*

65 add *v*
f additionner
i sommare
e sumar; adicionar
n optellen
d zusammenzählen; zusammenrechnen;
hinzurechnen

66 adding machine
f machine *f* à additionner
i addizionatrice *f*
e máquina *f* de sumar; sumadora *f*
n telmachine *f*
d Addiermaschine *f*

67 addition
f addition *f*; somme *f*
i addizione *f*; somma *f*
e adición *f*; suma *f*
n optelling *f*; som *f*
d Zusammenrechnung *f*; Addition *f*;
Zusammenzählung *f*

68 address
f adresse *f*
i indirizzo *m*
e dirección *f*
n adres *n*
d Adresse *f*

69 address *v*
f adresser; s'adresser
i indirizzare; rivolgere; rivolgersi
e dirigir; dirigirse
n adresseren; richten; zich richten
d adressieren; richten; sich richten

70 addressee
f destinataire *m*

i destinatario *m*
e destinatario *m*
n geadresseerde *m*
d Adressat *m*; Empfänger *m*

71 adjudication of bankruptcy
f jugement *m* déclaratif de faillite
i dichiarazione *f* di fallimento
e declaración *f* judicial de quiebra
n faillietverklaring *f*
d Konkurseröffnung *f*

* **adjuster** → 628

72 adjustment of claims *(insurance)*
f estimation *f* de dommages
i tassazione *f* dei danni; acertamento *m*
dei danni
e tasación *f* de daños; tasación *f* de
averías
n schadeopneming *f*; opmaking *f* der
schade
d Schadenfestsetzung *f*

* **administer** *v* → 1571

73 administrant; administrator
f administrateur *m*; gérant *m*
i amministratore *m*; direttore *m*
e administrador *m*; director *m*
n bestuurder *m*; beheerder *m*;
administrateur *m*
d Verwalter *m*

74 administration
f administration *f*; régie *f*
i amministrazione *f*
e administración *f*
n bestuur *n*; beheer *n*
d Verwaltung *f*

75 administrative
f administratif
i amministrativo
e administrativo
n beherend; bestuurs-
d Verwaltungs-

76 administrative budget
f budget *m* administratif
i bilancio *m* amministrativo
e presupuesto *m* administrativo
n administratieve begroting *f*
d Verwaltungsetat *m*

* **administrator** → 73

77 admission
f admission *f*

i ammissione *f*
e admisión *f*
n toelating *f*; aanvaarding *f*
d Zulassung *f*; Annahme *f*

78 ad valorem
f ad valorem; selon la valeur
i secondo il valore
e al valor; sobre el valor; ad valorem
n ad valorem; over de waarde; volgens de waarde
d dem Wert nach

79 ad valorem (customs) duty
f droit *m* (de douane) ad valorem
i diritti *mpl* doganali; dazio *m* ad valorem
e derecho *m* (aduanero) ad valorem
n ad valorem (invoer- of douane)recht *n*
d Wertzoll *n*; dem Wert entsprechender (Einfuhr)zoll *n*

80 advance *v*
f avancer; anticiper
i anticipare
e adelantar; anticipar
n voorschieten; vooruitbetalen
d vorschiessen

81 advance; advancement
f avance *f*
i anticipo *m*; anticipazione *f*
e adelanto *m*; anticipo *m*
n voorschot *n*
d Vorschuss *m*

82 advance
f hausse *f*
i aumento *m* dei prezzi
e alza *f*; aumento *m* de precio
n prijsstijging *f*
d Preiserhöhung *f*

83 advance deposit
f dépôt *m* préalable
i deposito *m* anticipato
e depósito *m* previo
n voorschotdeposito *n* (aanbetaling)
d Vorschussanzahlung *f*

84 advance deposit requirement (on imports)
f obligation *f* de constituer un dépôt préalable (à l'importation)
i richiesta *f* di deposito anticipato (sulle importazioni)
e requisito *m* de depósito previo (a la importación)
n vereiste *n* voor voorschotdeposito (invoer)

d im voraus verlangte Einlage *f* (Einfuhrgeschäfte)

* **advancement** → 81

* **advance payment** → 1804

85 advance repayment
f remboursement *m* anticipé
i rimborso *m* anticipato
e reembolso *m* anticipado
n voorschot-terugbetaling *f*; vooruitbetaald rembours *n*
d Vorschussrückzahlung *f*

86 adventure
f spéculation *f* hasardée; risque *m*
i speculazione *f*; rischio *m*
e especulación *f*; riesgo *m*
n gewaagde speculatie *f*; risico *n/f*
d Spekulationsgeschäft *n*; Risiko *n*

87 adviser
f conseiller *m*
i consulente *m*; consigliere *m*
e consejero *m*; asesor *m*
n raadgever *m*; adviseur *m*
d Berater *m*; Ratgeber *m*

88 affidavit
f affidavit *m*
i affidavit *m*
e affidavit *m*; declaración *f* jurada
n affidavit *n*; beëdigde verklaring *f*
d Affidavit *n*; schriftliche (eidliche) Erklärung *f*

89 affiliate
f institution *f* affiliée; filiale *f*
i società *f* affiliata; filiale *f*
e institución *f* afiliada; filial *f*
n filiaal *n*; aangesloten bedrijf *n*
d Tochtergesellschaft *f*; Filiale *f*

90 affreightment
f affrètement *m*; nolisement *m*
i noleggio *m*
e fletamento *m*
n bevrachting *f*
d Befrachtung *f*

91 afteracceptation
f acceptation *f* postérieure
i accettazione *f* posteriore
e aceptación *f* a posteriori
n latere acceptatie *f*
d spätere Annahme *f*

92 afteraccount
f compte *m* nouveau
i conto *m* nuovo
e cuenta *f* nueva
n nieuwe rekening *f*
d neue Rechnung *f*

93 aftercost
f coût *m* complémentaire
i costo *m* complementario; costo *m* addizionale
e costo *m* adicional; sobrecarga *f*
n bijkomende kosten *mpl*
d zusätzliche Unkosten *fpl*; Aufschlag *m*

94 agency
f institution *f*
i agenzia *f*; ufficio *m*
e organismo *m*
n agentschap *n*
d Dienststelle *f*

95 agenda
f ordre *m* du jour
i ordine *m* del giorno
e orden *m/f* del día
n agenda *f*; orde *f* van de dag
d Tagesordnung *f*

96 agent
f agent *m*
i agente *m*
e agente *m*
n vertegenwoordiger *m*
d Agent *m*; Vertreter *m*

97 aggregate
f agrégat *m*
i aggregato *m*; totale *m* aggregato; globale *m*
e agregado *m*; monto *m* global
n gezamenlijk bedrag *n*
d Gesamtsumme *f*

98 aggregate demand
f demande *f* globale
i domanda *f* aggregata
e demanda *f* global
n gezamenlijke vordering *f*
d Gesamtnachfrage *f*; Gesamtbedarf *m*

99 aggregative planning
f planification *f* globale
i pianificazione *f* aggregativa; programmazione *f* aggregativa
e planificación *f* global
n gezamenlijke planning *f*
d Gesamtplanung *f*

100 agio
f agio *m*
i aggio *m*
e agio *m*
n agio *n*; opgeld *n*
d Agio *n*; Aufgeld *n*

101 agree *v*
f être d'accord
i essere d'accordo; concordare
e estar de acuerdo
n overeenkomen; overeenstemmen
d einverstanden sein; übereinstimmen

102 agreement
f accord *m*; convention *f*
i accordo *m*; convenzione *f*
e acuerdo *m*; convenio *m*
n overeenstemming *f*; afspraak *f*; overeenkomst *f*
d Einverständnis *n*; Übereinstimmung *f*; Abkommen *n*

103 agroindustries; agribusiness
f agro-industries *fpl*
i industria *f* agricola
e agroindustrias *fpl*
n landbouw-industrieën *fpl*
d landwirtschaftliche Industrie *f*

104 alienable
f aliénable
i alienabile; trasferibile
e enajenable
n vervreemdbaar
d veräusserlich

105 alienate *v*
f aliéner; transférer
i alienare; trasferire
e enajenar; transferir
n vervreemden; overdragen
d entfremden; veräussern

106 alienation
f aliénation *f*
i alienazione *f*
e enajenación *f*
n vervreemding *f*
d Veräusserung *f*

107 alienee
f aliénataire *m*
i alienatario *m*
e beneficiario *m*; "enajenatario" *m*
n ontvanger *m*
d Erwerber *m*

108 allege v
  f alléguer
  i addurre
  e alegar
  n aanvoeren; beweren
  d anführen; behaupten

109 all-in insurance; all-inclusive insurance (US)
  f assurance f totale; assurance f tous-risques
  i assicurazione f generale
  e seguro m total
  n all-riskverzekering f
  d Allrisk-Versicherung f

110 allocate v
  f assigner; affecter
  i assegnare; destinare
  e adjudicar; asignar; destinar
  n toewijzen
  d zuweisen; zuteilen

111 allocation
  f affectation f
  i assegnazione f
  e asignación f; destino m
  n toewijzing f
  d Zuweisung f; Zuteilung f

112 allocation of proceeds (loan)
  f affectation f des fonds (du prêt)
  i allocazione f dei ricavi (del prestito)
  e asignación f del importe (del prestamo)
  n toewijzing f van de opbrengst (lening)
  d Bestimmung f des Betrags (Darlehen)

113 allocation of profits
  f affectation f des bénéfices
  i allocazione f dei profitti
  e asignación f de las utilidades
  n toewijzing f van de winsten
  d Bestimmung f des Gewinns

114 allocation of resources
  f répartition f de ressources
  i allocazione f delle risorse
  e distribución f de los recursos; asignación f de los recursos
  n toewijzing f van de geldmiddelen
  d Zuteilung f der Geldmittel; Zuweisung f der Geldmittel

115 allocatur
  f certificat m des frais alloués
  i certificato m di spese concesse
  e certificado m de autorización de gastos
  n certificaat n van toestemming voor uitgaven
  d Zustimmungsbescheinigung für Ausgaben

116 allonge
  f allonge f (d'une lettre de change)
  i talloncino m (della cambiale)
  e talón m (de letra de cambio)
  n aanvullingsstuk n (van een wissel)
  d Allonge f; Ansatzstück n

117 allot v
  f attribuer; assigner
  i assegnare
  e asignar; adjudicar
  n toewijzen
  d zuweisen

118 allot v
  f partager; distribuer
  i ripartire
  e distribuir
  n verdelen
  d zuteilen; verteilen

119 allot v
  f livrer
  i rimettere; consegnare
  e entregar
  n leveren
  d liefern

120 allotment
  f attribution f; assignation f
  i assegnazione f
  e asignación f; adjudicación f
  n toewijzing f
  d Zuweisung f

121 allotment
  f partage m
  i ripartizione f
  e distribución f; reparto m
  n verdeling f
  d Zuteilung f

122 allotment
  f livraison f
  i rimessa f; consegna f
  e entrega f
  n levering f
  d Lieferung f; Ablieferung f

* **allotment letter** → 1515

123 allow v
  f concéder; accorder
  i concedere
  e conceder; otorgar

n toewijzen
d bewilligen

124 allow *v*
f permettre
i permettere
e permitir
n toestaan
d zulassen

125 allowance
f compensation *f*; subside *m*; indemnité *f*
i compenso *m*; compensazione *f*; sussidio *m*; sovvenzione *f*
e compensación *f*; subsidio *m*; retribución *f*
n toelage *f*; toelaag *f*; subsidie *f/n*
d Zuschuss *m*; Vergütung *f*

126 allowance
f traitement *m*; salaire *m*
i stipendio *m*; salario *m*
e sueldo *m*
n salaris *n*
d Gehalt *n*

127 allowance
f concession *f*
i permesso *m*; concessione *f*
e concesión *f*; permiso *m*
n vergunning *f*
d Zulassung *f*

128 allowance
f rabais *m*
i ribasso *m*
e rebaja *f*
n korting *f*
d Abzug *m*; Rabatt *m*

129 alteration
f altération *f*; changement *m*
i alterazione *f*
e alteración *f*
n wijziging *f*; verandering *f*
d Änderung *f*; Veränderung *f*

130 alternative drawee
f tiré *m* alternatif
i trattario *m* alternativo
e librado *m* alternativo
n medetrassaat *m*; medebetrokkene *m*
d Alternativtrassat *m*

131 alternative payee
f bénéficiaire *m* alternatif
i beneficiario *m* alternativo
e beneficiario *m* alternativo

n medebegunstigde *m*; mede-inner *m*
d alternativer Begünstigter *m*

132 amortization; amortizement
f amortissement *m*
i ammortamento *m*
e amortización *f*
n amortisatie *f*; aflossing *f*
d Amortisation *f*; Schuldentilgung *f*; Tilgung *f*

133 amortization schedule
f calendrier *m* d'amortissement
i piano *m* di ammortamento
e plan *m* de amortización
n amortisatieplan *n*; afbetalingsplan *n*
d Amortisationstabelle *f*; Tilgungsplan *m*

134 amortize *v*
f amortir
i ammortizzare
e amortizar
n amortiseren; delgen
d amortisieren; tilgen

* **amortizement** → **132**

135 amount
f montant *m*; somme *f*
i importo *m*; somma *f*
e importe *m*; suma *f*; monto *m*
n bedrag *n*; som *f*
d Betrag *m*; Summe *f*

136 amount *v* **to**
f se monter à; s'élever à
i ammontare a
e ascender a
n bedragen; belopen; uitmaken
d sich belaufen auf

137 anatocism
f anatocisme *m*
i interesse *m* composto; interesse *m* usurario
e interés *m* compuesto; doble usura *f*
n woekerrente *m*; interest *m* op interest
d Wucherzins *m*

138 ancillary letter of credit
f lettre *f* de crédit complémentaire
i lettera *f* di credito addizionale; lettera *f* di credito sussidiaria
e carta *f* de crédito complementaria
n aanvullende kredietbrief *m*
d Hilfskreditbrief *m*

139 announce *v*
f annoncer

i annunziare
e anunciar
n aankondigen; bekendmaken; annonceren;
aanzeggen
d bekanntgeben; anzeigen

140 annual
f annuel
i annuale
e anual
n jaarlijks
d jährlich

141 annual report; annual return
f rapport *m* annuel
i relazione *f* annuale; rapporto *m* annuale
e informe *m* anual
n jaarverslag *n*
d Jahresbericht *m*; Jahresausweis *m*

142 annual return
f revenu *m* annuel
i profitto *m* annuale
e rédito *m* anual; ganancia *f* anual
n jaarlijkse opbrengst *f*
d Jahresgewinn *m*

* annual return → 141

143 annuitant
f bénéficiaire *m* d'une annuité; rentier *m*
i titolare *m* di una annualità;
reddituario *m*
e beneficiario *m* de una anualidad; rentista
m/f
n rentetrekker *m*; rentenier *m*
d Empfänger *m* einer Jahresrente;
Rentner *m*

144 annuity
f annuité *f*; rente *f* annuelle
i annualità *f*; rendita *f* annuale
e anualidad *f*; renta *f* anual
n annuïteit *f*; jaarlijkse aflossing *f*;
jaargeld *n*; rente *f*
d Annuität *f*; Jahresrente *f*

145 annuity bond
f obligation *f* de rente; obligation *f*
d'annuité
i titolo *m* senza scadenza
e bono *m* perpetuo; bono *m* sin
vencimiento
n niet aflosbare obligatie *f*
d Renteanleihe *f* ohne Tilgungszwang;
Rentenschuldverschreibung *f*

146 annul *v*
f annuler; déclarer nul

i annullare; cancellare
e anular; cancelar; dejar sin efecto
n annuleren; vernietigen; nietig verklaren;
opheffen
d annullieren; streichen; nichtig erklären;
aufheben

147 annulment
f annulation *f*
i annullamento *m*; cancellazione *f*
e anulación *f*; cancelación *f*
n annulering *f*; opheffing *f*
d Annullierung *f*; Aufhebung *f*;
Abschaffung *f*

148 answer
f réponse *f*
i risposta *f*
e respuesta *f*; contestación *f*
n antwoord *n*
d Antwort *f*; Beantwortung *f*

149 answer *v*
f répondre
i rispondere
e responder; contestar
n antwoorden; beantwoorden
d antworten; beantworten

150 answer *v* **for**
f répondre pour
i rispondere di; essere garante di
e responder por
n verantwoordelijk zijn voor; instaan voor
d einstehen für

151 antichresis
f antichrèse *f*
i anticresi *f*
e anticresis *f*
n antichresis *f*
d Antichresis *f*

* anticipated payment → 1804

152 anticyclical policy
f politique *f* anticyclique
i politica *f* anticiclica
e política *f* anticíclica
n anti-cyclische conjunctuurpolitiek *f*
d antizyklische Wirtschaftspolitik *f*

153 applicant
f postulant *m*; candidat *m*
i postulante *m*; richiedente *m*
e aspirante *m*; postulante *m*
n sollicitant *m*
d Bewerber *m*; Anwärter *m*; Antrag-
steller *m*

154 application
f demande f
i domanda f; richiesta f
e solicitud f
n aanvraag m; verzoek n
d Gesuch n; Bewerbung f; Antrag m

155 application form
f formulaire m de demande
i modulo m per domande
e formulario m de solicitud
n aanvraagformulier n
d Antragsformular n

156 application for membership
f demande f d'adhésion
i domanda f d'iscrizione
e solicitud f de ingreso
n aanmelding f voor lidmaatschap
d Mitgliedschaftsantrag m

157 application for withdrawal (from loan account)
f demande f de retrait (d'un compte de prêt)
i richiesta f di prelievo (da un conto di prestito)
e solicitud f de retiro de fondos (de una cuenta de préstamos)
n opvraging f van gelden (van een kredietrekening); uitbetalingsaanvraag f (van een kredietrekening)
d Auszahlungsantrag m (von einem Kreditkonto)

158 apply v for
f demander
i chiedere; domandare
e solicitar
n aanvragen
d verlangen; ansuchen um

159 apply v to
f s'adresser à
i rivolgersi a
e dirigirse a
n zich wenden tot; zich richten tot
d sich wenden an

160 appoint v
f nommer; désigner
i nominare
e nombrar; designar
n benoemen
d ernennen

161 appointee
f nommé m; désigné m
i nominato m

e nombrado m; designado m
n benoemde m
d Ernannte(r) m; Beauftragte(r) m

162 appointer
f celui qui nomme
i chi nomina
e el que nombra
n benoemer m
d Ernenner m

163 appointment
f nomination f; désignation f
i nomina f
e nombramiento m; designación f
n benoeming f
d Ernennung f

164 apportion v
f répartir; lotir
i ripartire; dividere
e repartir; distribuir; prorratear
n verdelen; toedelen
d verteilen

165 apportionment
f répartition f; partage m
i ripartizione f
e reparto m; distribución f
n verdeling f
d Verteilung f

166 appraisable
f évaluable
i valutabile; stimabile; tassabile
e avaluable; tasable
n waardeerbaar; te schatten
d abschätzbar; taxierbar

167 appraisal; appraisement; appreciation; apprisement
f évaluation f; estimation f; appréciation f; taxation f
i valutazione f; tassazione f; stima f; apprezzamento m
e avaluación f; tasación f; aforo m; estimación f; valoración f; avalúo m
n prijsbepaling f; schatting f; waardering f; taxatie f
d Bewertung f; Wertung f; Schätzung f; Taxierung f; Wertschätzung f

168 appraise v; appreciate v; apprise v
f estimer; évaluer; taxer
i stimare; valutare; tassare
e estimar; avaluar; tasar; valorar; aforar
n schatten; waarderen; taxeren
d abschätzen; schätzen; bewerten; taxieren

* **appraisement** → 167

169 appraiser; appreciator
f évaluateur *m*; estimateur *m*
i perito *m* stimatore; tassatore *m*
e avaluador *m*; tasador *m*; aforador *m*
n schatter *m*; taxateur *m*
d Schätzer *m*; Taxator *m*

* **appreciate** *v* → 168

* **appreciation** → 167

170 apprise *v*
f informer; notifier
i informare; notificare
e informar; dar parte de; notificar
n kennisgeven; berichten
d benachrichtigen; in Kenntnis setzen

* **apprise** *v* → 168

171 apprisement
f information *f*; notification *f*
i informazione *f*; notifica *f*
e información *f*; notificación *f*; aviso *m*
n aankondiging *f*; kennisgeving *f*
d Benachrichtigung *f*; Bekanntgabe *f*

* **apprisement** → 167

172 appropriate *v*
f s'approprier de
i appropriarsi di
e apropiarse de
n zich toeëigenen
d sich aneignen

173 appropriate *v*
f affecter; assigner
i assegnare; destinare
e asignar; destinar
n toewijzen
d zuweisen

174 appropriation
f appropriation *f*; prise *f* de possession
i appropriazione *f*
e apropiación *f*
n toeëigening *f*
d Aneignung *f*

175 appropriation
f affectation *f*; assignation *f*
i assegnazione *f*; destino *m*
e asignación *f*; destino *m*
n toewijzing *f*; bestemming *f*
d Zuweisung *f*; Bestimmung *f*; Verwendung *f*

176 approval
f approbation *f*; consentement *m*
i approvazione *f*
e aprobación *f*; conformidad *f*
n goedkeuring *f*; toestemming *f*
d Billigung *f*; Genehmigung *f*; Approbation *f*; Beifall *m*

177 approve *v*
f approuver
i approvare
e aprobar
n goedkeuren
d billigen

* **arbitrage** → 179

178 arbitrate *v*
f arbitrer; juger
i arbitrare
e arbitrar; juzgar; decidir
n arbitreren; beslechten
d entscheiden (durch Schiedsspruch); schlichten

179 arbitration; arbitrage
f arbitrage *m*
i arbitraggio *m*
e arbitraje *m*
n arbitrage *f*; scheidsrechterlijke uitspraak *f*; bemiddeling *f*
d Arbitrage *f*; schiedsrichterliche Entscheidung *f*; Schiedspruch *m*

180 arbitration of exchange; exchange arbitration
f arbitrage *m* de change
i arbitraggio *m* di cambio
e arbitraje *m* de cambio
n wisselarbitrage *f*; koersarbitrage *f*; deviezenarbitrage *f*
d Wechselarbitrage *f*; Kursarbitrage *f*; Devisenarbitrage *f*

181 arbitrator
f arbitre *m*; juge *m*
i arbitro *m*
e árbitro *m*; juez *m*
n scheidsrechter *m*
d Schiedsrichter *m*

182 arrange *v*
f arranger; convenir; régler
i sistemare; regolare; disporre; concertare; convenire
e arreglar; convenir; disponer
n regelen; schikken
d regeln; erledigen; schlichten; vereinbaren; abmachen

183 arrangement
f arrangement *m*; accord *m*; composition *f*
i sistemazione *f*; accordo *m*; convenzione *f*
e arreglo *m*; convenio *m*
n regeling *f*; schikking *f*; overeenkomst *f*
d Regelung *f*; Erledigung *f*; Abkommen *n*; Vereinbarung *f*

184 arrangement with creditors
f concordat *m*; composition *f* avec les créanciers
i accomodamento *m* con i creditori
e concordato *m* con (los) acreedores
n akkoord *n*; schikking *f* met schuldeisers
d Gläubigerausgleich *m*

185 arrears
f arriérés *mpl*
i arretrati *mpl*
e importe *m* atrasado; deuda *f* atrasada
n achterstallige schuld *f*; achterstand *m*
d Rückstände *mpl*

186 arson
f incendie *m* volontaire
i incendio *m* doloso
e incendio *m* intencional; incendio *m* doloso
n brandstichting *f*
d Brandstiftung *f*

187 article
f article *m*
i articolo *m*
e articulo *m*
n artikel *n*
d Artikel *m*

188 articles of association
f statuts *mpl* d'une société
i statuto *m* sociale
e estatutos *mpl* de una sociedad; reglamentos *mpl* de una sociedad
n statuten *npl* van een vennootschap
d Gesellschaftsstatuten *npl*

189 articles of partnership
f contrat *m* d'association
i atto *m* costitutivo (d'una società)
e contrato *m* de asociación
n contract *n* van vennootschap
d Gesellschaftsvertrag *m*

190 assemble *v*
f se réunir; se rassembler
i riunirsi
e reunirse

n bijeenkomen
d sich versammeln

191 assemble *v*
f convoquer
i convocare
e convocar
n oproepen; bijeenroepen
d vorladen; einberufen; zusammenrufen

192 assembly
f assemblée *f*; réunion *f*
i assemblea *f*
e asamblea *f*
n vergadering *f*; bijeenkomst *f*
d Versammlung *f*

193 assess *v*
f grever
i gravare
e gravar
n belasten; bezwaren
d belasten; besteuern

194 assess *v*
f évaluer; taxer
i valutare; stimare; tassare
e avaluar; tasar
n schatten; taxeren
d schätzen; taxieren

* **assessed income** → **2292**

195 assessment
f impôt *m*; charge *f*
i gravame *m*; imposta *f*
e gravamen *m*; impuesto *m*
n belasting *f*
d Belastung *f*; Besteuerung *f*

196 assessment
f évaluation *f*; taxation *f*
i valutazione *f*; tassazione *f*
e avalúo *m*; tasación *f*
n schatting *f*; taxatie *f*
d Schätzung *f*; Taxierung *f*

197 asset
f poste *m* de l'actif
i partita *f* attiva
e partida *f* del activo
n actiefpost *f*
d Aktivposten *m*

198 assets
f actif *m*
i attivo *m*
e activo *m*

n actief n
d Aktiva npl

199 assets side
f actif m
i attivo m
e activo m
n actiefzijde f
d Aktivseite f

200 assign v
f assigner
i assegnare
e asignar
n toewijzen
d zuweisen

201 assign v
f céder
i cedere
e ceder
n afstaan
d zedieren; abtreten

202 assign v
f transférer
i trasferire
e transferir
n overdragen
d übertragen

203 assignable
f assignable
i assegnabile
e asignable
n toewijsbaar
d zuweisbar

204 assignable
f transférable
i trasferibile
e transferible
n overdraagbaar
d übertragbar

205 assignable
f cessible
i cedibile
e cesible
n cedeerbaar
d zessionsfähig

206 assignation; assignment
f assignation f
i assegnazione f
e asignación f
n assignatie f; toewijzing f
d Zuweisung f

207 assignation; assignment
f transfert m
i trasferimento m
e traspaso m; transferencia f
n overdracht f
d Übertragung f

208 assignation; assignment
f cession f
i cessione f
e cesión f
n afstand m
d Zession f; Abtretung f

209 assigned account *(US)*
f compte m en garantie
i conto m in garanzia
e cuenta f en garantia
n garantierekening f
d Garantiekonto n

210 assignee
f cessionnaire m
i cessionario m
e cesionario m
n cessionaris m
d Zessionär m; Übernehmer m

211 assigner; assignor
f cédant m
i cedente m
e cesionista m
n cedent m
d Zedent m; Abtretender m

* **assignment** → 206, 207, 208

212 assignment agreement
f accord m de délégation de créance
i accordo m di cessione
e acuerdo m de cesión
n cessieverdrag n
d Zessionsvertrag m

* **assignor** → 211

213 assistant
f assistant m
i assistente m; collaboratore m
e asistente m; ayudante m
n assistent m; helper m
d Mitarbeiter m; Gehilfe m

214 associate v
f associer; s'associer
i associare; associarsi
e asociar; asociarse
n verbinden; zich verbinden; zich associëren

d verbinden; vereinigen; assozieren; sich
verbinden; sich vereinigen

215 association
f association f; société f
i associazione f
e asociación f; sociedad f
n vennootschap f; maatschappij f;
associatie f
d Vereinigung f; Gesellschaft f

216 assumpsit
f engagement m verbal
i promessa f verbale
e promesa f verbal
n mondelinge overeenkomst f
d mündliches Versprechen n

* **assurance** → **1410**

* **assure** v → **1416**

217 attach v
f saisir; confisquer
i confiscare; sequestrare
e embargar; decomisar
n in beslag nemen; embargo leggen op
d in Beschlag nehmen; belegen mit
Beschlag; beschlagnahmen

218 attach v
f joindre; attacher
i allegare; accludere
e adjuntar; agregar
n aanhechten
d beilegen; beifügen

219 attached account *(US)*
f compte m saisi
i conto m bloccato; conto m sequestrato
e cuenta f bloqueada; cuenta f intervenida
judicialmente
n geblokkeerde rekening f
d gesperrtes Konto n; blockiertes Konto m

220 attachment
f saisie f
i confisca f; sequestro m
e embargo m; decomiso m
n beslag n; embargo n
d Beschlagnahme f

221 attachment ledger *(US)*
f livre m des saisies
i libro m dei conti bloccati
e registro m de cuentas bloqueadas
n register n van geblokkeerde rekeningen
d Verzeichnis n von blockierten (gesperr-

ten) Konten; Verzeichnis n von blockierten (gesperrten) Rechnungen

222 attest
f témoignage m
i attestazione f
e testimonio m
n attestatie f; getuigenis f; verklaring f
d Beglaubigung f; Zeugnis n

223 attest v
f attester; certifier; déclarer
i attestare; certificare; dichiarare
e atestiguar; testimoniar; certificar;
declarar
n getuigen; betuigen; verklaren
d beglaubigen; bezeugen

224 attestor
f témoin m
i testimone m
e testigo m
n getuige m
d Zeuge m

225 attorney
f mandataire m; représentant m;
procureur m
i mandatario m; procuratore m
e apoderado m; poderhabiente m;
procurador m
n gemachtigde m; procureur m
d Bevollmächtigter m; Vertreter m

226 auction
f enchère f; encan m; vente f publique
i asta f
e subasta f; remate m; venta f pública
n vendu f; vendutie f; openbare
verkoping f; veiling f; auctie f
d Versteigerung f; Auktion f

227 auction v
f vendre aux enchères
i mettere all'asta
e subastar; rematar
n veilen; verkopen in het openbaar
d versteigern

228 auctioneer
f commissaire-priseur m; adjudicateur m;
vendeur m aux enchères
i tenitore m dell'asta; venditore m all'asta
e subastador m; rematador m;
martillero m
n veilinghouder m; veilingmeester m;
venduhouder m; vendumeester m; auctio-
naris m
d Auktionator m; Versteigerer m

229 audit *v*
f examiner (des comptes)
i esaminare (i conti); verificare (i conti)
e revisar (cuentas); intervenir (cuentas)
n (rekeningen) controleren
d revidieren; (Rechnungen) prüfen

230 audited statement of accounts
f état *m* vérifié des comptes
i bilancio *m* approvato
e estado *m* de cuentas certificado
n gecertificeerd rekening-
courantafschrift *n*
d geprüfter Rechnungsauszug *m*

231 auditing of accounts
f vérification f des comptes
i verificazione f dei conti
e intervención f de cuentas; revisión f de
cuentas
n onderzoek *n* van een boekhouding
d Rechnungsprüfung f; Bücherrevision f;
Prüfung f der Bücher

232 auditor
f vérificateur *m* aux comptes; expert-
comptable *m*
i revisore *m* (dei conti)
e síndico *m*; interventor *m*; revisor *m* de
cuentas
n accountant *m*
d Rechnungsprüfer *m*; Rechnungs-
revisor *m*; Bücherrevisor *m*

233 auditorship
f fonction f de vérificateur aux comptes
i funzione f del verificatore di conti
e función f de intervenir cuentas
n accountantsschap *n*
d Rechnungsprüferamt *n*

234 authenticate *v*
f authentiquer; certifier; valider
i autenticare; certificare
e autenticar; certificar; validar
n rechtsgeldig verklaren; legaliseren
d beglaubigen; bescheinigen

235 authentication
f certification f; validation f
i autenticazione f
e autenticación f
n staving f; waarmerking f
d Beglaubigung f

236 authorization
f autorisation f
i autorizzazione f
e autorización f; permiso *m*

n machtiging f
d Ermächtigung f; Bevollmächtigung f;
Autorisation f; Autorisierung f

237 authorize *v*
f autoriser
i autorizzare
e autorizar
n autoriseren; machtigen
d ermächtigen; bevollmächtigen; autorisie-
ren

238 authorized bank
f banque f agréée
i banca f autorizzata
e banco *m* autorizado
n geautoriseerde bank f
d bevollmächtigte Bank f

239 authorized capital
f capital *m* autorisé
i capitale *m* autorizzato
e capital *m* autorizado
n geautoriseerd kapitaal *n*; gewettigd
kapitaal *n*
d autorisiertes Kapital *n*; genehmigtes
Kapital *n*

240 authorized signature
f signature f autorisée
i firma f autorizzata
e firma f autorizada
n geldige ondertekening f
d berechtigte Unterschrift f

241 availability; availment
f disponibilité f
i disponibilità f
e disponibilidad f
n beschikbaarheid f
d Verfügbarkeit f

242 available
f disponible
i disponibile
e disponible
n beschikbaar; verkrijgbaar
d verfügbar; erhältlich

* **availment → 241**

243 avail(s)
f utilité f; profit *m*
i profitto *m*; reddito *m*
e utilidad f; beneficio *m*; producido *m*
n product *n*; baat f; opbrengst f
d Ertrag *m*

244 aval
f aval *m*
i avallo *m*
e aval *m*; garantía *f*
n aval *n*; wisselborgtocht *m*; garantie *f*
d Aval *m*; Wechselbürgschaft *f*

245 average
f avarie *f*
i avaria *f*
e avería *f*
n averij *f*
d Havarie *f*

246 average adjuster; average stater
f dispacheur *m*
i tassatore *m* di avarie marittime
e tasador *m* de averías; árbitro *m* de seguros marítimos
n dispacheur *m*
d Dispacheur *m*

247 average bond
f compromis *m* d'avarie
i compromesso *m* d'avaria
e fianza *f* de avería
n compromis *n* van averijgrosse
d Havarieschein *m*

248 average clause
f clause *f* d'avarie
i clausola *f* d'avaria
e cláusula *f* de avería
n averijclausule *f*
d Havarieklausel *f*; Freizeichnungsklausel *f*

249 average deposit
f dépôt *m* d'avarie
i deposito *m* per avaria
e depósito *m* por avería
n averijdeposito *n*
d Havarieeinlage *f*

250 average loss
f perte *f* par avarie
i perdita *f* per avaria
e pérdida *f* por avería
n verlies *n* door averij
d Havarieverlust *m*

* **average stater** → 246

251 avoid *v*
f annuler
i annullare
e anular
n annuleren; ongeldig verklaren
d annullieren

252 avoid *v*
f éviter
i evitare
e evitar
n vermijden
d vermeiden

253 avoidance
f annulation *f*
i annullamento *m*
e anulación *f*
n annulering *f*
d Annullierung *f*

254 avouch *v*
f déclarer; affirmer
i dichiarare; affermare
e declarar; afirmar; alegar
n verklaren; bevestigen
d erklären; zusichern

255 avouchment
f déclaration *f*
i dichiarazione *f*
e declaración *f*
n verklaring *f*
d Erklärung *f*

256 award
f sentence *f* arbitrale
i arbitraggio *m*
e laudo *m*; arbitraje *m*
n sententie *f*; uitspraak *f*; beslissing *f*
d Schiedsspruch *m*

B

257 back *v*
f endosser
i indossare
e endosar; certificar al dorso
n endosseren
d indossieren

* **back financing** → 2074

258 backwardation
f déport *m*
i deporto *m*
e prima *f* de aplazamiento
n deport *n*
d Deport *m*; Kursabschlag *m*

259 backward integration
f intégration *f* en amont
i integrazione *f* regressiva
e integración *f* regresiva
n teruglopende integratie *f*
d rückständige Integrierung *f*

260 bad debt
f créance *f* véreuse; mauvaise créance *f*
i debito *m* non riscuotibile
e deuda *f* incobrable
n oninbare schuld *f*
d uneinbringliche Schuld *f*

261 bail; bailment
f caution *f*; cautionnement *m*
i cauzione *f*
e caución *f*; fianza *f*
n borg *m*; borgtocht *m*; borgstelling *f*; onderpand *n*; cautie *f*
d Bürgschaft *f*; Kaution *f*

262 bail *v*
f cautionner
i prestare cauzione; garantire
e salir de fiador; caucionar
n borg staan voor; borg spreken voor
d Bürgschaft leisten; bürgen

263 bail bond
f engagement *m* signé par la caution
i scrittura *f* di garanzia
e compromiso *m* de fianza; fianza *f*
n borgtocht *m*; borgstelling *f*; akte *f* van borgtocht
d Bürgschaftsschein *m*

264 bailer; bailor
f caution *f*; garant *m*
i garante *m*

e fiador *m*; garante *m*
n borgsteller *m*; borg *m*
d Bürge *m*

* **bailment** → 261

265 balance
f bilan *m*; balance *f*
i bilancio *m*; pareggio *m*
e balance *m*
n balans *f*
d Bilanz *f*; Abschluss *m*

266 balance
f solde *m*
i saldo *m*
e saldo *m*
n saldo *n*; overschot *n*
d Saldo *m*

267 balance certificate
f certificat *m* de balance
i certificato *m* di bilancio
e certificado *m* de balance; comprobante *m* de balance
n balanscertificaat *n*
d Bilanzbescheinigung *f*

268 balance of account
f solde *m* de compte
i saldo *m* di conto
e saldo *m* de cuenta
n rekeningssaldo *n*
d Rechnungssaldo *m*

269 balance of payment
f solde *m* de paiement
i saldo *m* di pago
e saldo *m* de pago
n betalingssaldo *n*
d Zahlungssaldo *m*

270 balance of payments position
f position *f* de balance des paiements
i posizione *f* della bilancia dei pagamenti
e estado *m* de la balanza de pagos
n positie *f* van de betalingsbalans
d Zahlungsbilanzlage *f*

271 balance of securities
f bilan *m* des titres
i pareggio *m* di titoli
e balance *m* de títulos
n balans *f* van waardepapieren
d Bilanz *f* von Wertpapieren

272 balance of trade; trade balance
f balance *f* commerciale
i bilancia *f* commerciale

e balanza *f* comercial
n handelsbalans *f*
d Handelsbilanz *f*

273 balance sheet
f bilan *m* d'inventaire
i bilancio *m*; foglio *m* di bilancio
e hoja *f* de balance
n balansopstelling *f*; balansblad *n*
d Bilanzbogen *m*; Bilanzblatt *n*

274 bank
f banque *f*
i banca *f*
e banco *m*
n bank *f*
d Bank *f*

275 bank *v*
f déposer
i depositare
e depositar
n deponeren
d einlegen; deponieren

276 bank *v*
f réaliser des opérations bancaires
i fare operazioni di banca
e hacer negocios bancarios
n bankzaken doen
d Bankgeschäfte machen

277 bankable
f escomptable
i scontabile
e descontable
n disconteerbaar
d diskontierbar

278 bankable project
f projet *m* susceptible de bénéficier d'un
   concours de la banque
i progetto *m* finanziabile
e proyecto *m* financiable
n discontabel project *n*
d bankfähiges Projekt *n*

279 bank acceptance; banker's acceptance
f acceptation *f* de banque
i accettazione *f* bancaria
e aceptación *f* bancaria
n bankaccept *n*
d Bankakzept *n*

280 bank account
f compte *m* en banque
i conto *m* bancario
e cuenta *f* bancaria

n bankrekening *f*
d Bankkonto *n*

281 bank auditor
f auditeur *m*; syndic *m*
i revisore *m* di banca; sindaco *m* di banca
e sindico *m*; revisor *m* de banco
n bankcontroleur *m*; bankaccountant *m*
d Bankrevisor *m*

282 bank balances
f soldes *mpl* bancaires
i saldi *mpl* bancarios
e saldos *mpl* bancarios
n banksaldi *npl*
d Bankguthaben *n*

283 bank bill; bank draft
f traite *f*; lettre *f*
i cambiale *f*; tratta *f*
e letra *f* bancaria
n bankwissel *m*; banktraite *f*
d Banktratte *f*; Bankwechsel *m*

* **bank book** → **1779**

284 bank branch; branch bank
f filiale *f* de banque; succursale *f* de
   banque
i filiale *f* di banca; filiale *f* bancaria
e sucursal *f* de banco
n bijkantoor *n* van een bank; vestiging *f*
d Bankfiliale *f*; Bankzweigstelle *f*

285 bank call *(US)*
f demande *f* de bilan
i invito *m* alla presentazione del bilancio
   (della banca)
e solicitud *f* oficial de presentación del
   análisis financiero de un banco
n bevel *n* aan een bank om haar balans
   over te leggen
d Aufforderung *f* zur Vorlage des Bankaus-
   weises

286 bank cashier
f caissier *m* de banque
i cassiere *m* di banca
e cajero *m* de banco
n bankkassier *m*
d Bankkassierer *m*

287 bank charges
f frais *mpl* de banque
i spese *fpl* bancarie
e gastos *mpl* de banco; gastos *mpl*
   bancarios
n bankkosten *mpl*
d Bankspesen *fpl*; Bankkosten *fpl*

288 bank cheque; banker's cheque
f chèque *m* de banque
i assegno *m* bancario
e cheque *m* bancario; cheque *m* de banco
n bankcheque *m*
d Bankscheck *m*

289 bank commission
f commission f bancaire
i commissione f bancaria
e comisión f bancaria
n bankierscommissie f
d Bankprovision f

290 bank credit
f crédit *m* bancaire; crédit *m* de banque
i credito *m* bancario
e crédito *m* bancario
n bankkrediet *n*
d Bankkredit *m*

291 bank deposit
f dépôt *m* en banque; dépôt *m* bancaire
i deposito *m* bancario
e depósito *m* bancario
n bankdeposito *n*
d Bankeinlage f

292 bank director
f directeur *m* de banque
i direttore *m* di banca
e director *m* de banco
n bankdirecteur *m*
d Bankdirektor *m*

* **bank draft** → 283

293 bank employee
f employé *m* de banque
i impiegato *m* di banca; impiegato *m* bancario
e empleado *m* de banco; empleado *m* bancario; bancario *m*
n bankbediende *m*; bankemployé *m*
d Bankangestellter *m*

294 banker
f banquier *m*
i banchiere *m*
e banquero *m*
n bankier *m*
d Bankier *m*

* **banker's acceptance** → 279

* **banker's cheque** → 288

295 bank examination *(US)*
f inspection f officielle des banques

i ispezione f bancaria
e inspección f oficial de un banco
n bankinspectie f
d Bankrevision f

296 bank examiner *(US)*
f inspecteur *m* de banque
i ispettore *m* bancario
e inspector *m* oficial de bancos
n bankinspecteur *m*
d Bankrevisor *m*

297 bank guaranty
f garantie f bancaire; garantie f de banque
i garanzia f bancaria
e garantía f bancaria
n bankgarantie f
d Bankgarantie f

298 bank house
f maison f de banque
i casa f bancaria
e casa f de banca; casa f bancaria
n bankiershuis *n*
d Bankhaus *n*

299 banking
f banques *fpl*; système *m* bancaire
i banche *fpl*; sistema *m* bancario
e bancas *fpl*
n bankbedrijf *n*; bankwezen *n*
d Bankwesen *n*

300 bank ledger
f grand livre *m* de banque
i libro *m* mastro di banca
e libro *m* mayor
n bankgrootboek *n*
d Bankhauptbuch *n*

301 bank lien
f droit *m* bancaire de rétention
i gravame *m* bancario di protezione
e gravamen *m* bancario en prevención
n recht *n* van retentie van een bank
d Sicherheitsbelastung f der Bank

302 bank liquidity position
f position f de liquidité des banques
i posizione f della liquidità bancaria
e posición f de liquidez de los bancos
n bankliquiditeitspositie f
d Bankenliquiditätslage f

303 bank liquidity ratio
f ratio *m* de liquidité des banques
i coefficiente *m* di liquidità bancaria
e coeficiente *m* de liquidez bancaria

n bankliquiditeitsverhouding *f*
d Bankenliquiditätsverhältnis *n*

304 bank manager
f directeur *m* de banque
i gerente *m* di banca
e gerente *m* de banco
n bankdirecteur *m*
d Bankvorsteher *m*

305 bank money order
f mandat *m* de banque
i vaglia *m* bancario
e giro *m* bancario
n bankwissel *m*
d Zahlungsanweisung *f*; Bankanweisung *f*

306 bank note
f billet *m* de banque
i biglietto *m* di banca
e billete *m* de banco
n bankbiljet *n*; banknoot *f*
d Banknote *f*; Geldschein *m*

307 bank of circulation; bank of issue; issuing bank
f banque *f* d'émission
i banca *f* di emissione
e banco *m* de emisión; banco *m* emisor
n circulatiebank *f*; emissiebank *f*
d Emissionsbank *f*; Notenbank *f*

* **bank of deposit** → **945**

308 bank official
f haut employé *m* bancaire
i alto funzionario *m* bancario
e alto empleado *m* de banco; jefe *m* de banco
n leidinggevende bankfunctionaris *m*
d hoher Bankbeamter *m*

* **bank of issue** → **307**

309 bank paper
f valeurs *mpl* bancaires
i valori *mpl* bancari
e valores *mpl* bancarios
n bankpapier *n*
d Bankwerte *mpl*

310 bank rate of discount; bank rate
f taux *m* d'escompte bancaire; taux *m* officiel d'escompte; escompte *m* officiel
i saggio *m* di sconto; tasso *m* ufficiale di banca
e tasa *f* de descuento bancario; tipo *m* de descuento bancario; tipo *m* bancario
n tarief *n* van het bankdisconto;

bankdisconto *n*; officieel disconto *n*
d Bankdiskontsatz *m*; Banksatz *m*; Bankdiskont *m*; Diskontsatz *m*; Bankrate *f*

311 bank reserve
f fonds *mpl* de réserve (d'une banque)
i riserva *f* bancaria
e reserva *f* bancaria; fondos *mpl* de reserva
n bankreserve *f*
d Bankreserve *f*

312 bankrupt
f en faillite; failli
i in fallimento; in bancarotta; fallito
e en bancarrota; en quiebra; fallido; quebrado
n in staat van faillissement; failliet; in staat van bankroet; bankroet
d in Konkurs; bank(e)rott

313 bankrupt *v*
f mettre en faillite; réduire à la faillite
i mandare in fallimento; fare fallire
e poner en bancarrota; hacer quebrar
n failliet doen gaan; bankroet doen gaan
d in Konkurs setzen

314 bankrupt acceptor
f acceptant *m* en faillite
i accettante *m* fallito
e aceptante *m* (de una letra) fallido
n bankroete acceptant *m*
d bank(e)rottgegangener Akzeptant *m*

315 bankrupt agent
f agent *m* de banqueroutier
i agente *m* di bancarottiere; agente *m* fallimentare; agente *m* di fallito
e agente *m* de(l) fallido
n vertegenwoordiger *m* van de gefailleerde
d Agent *m* des Bankrotteurs

316 bankruptcy
f faillite *f*; banqueroute *f*
i fallimento *m*; bancarotta *f*
e quiebra *f*; bancarrota *f*
n faillissement *n*; bankroet *n*
d Konkurs *m*; Bank(e)rott *m*

317 bankruptcy creditor
f créancier *m* d'une société en faillite
i creditore *m* del fallito
e acreedor *m* de bancarrota
n crediteur *m* in een faillissement; crediteur *m* in een bankroet
d Konkursgläubiger *m*

318 bankruptcy notice
f avis *m* de banqueroute
i annunzio *m* di fallimento
e aviso *m* de quiebra
n kennisgeving *f* van faillissement
d Konkursanmeldung *f*; Konkurserklärung *f*

319 bankruptcy petition; petition
f pétition *f* de faillite
i petizione *f* di bancarotta
e petición *f* de quiebra
n faillissementsaanvrage *f*; verzoek *n* tot faillietverklaring
d Konkursantrag *m*

320 bankrupt drawee
f accepteur *m* en faillite; tiré *m* en faillite
i trattario *m* in fallimento
e librado *m* en bancarrota
n bankroete betrokkene *m*; bankroete wisselschuldenaar *m*
d bank(e)rottgegangener Trassat *m*

321 bankrupt drawer
f tireur *m* en faillite
i trattante *m* in fallimento
e librador *m* en bancarrota; girador *m* en bancarrota
n bankroete trekker *m*
d bank(e)rottgegangener Trassant *m*

322 bankrupt firm
f société *f* en faillite
i ditta *f* in fallimento; ditta *f* fallita
e firma *f* en bancarrota
n failliete firma *f*
d bank(e)rottgegangene Firma *f*; Firma *f* in Konkurs

323 bankrupt partner
f associé *m* en faillite
i socio *m* fallimentare; socio *m* in fallimento
e socio *m* en bancarrota
n bankroete compagnon *m*
d bank(e)rottgegangener Teilhaber *m*

324 bankrupt person
f failli *m*; banqueroutier *m*
i bancarottiere *m*; fallito *m*
e fallido *m*; quebrado *m*
n gefailleerde *m*; bankroetier *m*
d Bankrotteur *m*

325 bankrupt's estate
f masse *f* de la faillite
i massa *f* fallimentare
e masa *f* de la quiebra; cuerpo *m* de bienes de un quebrado
n failliete boedel *m*
d Konkursmasse *f*

326 bankrupt surety
f garant *m* en faillite
i garante *m* in fallimento
e fiador *m* en bancarrota; fiador *m* en quiebra
n bankroete borg *m*
d bank(e)rottgegangener Bürge *m*

327 bankrupt trustee
f syndic *m* en faillite
i fiduciario *m* in fallimento
e síndico *m* en bancarrota; síndico *m* en quiebra
n bankroete beheerder *m*
d bank(e)rottgegangener Treuhänder *m*

328 bank share
f titre *m* de banque; action *f* de banque
i azione *f* bancaria
e acción *f* bancaria
n bankaandeel *n*
d Bankaktie *f*

329 bank transfer
f virement *m*
i rimessa *f* bancaria
e transferencia *f* bancaria
n bankoverboeking *f*
d Banküberweisung *f*

330 bank vault
f trésor *m*
i arche *fpl* della banca
e tesoro *m* del banco
n bankkluis *f*
d Banktresor *m*

331 bargain
f accord *m*; arrangement *m*
i accordo *m*; convenzione *f*
e convenio *m*; trato *m*
n overeenkomst *f*
d Übereinkunft *f*

332 bargain *v*
f négocier; trafiquer
i negoziare
e negociar; tratar
n handelen; onderhandelen
d handeln

333 bargain
f bonne affaire *f*
i buon affare *m*

n koopje n
d Gelegenheitskauf m

334 bargain v
f marchander
i tirare nel prezzo
e regatear
n dingen; afdingen
d den Preis herunterhandeln

335 barratry
f baraterie f
i baratteria f
e baratería f
n baraterie f
d Baratterie f

336 barren money
f fonds mpl improductifs
i denaro m improduttivo
e dinero m improductivo
n renteloze gelden npl
d unverzinsliches Geld n

337 barter
f troc m; échange m
i cambio m; baratto m
e trueque m; cambio m; negocio m de
   trueque
n ruilhandel m; ruil m
d Tausch m; Tauschhandel m

338 barter v
f échanger; troquer
i cambiare; barattare
e cambiar; trocar; hacer negocios de
   trueque
n ruilen; ruilhandel drijven
d tauschen; Tauschhandel treiben

339 base coin; counterfeit coin
f fausse monnaie f
i moneta f falsa
e moneda f falsa
n valse munt f
d falsche Münze f

340 baseline costs
f coûts mpl initiaux
i costi mpl di base
e costos mpl iniciales
n initiële kosten mpl
d Grundkosten fpl; Ausgangskosten fpl

341 base year
f année f de référence
i anno m base
e año m base

n basisjaar n
d Vergleichsjahr n

342 basic account
f compte m de base
i conto m di base
e cuenta f básica
n basisrekening f
d Grundkonto n

343 batch (US); block
f groupe m de dépôts à l'inspection
i gruppo m di depositi riuniti per controllo
e grupo m de depósitos reunidos con fines
   de control
n groep f deposito's verzameld voor
   controle-doeleinden
d Depositenstoss m für Kontrollzwecke

344 bear v
f spéculer à la baisse; jouer à la baisse
i speculare al ribasso
e especular a la baja
n speculeren à la baisse
d spekulieren auf Baisse

345 bear
f baissier m; spéculateur m à la baisse
i ribassista m; speculatore m al ribasso
e bajista m; especulador m a la baja
n baissier m; baissespeculant m; speculant
   m à la baisse
d Baissespekulant m; Baissier m

346 bear account
f compte m des spéculations à la baisse
i conto m di speculazioni al ribasso
e cuenta f de especulaciones a la baja
n baisserekening f
d Baissekonto n

347 bearer
f porteur m; titulaire m
i portatore m; latore m
e portador m; titular m
n houder m; toonder m
d Überbringer m; Inhaber m

348 bearer bond; coupon bond
f obligation f au porteur
i obbligazione f al portatore
e título m al portador
n obligatie f aan toonder
d Inhaberobligation f

349 bearer instrument
f instrument m au porteur
i documento m al portatore
e instrumento m al portador

n akte *f* aan toonder
d Inhaberpapier *n*

350 bearer securities
f titres *mpl* au porteur
i titoli *mpl* al portatore
e valores *mpl* al portador
n waardepapieren *npl* aan toonder
d Inhabereffekten *npl*

351 bear *v* interest
f porter intérêt; produire intérêt
i produrre interessi; fruttare interessi
e devengar interés; dar interés; producir interés; rendir interés
n rente dragen; rente geven; rente opbrengen
d Zinsen tragen; Zinsen bringen

352 bear market
f marché *m* baissier
i mercato *m* al ribasso
e mercado *m* bajista
n baissemarkt *f*
d Effektenmarkt *m* à la Baisse

353 bear operation
f spéculation *f* à la baisse
i speculazione *f* al ribasso
e especulación *f* a la baja
n baissespeculatie *f*; baissetransactie *f*
d Baissespekulation *f*

354 become *v* bankrupt
f faire faillite
i fallire; far(e) fallimento
e quebrar; dar quiebra; hacer bancarrota
n failliet gaan; bankroet gaan
d in Konkurs gehen; in Konkurs geraten; Bank(e)rott machen

355 beggar-my-neighbor policy
f politique *f* d'égoïsme sacré
i politica *f* di sfruttamento del vicino
e política *f* de empobrecer al vecino
n naaste-buren-armoede-politiek *f*
d Nachbarnpumpenpolitik *f*

356 beneficiary
f bénéficiaire *m*
i beneficiario *m*
e beneficiario *m*
n begunstigde *m*
d Begünstigter *m*; Benefizient *m*

357 benefit
f utilité *f*; profit *m*; gain *m*
i profitto *m*; utilità *f*; guadagno *m*
e beneficio *m*; utilidad *f*; ganancia *f*

n nut *n*; baat *f*; winst *f*
d Nutzen *m*; Gewinn *m*

358 bequeath *v*
f léguer
i legare
e legar
n vermaken; nalaten
d vermachen

359 bequeather
f testateur *m*
i testatore *m*; legatario *m*
e testador *m*
n erflater *m*
d Erblasser *m*

360 bequest
f legs *m*
i legato *m*; disposizione *f* testamentaria
e legado *m*
n legaat *n*; testamentaire beschikking *f*
d Vermächtnis *n*; Legat *n*

361 bestow *v*
f conférer; donner
i concedere; accordare
e conferir; otorgar
n schenken; verlenen
d gewähren; verleihen; geben

362 betterment levy
f prélèvement *m* sur la plus-value
i imposta *f* sul plusvalore
e impuesto *m* sobre la plusvalía
n waardevermeerderingsbelasting *f*
d Wertzuwachssteuer *m*

363 biannual
f semestriel
i semestrale
e semestral
n halfjaarlijks
d halbjährlich

364 bid *v*
f offrir
i offrire
e ofrecer; licitar
n bieden
d bieten

365 bid
f offre *f*
i offerta *f*
e oferta *f*; licitación *f*
n bod *n*; aanbod *n*; offerte *f*
d Angebot *n*; Gebot *n*

366 bid bond
f caution f de soumissionnaire
i cauzione f per concorrere a una gara
e fianza f de licitación
n opbodobligatie f
d Bietungsgarantie f; Angebotsgarantie f

367 bidder
f enchérisseur m; offrant m;
　soumissionnaire m
i offerente m
e postor m; licitante m
n bieder m; biedende m
d Bietender m

368 bidding
f offre f
i offerta f (ad un'asta)
e licitación f; postura f; oferta f
n bod n
d Gebot n

369 bidding documents
f documents mpl du marché; dossier m
　d'appel d'offres
i documenti mpl di offerta
e documentos mpl de licitación
n opboddocumenten npl
d Angebotsdokumente npl

370 bill
f compte m; facture f
i conto m; fattura f
e cuenta f; factura f
n rekening f; factuur f
d Rechnung f

371 bill
f lettre f
i cambiale f
e letra f
n wissel m
d Wechsel m

372 bill
f note f; document m; effet m
i titolo m; effetto m
e documento m
n nota f
d Dokument n

373 bill
f billet m de banque
i biglietto m di banca; banconota f
e billete m de banco
n bankbiljet n; banknoot f
d Papiergeld n; Banknote f

* **bill book → 375**

374 bill broker
f courtier m de change; agent m de
　change
i sensale m di cambio; agente m di
　cambio
e corredor m de cambios
n wisselmakelaar m
d Wechselmakler m

375 bill diary; bill book
f carnet m d'échéances
i scadenzario m
e registro m de letras
n wisselboek n
d Verfallbuch n; Wechselbuch n

376 bill for collection
f lettre f à encaisser
i cambiale f all'incasso
e letra f al cobro
n te innen wissel m
d Inkassowechsel m

377 bill holder
f porteur m d'une lettre
i possessore m di una cambiale
e tenedor m de una letra
n wisselhouder m
d Wechselinhaber m

* **bill of credit → 1516**

378 bill of debt
f billet m à ordre
i nota f di debito; lettera f di debito
e pagaré m
n schuldbrief m
d Schuldschein m; Solawechsel m;
　Schuldanerkennung f

379 bill of exchange
f lettre f de change
i cambiale f; tratta f
e letra f de cambio
n wisselbrief m; wissel m
d Wechsel m

380 bill of freight
f lettre f de voiture
i lettera f di vettura; lettera f di porto
e carta f de porte; carta f de acarreo
n vrachtbrief m; cognossement n;
　connossement n
d Frachtbrief m

381 bill of lading
f connaissement m; feuille f de
　chargement; bulletin m de chargement
i polizza f di carico

e conocimiento *m* de embarque
n vrachtbrief *m*; cognossement *n*;
  connossement *n*
d Konnossement *n*; Seefrachtbrief *m*

382 bill of quantities
f devis *m* quantitatif
i preventivo *m* di costruzione
e estimación *f* cuantitativa
n voorlopige aanslag *m*
d Voranschlag *m*

383 bill of sale
f contrat *m* de vente
i scrittura *f* di vendita
e escritura *f* de venta
n koopbrief *m*
d Kaufbrief *m*; Kaufvertrag *m*

384 bill of weight
f note *f* du poids
i nota *f* di peso
e nota *f* de peso
n gewichtslijst *f*
d Gewichtschein *m*; Gewichtsnota *f*

385 bill payable
f lettre *f* à payer
i cambiale *f* da pagare
e letra *f* a pagar
n te betalen wissel *m*
d fälliger Wechsel *m*

386 bill receivable
f effet *m* à recevoir
i effetto *m* all'incasso; cambiale *f*
  all'incasso
e letra *f* a cobrar; letra *f* al cobro
n te innen wissel *m*
d einzulösender Wechsel *m*

387 bill register; discount register
f registre *m* des lettres
i registro *m* delle cambiali
e registro *m* de letras
n wisselregister *n*
d Wechselregister *n*

388 bind *v*
f obliger; engager
i obbligare
e obligar; comprometer
n binden; verplichten
d verpflichten

389 bisque clause
f clause *f* de dérogation temporaire
i clausola *f* di derogazione provvisoria
e cláusula *f* de excepción provisional

n tijdelijke ontheffingsclausule *f*
d vorläufige Abänderungsklausel *f*

390 black bourse
f bourse *f* noire
i borsa *f* nera
e bolsa *f* negra
n zwarte beurs *f*
d schwarze Börse *f*

391 black market
f marché *m* noir
i mercato *m* nero
e mercado *m* negro; estraperlo *m*
n zwarte markt *f*
d schwarzer Markt *m*; Schwarzmarkt *m*

392 blank
f en blanc
i in bianco
e en blanco
n in blanco; blanco
d Blanko-; blanko

393 blank acceptance
f acceptation *f* en blanc
i accettazione *f* in bianco
e aceptación *f* en blanco
n blanco-accept *n*; blanco-acceptatie *f*
d Blankoakzept *n*

394 blank cheque
f chèque *m* en blanc
i assegno *m* in bianco
e cheque *m* en blanco
n blanco-cheque *m*
d Blankoscheck *m*

395 blank credit
f crédit *m* en blanc; avance *f* à découvert
i credito *m* in bianco; credito *m* allo
  scoperto
e crédito *m* en blanco; crédito *m* al
  descubierto
n blanco-krediet *n*
d Blankkredit *m*; Blankokredit *m*

396 blank endorsement
f endossement *m* en blanc
i girata *f* in bianco
e endoso *m* en blanco
n blanco-endossement *n*
d Blankoindossament *n*

397 blanket
f général; total; global
i generale; complessivo
e general; total

n overkoepelend
d General-; Gesamt-

398 blanket clause
f condition *f* générale
i clausola *f* generale
e cláusula *f* general
n overkoepelende voorwaarde *f*
d Generalklausel *f*

399 blanket mortgage
f hypothèque *f* générale
i ipoteca *f* generale
e hipoteca *f* general; hipoteca *f* colectiva
n overkoepelende hypotheek *f*
d gemeinsame Hypothek *f*

400 blank form
f formulaire *m* en blanc
i modulo *m* in bianco
e formulario *m* en blanco
n blanco-formulier *n*; oningevuld
    formulier *n*
d Blankoformular *n*

401 blank signature
f signature *f* en blanc
i firma *f* in bianco
e firma *f* en blanco
n blanco-ondertekening *f*
d Blankounterschrift *f*

402 blank transfer
f transfert *m* en blanc
i rimessa *f* in bianco
e transferencia *f* en blanco
n blanco-overdracht *m*
d Blankogiro *n*

403 blend country
f pays *m* pouvant prétendre à un
    financement mixte
i paese *m* che può ottenere finanziamenti
    combinati
e país *m* con posibilidades de
    financiamientos combinados
n land *n* met gemengde
    financieringsmogelijkheden
d Land *n* welches eine gemischte Finan-
    zierung bekommen kann

404 blend financing
f financement *m* mixte
i finanziamento *m* combinato
e financiamiento *m* combinado
n gemengde financiering *f*
d gemischte Finanzierung *f*; Misch-
    finanzierung *f*

405 block *v*
f bloquer
i bloccare
e bloquear
n blokkeren
d blockieren

* **block → 343**

406 blocked account
f compte *m* bloqué
i conto *m* bloccato
e cuenta *f* bloqueada
n geblokkeerde rekening *f*
d blockiertes Konto *n*; gesperrtes Konto *n*

407 blocked balances
f fonds *mpl* bloqués
i saldi *mpl* bloccati
e saldos *mpl* bloqueados
n geblokkeerd saldo *n*
d gesperrter Saldo *m*

408 blocked currencies
f devises *fpl* bloquées
i valute *fpl* bloccate
e divisas *fpl* bloqueadas
n geblokkeerde deviezen *npl*
d blockierte Devisen *fpl*

409 blocked funds
f fonds *mpl* bloqués
i fondi *mpl* bloccati
e fondos *mpl* bloqueados
n geblokkeerde fondsen *npl*
d blockiertes Kapital *n*; blockierte Fonds
    mpl

410 blotter *(US)*
f brouillard *m*
i brogliaccio *m*
e libro *m* borrador
n kladboek *n*
d Tageberichtsbuch *n*

**411 blue chip stock *(US)*; blue chips; gilt-
    edged securities**
f effets *mpl* très solides; titres *mpl* de
    premier ordre
i valori *mpl* solidissimi; titoli *mpl* di
    prima classe
e valores *mpl* solidísimos; títulos *mpl* de
    primera clase
n eersteklaswaardepapieren *npl*;
    goudgerande waarden *fpl*
d erstklassige Werte *mpl*; goldgeränderte
    Wertpapiere *npl*

412 board of directors
f conseil *m* d'administration
i consiglio *m* di amministrazione
e directorio *m*; consejo *m* directivo
n raad *m* van commissarissen
d Aufsichtsrat *m*

413 body corporate; corporate body
f personne *f* morale
i persona *f* giuridica
e persona *f* jurídica
n rechtspersoon *m*
d juristische Person *f*; Körperschaft *f*

414 bona fide holder; bona fide holder for value; holder for value; holder in due course
f porteur *m* de bonne foi
i titolare *m* in buona fede
e tenedor *m* en buena fe
n bona-fidehouder *m*; houder *m* te goeder trouw
d gutgläubiger Besitzer *m*

415 bond
f obligation *f*; bon *m*; titre *m*
i obbligazione *f*; buono *m*; titolo *m*
e obligación *f*; bono *m*; título *m*
n obligatie *f*; schuldbewijs *n*
d Obligation *f*; Schuldverschreibung *f*; Schuldschein *m*

416 bond
f caution *f*
i cauzione *f*
e caución *f*
n onderpand *n*; borg *m*
d Kaution *f*

417 bond creditor
f créancier *m* garanti
i creditore *m* garantito; creditore *m* con garanzia
e acreedor *m* con caución
n crediteur *m* onder borg
d garantierter Gläubiger *m*

418 bonded
f garanti par une obligation
i garantito da una obbligazione
e garantido por obligación escrita
n gedekt door obligaties
d gesichert durch Schuldverschreibung

419 bonded goods
f merchandises *fpl* entreposées en douane
i merci *fpl* in deposito doganale
e mercancías *fpl* en depósito de aduana

n goederen *npl* in douane-entrepot
d Zollagergüter *npl*

420 bonded warehouse
f entrepôt *m* de douane
i magazzino *m* doganale
e depósito *m* de aduana
n douane-entrepot *n*
d Zollager *n*

421 bond holder
f propriétaire *m* d'obligations; titulaire *m* d'obligations; obligataire *m*
i possessore *m* d'obbligazioni
e tenedor *m* de obligaciones; tenedor *m* de títulos
n obligatiehouder *m*
d Obligationsinhaber *m*; Obligationär *m*

422 bond issue
f émission *f* d'obligations; émission *f* de bons
i emissione *f* di obbligazioni
e emisión *f* de títulos; emisión *f* de bonos
n uitgifte *f* van obligaties; obligatie-emissie *f*
d Ausgabe *f* von Obligationen

423 bond of indemnity; indemnity bond
f garantie *f* d'indemnité
i garanzia *f* di indennizzo
e fianza *f* de indemnización
n garantie *f* van schadeloosstelling
d Garantie *f* auf Schadloshaltung

424 bondsman
f garant *m*; caution *f*
i garante *m*
e fiador *m*; garantia *f*
n borg *m*
d Bürge *m*

425 bonus
f gratification *f*; sursalaire *m*
i gratificazione *f*
e gratificación *f*; aguinaldo *m*; premio *m*
n gratificatie *f*; extrabetaling *f*
d Gratifikation *f*

426 bonus
f dividende *m* extraordinaire
i dividendo *m* supplementare
e dividendo *m* extraordinario
n bonus *m*; bonus-uitkering *f*; extra-uitkering *f*
d Extradividende *f*

427 bonus issue
f distribution *f* d'actions gratuites

i dividendo *m* in azioni
e dividendo *m* en acciones
n emissie *f* van gratis aandelen; uitgifte *f* van gratis aandelen
d Ausgabe *f* von Gratisaktien

428 bonus shares
  f actions *fpl* données en prime; actions *fpl* gratuites
  i azioni *fpl* di godimento
  e acciones *fpl* en premio; acciones *fpl* extraordinarias
  n bonusaandelen *npl*; gratisaandelen *npl*
  d Genussaktien *fpl*; Gratisaktien *fpl*

429 book debt
  f dette *f* comptable
  i debito *m* contabile
  e deuda *f* contabilizada
  n boekschuld *f*
  d Buchschuld *f*

430 bookkeeper
  f teneur *m* de livres; comptable *m*
  i computista *m*; ragioniere *m*; contabile *m*
  e tenedor *m* de libros
  n boekhouder *m*
  d Buchhalter *m*; Buchführer *m*

431 bookkeeping
  f comptabilité *f*; tenue *f* des livres
  i computisteria *f*; contabilità *f*
  e teneduría *f* de libros
  n boekhouding *f*; boekhouden *n*
  d Buchhaltung *f*

432 book rate of a currency
  f taux *m* comptable d'une monnaie
  i tipo *m* di cambio contabile
  e tipo *m* de cambio contable
  n boekhoudkundige deviezenkoers *m*
  d buchmässiger Devisenkurs *m*

433 book value
  f valeur *f* comptable
  i valore *m* contabile
  e valor *m* contabilizable
  n boekwaarde *f*
  d Buchwert *m*

434 boom
  f hausse *f*
  i rialzo *m*
  e auge *m*
  n hausse *f*
  d Hausse *f*

435 border taxes
  f taxation *f* aux frontières

i imposte *fpl* di frontiera
e impuestos *mpl* fronterizos
n grensbelastingen *fpl*
d Grenzsteuern *fpl*

436 borrow v
  f emprunter
  i prendere in prestito
  e tomar en préstamo; recibir en préstamo
  n lenen
  d leihen; entleihen; entlehnen; aufnehmen

437 borrower
  f emprunteur *m*
  i mutuatario *m*; prestatatorio *m*
  e prestatario *m*; el que recibe en préstamo
  n lener *m*; borger *m*
  d Entleiher *m*; Entlehner *m*

438 borrowing capacity
  f capacité *f* d'emprunt; capacité *f* d'endettement
  i capacità *f* d'indebitamento
  e capacidad *f* de endeudamiento
  n leningsbevoegdheid *f*
  d Verschuldungsfähigkeit *f*

439 bottleneck
  f goulet *m* d'étranglement
  i strangolamento *m*
  e estrangulamiento *m*; cuello *m* de botella
  n flessehals *m*
  d Engpass *m*

440 bottomry
  f bômerie *f*; prêt *m* à la grosse aventure; hypothèque *f* sur un navire
  i prestito *m* marittimo; prestito *m* alla grossa
  e préstamo *m* a la gruesa
  n bodemerij *f*
  d Bodmerei *f*; Schiffsverpfändung *f*

441 bottomry bond
  f contrat *m* à la grosse (aventure)
  i contratto *m* di prestito marittimo; contratto *m* di prestito alla grossa
  e contrato *m* de préstamo a la gruesa; contrato *m* a la gruesa
  n bodemerijbrief *m*; bodemerijwissel *m*
  d Bodmereibrief *m*

442 bourse
  f bourse *f*
  i borsa *f*
  e bolsa *f*
  n beurs *f*
  d Börse *f*; Geldmarkt *m*

443 bracket progression *(taxes)*
f progression f par tranches
i progressione f scalonata
e progresión f escalonada
n schijvenprogressie f
d gestaffelte Steuerbelastung f

444 brain drain
f exode m des cerveaux
i esodo m di cervelli
e éxodo m de cerebros; éxodo m de profesionales
n intellectuelenvlucht f
d Abwanderung f der Intellektuellen

445 branch
f succursale f; filiale f
i succursale f; filiale f
e sucursal f; filial f
n bijkantoor n; filiaal n; vestiging f
d Filiale f; Zweigstelle f; Zweiggeschäft n

* **branch bank** → 284

446 branches ledger
f registre m des succursales
i libro m mastro delle filiali
e libro m mayor de sucursales
n bijkantorengrootboek n
d Filialenhauptbuch n

447 brand
f marque f
i marca f
e marca f
n merk n
d Marke f

448 breadwinner
f soutien m de famille
i sostegno m di famiglia
e sostén m de familia
n kostwinner m
d Ernährer m

449 breakdown
f classification f; distribution f
i classificazione f; distribuzione f; ripartizione f
e desglose m; distribución f
n classificatie f; uitsplitsing f
d Aufschlüsselung f; Aufgliederung f; Analyse f

450 break-even point
f seuil m de rentabilité
i punto m di equilibrio
e punto m muerto; punto m de equilibrio

n break-even point n; dood punt n
d Nutzenschwelle f; Rentabilitätsschwelle f

451 bridge-over
f crédit m provisoire
i credito m provvisorio; credito m anticipato
e crédito m provisional
n overbruggingskrediet n
d vorläufiger Kredit m; Vorschusskredit m

452 broker
f courtier m; agent m de change
i agente m; sensale m
e corredor m
n makelaar m
d Makler m

453 brokerage
f courtage m
i senseria f; mediazione f
e corretaje m
n courtage f; makelaarsloon n; makelaardij f; makelarij f
d Courtage f; Maklergeschäft n

454 brokerage charges
f frais mpl de courtage
i spese fpl di senseria
e gastos mpl de corretaje
n makelaarskosten mpl; courtage f
d Maklergebühr f

455 bucket shop *(US)*
f officine f du coulissier marron
i borsa f illegale
e bolsa f ilegal; bolsa f clandestina; oficina f clandestina de operaciones bursátiles
n gokkantoor n; ongeregistreerd meestal fraudulent kantoor n voor handel in effecten
d Winkelbörse f

456 budget
f budget m
i bilancio m
e presupuesto m
n budget n; begroting f
d Budget n; Etat m; Spesenvoranschlag m

457 budget appropriation
f crédit m budgétaire
i assegnazione f di bilancio
e asignación f presupuestaria; crédito m presupuestario
n begrotingskrediet n; begrotingstoewijzing f
d Haushaltsbewilligung f

458 budgetary
f budgétaire
i relativo al bilancio
e presupuestal; relativo al presupuesto
n budgetair; begrotings-; budget-
d das Budget betreffend; Budgets-; Etats-

459 budgetary gap
f déficit *m* budgétaire
i deficit *m* di bilancio
e déficit *m* presupuestario
n begrotingstekort *n*
d Haushaltsdefizit *n*

460 budget surplus
f excédent *m* budgétaire
i eccedenza *f* di bilancio
e superávit *m* presupuestal; superávit *m* presupuestario
n begrotingsoverschot *n*
d Haushaltsüberschuss *m*

461 buffer fund; buffer stock *(US)*
f fonds *m* régulateur
i fondo *m* di regolazione
e fondo *m* de regulación
n bufferfonds *n*
d Pufferstock *m*; Marktausgleichslager *n*

462 buffer stock agency
f organisme *m* chargé de l'administration du fonds régulateur
i organismo *m* incaricato di amministrare il fondo regolatore
e organismo *m* administrador del fondo de regulación
n beheerkantoor *n* voor het bufferfonds
d Pufferstock-Verwaltungsamt *n*; Verwaltungsamt *n* für ein Marktausgleichslager

463 buffer stock arrangements
f dispositions *fpl* relatives au fonds régulateur
i accordi *mpl* relativi al fondo regolatore
e acuerdos *mpl* sobre fondos de regulación
n bufferfondsovereenkomsten *fpl*
d Abkommen *n* über den Pufferstock

464 buffer stock scheme
f dispositif *m* du fonds régulateur
i piano *m* dei fondi di regolazione
e plan *m* de fondos de regulación
n bufferfondsontwerp *n*
d Plan *m* des Pufferstocks; Anwendungs-schema *n* des Pufferstocks

465 bulk of profit
f profit *m* total

i profitto *m* globale
e volumen *m* de ganancias
n winsttotaal *n*
d Hauptgewinn *m*

466 bull
f haussier *m*; spéculateur *m* à la hausse
i rialzista *m*
e alcista *m*
n haussespeculant *m*; haussier *m*
d Haussespekulant *m*; Haussier *m*

467 bull buying; bull purchase *(US)*
f achat *m* à la hausse
i acquisto *m* al rialzo; compera *f* al rialzo
e compra *f* de alcista
n hausse-aankoop *m*; koop *m* in verwachting van hausse
d Hausseankauf *m*

468 bullion
f barres *fpl* d'or ou d'argent; or *m* ou argent *m* en barres
i oro *m* ed argento *m* in verghe
e oro *m* en tejos y plata *f* en lingotes; oro *m* y plata *f* sin acuñar
n staafgoud *n*; staafzilver *n*; goud *n* en zilver *n* in staven; ongemunt goud *n* en zilver *n*
d Gold- und Silberbarren *fpl*; unge-münztes Gold *n* und Silber *n*

* **bullion points** → 1297

469 bullish
f à la hausse
i che ha tendenza al rialzo
e en alza
n met stijgende tendens
d in Hausse

470 bullish tendency
f tendance *f* à la hausse
i tendenza *f* al rialzo
e tendencia *f* al alza
n haussetendens *f*; haussebeweging *f*; tendens *f* tot stijgen
d Haussestimmung *f*; Haussetendenz *f*

471 bull market
f marché *m* haussier
i mercato *m* in rialzo
e mercado *m* alcista
n haussemarkt *f*
d Börse *f* in der Hausse; Haussebörse *f*

* **bull purchase** *(US)* → 467

472 buoyant demand
 f haute conjoncture f
 i domanda f attiva
 e demanda f intensa
 n levendige vraag f
 d starke Nachfrage f; steigende Nachfrage f

* **burden** v → 2290

473 burdened with mortgages
 f grevé d'hypothèques
 i gravato di ipoteche
 e gravado con hipotecas
 n belast met hypotheken; bezwaard met hypotheken
 d belastet mit Hypotheken

474 burden v with taxes
 f grever d'impôts
 i gravare da imposte
 e gravar con impuestos
 n belasten; belasting leggen op; belasting heffen van
 d belegen mit Steuern; besteuern

475 burglary insurance
 f assurance f contre le vol avec effraction; assurance f contre le cambriolage
 i assicurazione f contro il furto
 e seguro m contra robos
 n inbraakverzekering f; verzekering f tegen inbraak
 d Diebstahlversicherung f; Einbruchsversicherung f

476 business
 f affaires fpl; affaire f; commerce m
 i affari mpl; commercio m
 e negocios mpl; negocio m; comercio m
 n zaken fpl; zaak f; bedrijf n
 d Geschäft n; Handel m; Handelsbetrieb m

477 business account
 f compte m d'affaires
 i conto m d'affari; conto m di negozi
 e cuenta f de negocios
 n zakenrekening f
 d Geschäftskonto n

478 business community
 f milieux mpl d'affaires
 i circoli mpl impresariali; centro m d'affari
 e medios mpl empresariales
 n handelsgemeenschap f
 d Handelskreise mpl

479 business cycle
 f cycle m économique
 i ciclo m economico; ciclo m d'affari
 e ciclo m económico
 n conjunctuurcyclus m
 d Konjunkturzyklus m

480 business day
 f jour m ouvrable
 i giorno m lavorativo
 e día m hábil; día m laborable
 n werkdag m
 d Werktag m

481 businessman
 f homme m d'affaires
 i uomo m d'affari
 e hombre m de negocios; comerciante m
 n zakenman m
 d Geschäftsmann m

482 business transaction
 f opération f commerciale
 i transazione f comerciale
 e transacción f comercial
 n handelstransactie f
 d Geschäftsabschluss m

483 buy v
 f acheter
 i comprare
 e comprar
 n kopen
 d kaufen

484 buyer
 f acheteur m
 i compratore m
 e comprador m
 n koper m
 d Käufer m

485 buyers' credit
 f crédit-acheteur m
 i credito m ai compratori
 e crédito m de compradores
 n koperskrediet m
 d Käuferkredit m

486 buyers' market
 f marché m favorable à l'acheteur
 i mercato m favorevole ai compratori
 e mercado m de compradores
 n kopersmarkt f
 d Käufermarkt m

487 buy v for cash
 f acheter au comptant
 i comperare a contanti

 e comprar al contado
 n contant kopen; kopen tegen contante
  betaling
 d kaufen gegen bar

488 buy *v* for the rise
 f spéculer à la hausse
 i speculare al rialzo
 e especular al alza; jugar al alza
 n speculeren à la hausse
 d spekulieren auf Hausse

489 buying rate of exchange
 f taux *m* d'achat
 i tasso *m* per la compera di valute
 e tipo *m* de compra de divisas
 n aankoopkoers *m*
 d Ankaufskurs *m*

490 by-laws
 f règlement *m*
 i regolamenti *mpl*
 e reglamento *m*
 n reglement *n*; verordening *f*
 d Reglement *n*; Verordnung *f*

C

491 **cable transfer; telegraphic transfer**
f virement m télégraphique
i trasferimento m per cablogramma
e transferencia f cablegráfica
n telegrafische overmaking f; telegrafische
overboeking f
d Kabelauszahlung f

492 **calculate** v
f calculer
i calcolare
e calcular
n rekenen; berekenen
d rechnen; berechnen; ausrechnen;
kalkulieren

493 **calculation**
f calcul m
i calcolo m; calcolazione f
e cálculo m
n berekening f; rekening f; calculatie f
d Berechnung f; Ausrechnung f;
Kalkulation f

494 **calendar**
f calendrier m
i calendario m
e calendario m; almanaque m
n kalender m
d Kalender m

495 **calender year**
f année f civile
i anno m civile
e año m civil
n kalenderjaar n
d Kalenderjahr n

496 **call** v
f exiger
i richiamare
e exigir; demandar
n vorderen; opeisen
d fordern; auffordern

497 **call**
f appel m; convocation f
i chiamata f; convocazione f
e llamado m
n appel n
d Appell m; Aufruf m

498 **call**
f demande f; réclamation f
i domanda f
e solicitud f; demanda f

n sommatie f; vordering f
d Antrag m; Forderung f

499 **call** v **in a loan**
f demander le remboursement d'un prêt
i esigere il rimborso di un prestito
e exigir el reembolso de un préstamo
n een lening opzeggen
d einen Kredit kündigen

500 **call loan**
f emprunt m (payable) sur demande; prêt
m sur demande; emprunt m à courte
échéance
i prestito m pagabile a richiesta; prestito
m a breve scadenza
e préstamo m pagadero a solicitud;
préstamo m pagadero a corto plazo
n daggeldlening f; lening f op korte
termijn
d kündbares Darlehen n; kurzfristiges Darlehen n

501 **call money; money at call; day-to-day
money; demand loan**
f argent m au jour le jour
i denaro m a breve
e dinero m pagadero a corto plazo; dinero
m pagadero a solicitud
n daggeld n; callgeld n
d tägliches Geld n; Geld n auf Aufruf

502 **call rate**
f taux m d'intérêt sur les prêts à courte
échéance
i tasso m d'interesse su prestiti a breve
scadenza
e tasa f de interés sobre préstamos a corto
plazo
n rentetarief n van direct opvorderbaar
geld
d Zinssatz m für Tagesgeld; Tagesgeldzins-
satz m

503 **cambist**
f cambiste m
i cambista m
e cambista m
n geldwisselaar m
d Geldwechsler m

504 **cancel** v
f annuler
i cancellare; annullare
e cancelar; anular
n annuleren
d annullieren; streichen

505 cancellation
f annulation f; résiliation f
i cancellazione f; annullamento m
e cancelación f; anulación f
n annulering f
d Annullierung f

506 cancelled debt
f dette f annulée
i debito m cancellato
e deuda f anulada
n geannuleerde schuld f
d annullierte Schuld f

507 capital; principal
f capital m
i capitale m
e capital m
n kapitaal n; hoofdsom f
d Kapital n

508 capital account
f compte-capital m; compte m de capital
i conto m di capitale
e cuenta f de capital
n kapitaalrekening f
d Kapitalkonto n

509 capital assets
f biens mpl de capital
i beni mpl di capitale
e bienes mpl de capital
n vaste activa npl; vastliggend kapitaal n
d Kapitalvermögen n; Anlagevermögen n;
   Kapitalanlagegüter npl

510 capital budget
f budget m d'équipement; budget m
   d'investissement
i bilancio m di capitale
e presupuesto m de capital
n investeringsbegroting f;
   kapitaalbegroting f
d Investitionsrechnung f

511 capital cost
f dépense f d'investissement
i costo m di investimento
e costo m de inversión
n kapitaalkosten mpl
d Investitionskosten fpl

512 capital deepening
f intensification f du capital
i aumento m del rapporto capital-lavoro
e aumento m de la relación capital-trabajo
n verhoging f van de verhouding kapitaal-
   werk
d Kapitalerweiterung f

513 capital efficiency
f productivité f du capital
i produttività f del capitale
e productividad f del capital
n productiviteit f van het kapitaal
d Leistungsfähigkeit f des Kapitals

514 capital equipment
f biens mpl de capital; biens mpl
   d'équipement
i beni mpl di capitale
e bienes mpl de capital; bienes mpl de
   equipo
n kapitaalgoederen npl
d Kapitalgüter npl

515 capital expenditure
f dépense f d'investissement
i spese fpl di capitale
e gastos mpl de capital; inversión f en
   capital fijo
n kapitaaluitgave f
d Kapitalausgaben fpl

516 capital flight; drain of bullion
f fuite f de capitaux; exode m de capitaux;
   évasion f de capitaux
i fuga f di capitali; esodo m di capitali
e fuga f de capitales; evasión f de capitales
n kapitaalvlucht f
d Kapitalflucht f; Kapitalabwanderung f

517 capital flow
f flux m de capital; mouvement m de
   capital
i flusso m di capitale
e corriente f de capital; flujo m de capital
n kapitaalverplaatsing f
d Kapitalfluss m; Kapitalbewegung f

518 capital formation
f formation f de capital
i formazione f di capitale
e formación f de capital
n kapitaalvorming f
d Kapitalbildung f

519 capital gain
f gain m en capital; plus-value f
i guadagno m di capitale
e incremento m de capital; ganancia f de
   capital
n kapitaalwinst f; vermogensaanwas m
d Kapitalgewinn m

520 capital gains tax
f impôt m sur le gain en capital; impôt m
   sur les plus-values
i imposta f sull' aumento del capitale

e impuesto *m* sobre las ganancias de
capital; impuesto *m* sobre la plusvalía de
capital
n kapitaalwinstbelasting *f*; vermogens-
aanwasbelasting *f*
d Kapitalgewinnsteuer *f*; Kapitalzuwachs-
steuer *f*

521 capital goods
f biens *mpl* d'équipement
i beni *mpl* di equipaggiamento
e bienes *mpl* de equipo
n investeringsgoederen *npl*;
kapitaalgoederen *npl*
d Investitionsgüter *npl*; Kapitalgüter *npl*

* **capital inflow** → 1393

522 capital intensity
f intensité *f* de capital
i intensità *f* del capitale
e intensidad *f* de capital
n kapitaalintensiteit *f*
d Kapitalstärke *f*; Kapitalintensität *f*

523 capital-intensive
f capitalistique
i capitalistico; con uso intensivo di capitale
e con gran intensidad de capital; con uso
intensivo de capital
n kapitaalintensief
d kapitalintensiv

524 capitalist
f capitaliste *m*
i capitalista *m*
e capitalista *m*
n kapitalist *m*; kapitaalbezitter *m*
d Kapitalist *m*

525 capitalization
f capitalisation *f*
i capitalizzazione *f*
e capitalización *f*
n kapitalisatie *f*
d Kapitalisierung *f*

526 capitalize *v*
f capitaliser
i capitalizzare
e capitalizar
n kapitaliseren
d kapitalisieren

527 capitalized value
f valeur *f* capitalisée
i valore *m* capitalizzato
e valor *m* capitalizado

n gekapitaliseerde waarde *f*
d kapitalisierter Wert *m*

528 capital-labor ratio
f rapport *m* capital-travail
i relazione *f* capitale-lavoro
e relación *f* capital-trabajo
n verhouding *f* tussen kapitaal en
arbeidskracht
d Verhältnis *n* zwischen Kapital und
Arbeitskraft

529 capital levy
f prélèvement *m* sur le capital
i imposta *f* sul capitale
e impuesto *m* sobre el capital
n kapitaalheffing *f*
d Kapitalsteuer *f*

530 capital loss
f perte *f* en capital; moins-value *f*
i perdita *f* di capitale
e pérdida *f* de capital
n kapitaalverlies *n*
d Kapitalverlust *f*

531 capital market
f marché *m* des capitaux
i mercato *m* dei capitali
e mercado *m* de capitales
n kapitaalmarkt *f*
d Kapitalmarkt *m*

532 capital movements
f mouvements *mpl* de capitaux
i movimenti *mpl* di capitale
e movimientos *mpl* de capital
n kapitaalbewegingen *fpl*;
kapitaalomzet *m*
d Kapitalverkehr *m*; Kapitalbewegungen
fpl

533 capital outlays
f dépenses *fpl* d'équipement
i investimenti *mpl* in beni di capitale;
sborso *m* di capitali
e inversiones *fpl* en bienes de capital;
desembolsos *mpl* de capital
n kapitaaluitgaven *fpl*; investering *f* in
kapitaalgoederen
d Investitionen *fpl*; Kapitalaufwand *m*

534 capital-output ratio
f coefficient *m* d'intensité de capital
i relazione *f* capitale-produzione
e relación *f* capital-producto
n kapitaal-omzet-verhouding *f*
d Kapitalkoeffizient *m*

535 capital reserve
f réserve f de capital
i riserva f di capitale
e reserva f de capital
n kapitaalreserve f
d Kapitalreserve f

* **capital stock** *(US)* → **2160**

536 capital stock of a nation
f capital m national
i capitale m nazionale
e capital m nacional
n nationaal vermogen n
d Staatskapital n

537 capital structure
f structure f financière
i struttura f del capitale
e estructura f de capital
n kapitaalstructuur f
d Kapitalstruktur f; Kapitalzusammen-
setzung f

538 capital supply
f offre f de capitaux
i somministrazione f di capitale; offerta f
di capitale
e oferta f de capital
n kapitaalaanbod n
d Kapitalangebot n

539 capital surplus
f excédent m de capital
i eccedenza f di capitale
e excedente m de capital
n kapitaaloverschot n; kapitaalsurplus n
d Kapitalüberschuss m

540 capital transactions
f transactions fpl de capital
i transazioni fpl in capitali
e transacciones fpl de capital
n kapitaalverkeer n
d Kapitalverkehr m

541 capital transfer
f transfert m de capital
i trasferimento m di capitali
e transferencia f de capital
n kapitaaloverdracht f
d Kapitalübertragung f

542 capital turnover
f circulation f des capitaux; rotation f des
capitaux
i giro m dei capitali
e giro m del capital

n kapitaalomzet m
d Kapitalumsatz m

543 capitation; poll tax
f impôt m personnel; impôt m de
capitation
i imposta f di capitazione
e impuesto m de capitación; capitación f
n hoofdgeld n; premie f per hoofd;
hoofdelijke belasting f
d Kopfsteuer f

544 carat
f carat m
i carato m
e quilate m
n karaat n
d Karat n

545 carrying cost of capital
f coût m d'inactivité de capitaux
i costo m di inattività di capitale
e costo m de inactividad del capital
n kosten mpl van braakliggend kapitaal
d Kosten fpl brachliegenden Kapitals

546 carry v over
f transférer
i riportare
e trasladar; pasar a otra cuenta
n overbrengen; transporteren
d übertragen; Übertrag m machen

547 cash
f caisse f
i cassa f
e caja f
n kas f
d Kasse f

548 cash v
f toucher; encaisser
i incassare
e cobrar; hacer efectivo
n innen; incasseren
d einkassieren; einlösen

549 cash
f argent m comptant
i contante m
e dinero m contante
n gereed geld n; contanten npl
d Bargeld n

550 cash v
f changer
i cambiare
e cambiar

n wisselen; verzilveren
d wechseln

551 cash
f au comptant
i in contanti; per contanti
e al contado
n contant; in baar
d bar

552 cash account
f compte m de caisse
i conto m (di) cassa
e cuenta f de caja
n kasrekening f
d Kassenkonto n; Kassakonto n

553 cash account
f crédit m
i credito m
e crédito m
n krediet n
d Kredit m

554 cash balance
f solde m de trésorerie; liquidités fpl en caisse; encaisse f
i saldo m di cassa
e saldo m de caja
n kassaldo n
d Kassenbestand m

555 cash basis accounting
f comptabilité f de gestion; comptabilité f de caisse
i contabilità f basata sul criterio di registro di cassa; contabilità f di gestione di cassa
e contabilidad f según el criterio de registro de caja
n kasregisterboekhouding f
d kassenbasierte Buchführung f

556 cash bonus
f dividende m supplémentaire en espèces
i dividendo m supplementare
e dividendo m extraordinario en efectivo
n extra-uitkering f in contanten
d Extrabarausschüttung f

557 cash book
f livre m de caisse; journal m de caisse
i libro m di cassa; giornale m di cassa
e libro m de caja
n kasboek n
d Kassenbuch n

558 cash budget
f budget m de gestion; budget m de

trésorerie
i bilancio m di cassa
e presupuesto m de caja
n kasbegroting f
d Kassenbudget m

559 cash credit
f crédit m à la caisse
i credito m di cassa
e crédito m de caja
n kaskrediet n
d Kassenkredit m

560 cash crop
f culture f de rapport; culture f commerciale
i coltivazione f commerciale
e cultivo m comercial
n handelsbevordering f; handelsteelt m
d Handelspflege f

561 cash deficit
f déficit m de trésorerie; découvert m de trésorerie
i deficit m di cassa
e déficit m de caja
n kasdeficit n; kastekort n
d Kassendefizit n

562 cash discount
f escompte m au comptant
i sconto m per pronta cassa
e descuento m de caja; descuento m para pago al contado
n korting f voor contante betaling
d Kassaskonto m; Barrabatt m

563 cash flow
f marge f brute
i flusso m di fondi
e corriente f de fondos; flujo m de fondos
n cashflow m
d Kapitalfluss m

564 cash holdings
f avoirs mpl en caisse; avoirs mpl en numéraire
i effettivo m in cassa
e efectivo m en caja
n kasgeld n
d Barmittel npl; Barbestand m

565 cashier *(US)*
f haut fonctionnaire m de banque
i alto impiegato m di banca
e alto funcionario m de banco
n hoge bankfunctionaris m
d höherer Bankangestellter m

566 cashier *(GB)*
f caissier *m*
i cassiere *m*
e cajero *m*
n kassier *m*
d Kassierer *m*

567 cashier's book
f livre *m* de caisse
i libro *m* di cassa
e libro *m* del cajero
n kasboek *n*; kassiersboek *n*
d Kassabuch *n*; Kassenbuch *n*

568 cash income
f revenu *m* monétaire
i entrata *f* monetaria
e ingresos *mpl* monetarios
n kasinkomsten *fpl*
d Bareinkommen *n*

569 cash on delivery
f livraison *f* contre remboursement
i pagamento *m* contro consegna
e entrega *f* contra reembolso
n levering *f* tegen contante betaling
d Lieferung *f* gegen Nachnahme des
   Betrages

570 cash order
f commande *f* à paiement comptant
i ordine *m* per pagamento in contanti
e orden *f* al contado; pedido *m* al contado
n bestelling *f* à contant
d Auftrag *m* mit sofortiger Barzahlung;
   Barzahlungsauftrag *m*

571 cash payment
f paiement *m* comptant
i pagamento *m* per contanti; pagamento
   m a pronta cassa
e pago *m* al contado
n contante betaling *f*
d Barzahlung *f*; sofortige Zahlung *f*

572 cash position
f argent *m* en caisse
i effettivo *m* in cassa; consistenza *f* in
   cassa; cassa *f*
e dinero *m* efectivo en caja
n kaspositie *f*; beschikbare contanten *npl*
d Kassenbestand *m*; Barbestand *m*;
   Kassa *f*

573 cash projections
f projections *fpl* de trésorerie
i calcolo *m* del flusso di fondi
e proyección *f* del flujo de fondos
n cashflow-projectie *f*

d Berechnung *f* von Kapitalfluss;
   Voraussicht *f* von Kapitalfluss

574 cash register
f caisse *f* enregistreuse
i registratore *m* di cassa
e caja *f* registradora
n kasregister *n*
d Registrierkasse *f*

575 cash reserve
f réserves *fpl* d'argent liquide
i riserva *f* in contanti
e reserva *f* en efectivo
n kasreserve *f*; contante reserve *f*
d bare Reserve *f*; Kassenreserve *f*

576 cash shorts and overs
f différences *fpl* de caisse
i deficit *m* ed eccedenze *f* di cassa
e déficit *m* y excedentes *mpl* de caja
n kasverschillen *npl*
d Kassendefizit *n* und Kassenüber-
   schuss *m*

577 cash surrender value
f valeur *f* de rachat au comptant
i valore *m* di ricupero in contanti
e valor *m* de rescate al contado
n afkoopwaarde *f*
d Barrückkaufwert *m*

578 caution
f caution *f*
i cauzione *f*
e caución *f*; garantía *f*
n cautie *f*; borgtocht *m*
d Kaution *f*; Bürgschaft *f*

579 cautioner
f garant *m*; répondant *m*
i mallevadore *m*; garante *m*; avvallante *m*
e fiador *m*; garante *m*
n borgsteller *m*; borg *m*
d Bürge *m*

580 ceiling
f plafond *m*
i livello *m* massimo; limite *m* massimo
e tope *m*; límite *m* máximo
n plafond *n*
d Höchstgrenze *f*; Limit *n*

581 ceiling price
f prix *m* plafond
i prezzo *m* massimo
e precio *m* tope; máximo *m*
n maximum prijs *m*
d Höchstpreis *m*

582 central bank
f banque f centrale
i banca f centrale
e banco m central
n centrale bank f
d Zentralbank f

583 centrally planned economy
f économie f planifiée
i economia f centralizzata; economia f
  pianificata
e economía f de planificación centralizada
n centraal geplande economie f
d Zentralverwaltungswirtschaft f

584 central rate
f taux m central
i tipo m di cambio centrale
e tipo m de cambio central
n middenkoers m
d Leitkurs m

585 certificate
f certificat m; attestation f
i certificato m; attestato m
e certificado m
n certificaat n; verklaring f
d Bescheinigung f; Zeugnis n; Zertifikat n

586 certificated bankrupt
f failli m concordataire
i fallito m riabilitato; fallito m risolto da
  un concordato
e fallido m rehabilitado
n gerehabiliteerd bankroetier m
d rehabilitierter Bankrottierer m

587 certificate of deposit
f certificat m de dépôt
i certificato m di deposito
e certificado m de depósito
n depositocertificaat n
d Depositenschein m

588 certificate of insurance
f certificat m d'assurance
i certificato m di assicurazione
e certificado m de seguro
n verzekeringscertificaat n
d Versicherungsurkunde f

589 certificate of protest
f certificat m de protêt
i certificato m di protesto
e certificado m de protesto
n certificaat n van protest
d Protestschein m; Protesturkunde f

* **certificate of stock** → **2161**

590 certification of transfer
f certification f de transfert
i certificato m di rimessa
e certificado m de transferencia
n verklaring f van overmaking
d Überweisungsausweis m

591 certified bill of lading
f connaissement m certifié
i polizza f d'imbarco certificata
e conocimiento m de embarque certificado
n gecertificeerd connossement n
d beglaubigtes Konnossement n

592 certified cheque
f chèque m visé
i assegno m approvato; assegno m
  raccomandato
e cheque m certificado
n gewaarmerkte cheque m
d beglaubigter Scheck m

593 certify v
f certifier
i certificare
e certificar
n garanderen; certificeren; schriftelijk
  verklaren; attesteren
d bescheinigen; beglaubigen; beurkunden

594 cession
f cession f; abandon m
i cessione f
e cesión f; traspaso m
n cessie f; afstand m
d Abtretung f; Zession f; Überlassung f;
  Verzicht m

595 cessionary
f cessionnaire m
i cessionario m
e cesionario m
n cessionaris m
d Zessionär m; Übernehmer m (eines abge-
  tretenen Rechts)

596 chain banking
f système m de banques associées
i sistema m di banche associate
e sistema m de bancos associados
n systeem n van aangesloten banken
d Zusammenschluss m von Banken;
  Kettenbankwesen n

597 change v
f changer
i cambiare
e cambiar
n wisselen; omwisselen

d wechseln; tauschen; austauschen; vertauschen

598 change
f monnaie *f*
i moneta *f* spicciola
e cambio *m*; calderilla *f*; vuelto *m*
n kleingeld *n*; wisselgeld *n*
d Kleingeld *n*; Wechselgeld *n*

599 charge *v*
f débiter; passer au débit; mettre au compte; charger
i addebitare; mettere in conto
e debitar; poner en cuenta; cargar
n debiteren; in rekening brengen; belasten
d debitieren; in Rechnung stellen; belasten; anschreiben

600 charge account
f compte *m* d'achats au crédit
i conto *m* (di) acquisti a credito
e cuenta *f* de compras a crédito
n rekening *f* voor inkopen op krediet
d Anschreibungskonto *n*

601 charge(s)
f coût *m*
i costi *mpl*
e costo *m*
n kosten *mpl*
d Kosten *fpl*; Spesen *fpl*

602 charge(s)
f débit *m*
i addebito *m*
e débito *m*
n debet *n*
d Debet *n*

* **charge ticket** → **871**

603 charter
f affrètement *m*
i noleggio *m*
e fletamento *m*
n charter *n*
d Befrachtung *f*

604 charter *v*
f affréter; fréter; noliser
i noleggiare
e fletar
n charteren
d befrachten; chartern

605 chartered bank
f banque *f* privilégiée
i banca *f* privilegiata

e banco *m* con privilegios
n monopoliebank *f*
d privilegierte Bank *f*; konzessionierte Bank *f*

606 charter party
f contrat *m* d'affrètement; charte-partie *f*
i contratto *m* di noleggio
e contrato *m* de fletamento
n chertepartij *f*; chartercontract *n*
d Chartepartie *f*; Frachtvertrag *m*

607 chattel mortgage *(US)*
f hypothèque *f* mobilière
i ipoteca *f* su beni mobili
e hipoteca *f* sobre bienes muebles
n hypotheek *f* op roerende goederen
d Mobiliarhypothek *f*

608 chattels
f biens *mpl* meubles
i beni mobili *mpl*; mobili *mpl*
e bienes *mpl* muebles
n roerend bezit *n*; roerende goederen *npl*
d bewegliche Güter *npl*; Mobilien *fpl*

609 cheap money
f argent *m* à bon marché
i denaro *m* a basso interesse
e dinero *m* barato
n goedkoop geld *n*
d billiges Geld *n*

610 check *v*
f contrôler; vérifier
i controllare; verificare
e controlar; fiscalizar; verificar
n controleren
d kontrollieren; nachprüfen; überprüfen

* **check** *(US)* → **612**

* **checking account** *(US)* → **820**

611 checking deposit
f dépôt *m* à vue
i deposito *m* a vista
e depósito *m* a la vista; depósito *m* en cuenta corriente
n zichtdeposito *n*; rekening-courant-deposito *n*
d Sichteinlagen *fpl*; Kontokorrenteinlagen *fpl*

612 cheque *(GB)*; **check** *(US)*
f chèque *m*
i assegno *m*
e cheque *m*

n cheque *m*
d Scheck *m*; Bankweisung *f*

613 cheque book
f carnet *m* de chèques; chéquier *m*
i libretto *m* (di) assegni
e libreta *f* de cheques; talonario *m* de cheques
n chequeboek *n*
d Scheckbuch *n*

614 cheque ledger
f grand livre *m* de mouvement de chèques
i libro *m* mastro di controllo
e libro *m* de registro de cheques
n chequegrootboek *n*
d Scheckhauptbuch *n*

615 cheque rate
f cours *m* pour les chèques
i cambio *m* per gli assegni
e cotización *f* para cheques
n chequekoers *m*
d Scheckkurs *m*; Umrechnungskurs *m* für Schecks

616 cheque register
f registre *m* des chèques
i registro *m* degli assegni
e registro *m* de cheques
n chequeregister *n*
d Scheckeingangsbuch *n*

617 cheque stub
f talon *m* de chèque
i talloncino *m*
e talón *m* de cheque
n chequetalon *m*
d Schecktalon *m*

618 cheque to bearer
f chèque *m* au porteur
i assegno *m* al portatore
e cheque *m* al portador
n cheque *m* aan toonder
d Inhaberscheck *m*; Überbringerscheck *m*

619 chink *(pop.)*
f fric *m*
i denaro *m*
e plata *f*
n centen *mpl*
d Moneten *fpl*

620 c.i.f.
f c.i.f.; coût, fret et assurance
i c.i.f.; costo, assicurazione e nolo
e c.i.f.; costo, seguros y flete

n c.i.f.; kostprijs, verzekering en vracht
d c.i.f.; Kosten, Versicherung, Fracht

621 circular capital
f capital *m* circulant; capital *m* flottant
i capitale *m* circolante
e capital *m* circulante; capital *m* en giro
n werkkapitaal *n*
d Umlaufskapital *n*

* **circular cheques** → 2339

622 circular flow
f flux *m* circulaire; circuit *m*
i flusso *m* circolare
e corriente *f* circular
n circulaire geldstroom *m*
d Zirkulargeldfluss *m*

* **circular notes** → 2339

623 circulation
f circulation *f*
i circolazione *f*
e circulación *f*
n omloop *m*
d Umlauf *m*

624 civil service
f fonction *f* publique
i amministrazione *f* pubblica
e administración *f* pública
n ambtelijke dienst *m*; overheidsdienst *m*
d Staatsverwaltungsdienst *m*

625 claim *v*
f réclamer
i reclamare; richiamare
e reclamar
n vorderen; opeisen; eisen; aanspraak maken op
d fordern; beanstanden; reklamieren; Anspruch erheben auf

626 claim
f réclamation *f*; demande *f*
i reclamo *m*; richiesta *f*
e reclamo *m*; reclamación *f*
n vordering *f*; eis *m*
d Forderung *f*; Beanstandung *f*; Anspruch *m*

627 claimable
f exigible; revendicable
i che può essere reclamato
e reclamable
n vorderbaar; opeisbaar
d reklamierbar; einzufordernd

628 claim adjuster; adjuster
f répartiteur *m* d'avaries
i tassatore *m* di danni
e tasador *m* de daños; tasador *m* de
  averías
n schadeopnemer *m*; schadebepaler *m*;
  schatter *m* van averij
d Schadenschätzer *m*; Scha-
  denregulierer *m*; Havariesachverstän-
  diger *m*

629 clean acceptance
f acceptation *f* pure et simple
i accettazione *f* incondizionata
e aceptación *f* absoluta
n onvoorwaardelijke acceptatie *f*
d absolutes Akzept *n*; bedingungsloses
  Akzept *n*

630 clean bill of lading
f connaissement *m* sans réserves
i polizza *f* di carico netta (senza riserve)
e conocimiento *m* de embarque sin
  restricciones; conocimiento *m* limpio
n schoon connossement *n*; onbeperkt
  connossement *n*
d reines Konnossement *n*; echtes
  Konnossement *n*

631 clean credit
f crédit *m* sans réserve
i credito *m* incondizionato
e crédito *m* simple; crédito *m* sin
  condiciones
n krediet *n* zonder beperking
d bedingungsloser Kredit *m*

632 clean draft
f traite *f* sans réserve
i cambiale *f* incondizionata
e letra *f* sin condiciones; giro *m* simple
n wissel *m* zonder beperking
d Wechsel *m* ohne Dokumentensicherung

633 clean letter of credit
f lettre *f* de crédit sans réserve
i lettera *f* di credito incondizionata
e carta *f* de crédito simple
n kredietbrief *m* zonder beperking
d Kreditbrief *m* ohne Dokumentensicherung

634 clear v
f dédouaner
i sdoganare
e despachar (en la aduana)
n uitklaren
d klarieren; verzollen

635 clear v
f liquider des dettes; acquitter des dettes
i liquidare conti
e liquidar cuentas
n vereffenen; verrekenen; clearen
d verrechnen

636 clearance
f dédouanement *m*; dédouanage *m*
i sdoganamento *m*
e despacho *m* de aduana
n inklaring *f*
d Verzollung *f*; Zollabfertigung *f*

637 clear annuity
f annuité *f* sans impôts
i annualità *f* esente da tasse
e anualidad *f* libre de impuestos
n belastingvrije annuïteit *f*
d steuerfreie Annuität *f*

638 clearing
f liquidation *f* de comptes; règlement *m*
  de comptes
i clearing *m*; operazione *f* di
  compensazione; operazione *f* di clearing
e liquidación *f* de balances; clearing *m*
n clearing *f*; vereffening *f*; onderlinge
  verrekening *f*
d Clearing *n*; Clearing-Verkehr *m*

**639 clearing agreement; clearing
  arrangement**
f accord *m* de compensation
i accordo *m* di compensazione
e convenio *m* de liquidación; convenio *m*
  de compensación
n clearingovereenkomst *f*; compensatie-
  overeenkomst *f*
d Verrechnungsabkommen *n*; Clearing-
  Abkommen *n*

640 clearing bank
f banque *f* de compensation
i banca *f* di compensazione
e banco *m* de compensación
n clearingbank *f*
d Clearing-Bank *f*

641 clearing facilities
f mécanisme *m* de compensation
i sistema *m* di compensazione
e sistema *m* de compensación
n clearingsysteem *n*
d Clearing-Verkehr-System *n*; Clearing-
  System *n*

642 clearing house
f chambre *f* de compensation; office *m* de

compensation
i stanza *f* di compensazione; camera *f* di
compensazione
e cámara *f* de compensación
n clearingkantoor *n*
d Clearing-Haus *n*; Clearing-Stelle *f*; Ver-
rechnungsstelle *f*

643 clearing sale
f vente *f* de liquidation; liquidation *f*
i vendita *f* di liquidazione; liquidazione *f*
e venta *f* de liquidación; liquidación *f*
n uitverkoop *m*; liquidatie *f*
d Ausverkauf *m*; Liquidation *f*

644 clear profit
f bénéfice *m* net
i guadagno *m* netto
e beneficio *m* liquido; ganancia *f* neta
n nettowinst *f*
d Nettogewinn *m*

645 clear value
f valeur *f* nette
i valore *m* netto
e valor *m* neto
n nettowaarde *f*
d Nettowert *m*

646 close corporation
f société *f* privée
i società *f* i cui dirigenti soni i padroni
delle azioni
e sociedad *f* cuyos dirigentes poseen todas
las acciones
n gesloten naamloze vennootschap *f*
d Privat-Aktiengesellschaft *f*; geschlossene
Aktiengesellschaft *f*

647 closed economy
f économie *f* fermée
i economia *f* chiusa
e economía *f* cerrada
n besloten economie *f*
d geschlossener Markt *m*

648 closed-end investment company
f société *f* d'investissement à capital fixe
i società *f* di investimenti con portafoglio
composto fisso
e sociedad *f* de inversión con cartera de
composición fija
n beleggingsmaatschappij *f* met vast
kapitaal
d Investitionsgesellschaft *f* mit festem
Kapital

649 closed mortgage
f hypothèque *f* purgée

i ipoteca *f* liquidata
e hipoteca *f* cancelada; hipoteca *f* cerrada
n afgeloste hypotheek *f*
d eingelöste Hypothek *f*

650 closing date
f date *f* de clôture
i data *f* di chiusura
e fecha *f* de cierre
n sluitingsdatum *m*
d Schlusstag *m*

651 closing price
f cours *m* de clôture
i prezzo *m* di chiusura; quotazione *f* di
chiusura
e precio *m* de cierre; cotización *f* de
cierre; cotización *f* al cierre
n slotprijs *m*
d Schlusspreis *m*; Schlusskurs *m*; Schlussnotierung *f*

652 closing quotation
f cote *f* de clôture
i quotazione *f* di chiusura
e cotización *f* de cierre
n slotnotering *f*
d Schlussnotierung *f*

* **cocreditor** → **1474**

653 coded account
f compte *m* codifié
i conto *m* codificato
e cuenta *f* codificada
n code-rekening *f*; gecodeerde rekening *f*
d kodifiziertes Konto *n*; kodiertes Konto *n*

654 cognovit note *(US)*
f reconnaissance *f* formelle d'une dette
i riconoscimento *m* formale di un debito
e reconocimiento *m* formal de una deuda
n formele schuldbekentenis *f*
d schriftliches Schuldanerkenntnis *n*

655 coin
f monnaie *f* métallique; pièce *f* de
monnaie
i moneta *f*
e moneda *f*
n munt *f*; muntstuk *n*
d Münze *f*; Geldstück *n*; Hartgeld *n*

656 coin *v*
f monnayer
i coinare
e acuñar
n aanmunten; munten
d münzen; prägen

657 coinage
  f frappe f; monnayage m
  i coniazione f; coniatura f; monetazione f
  e acuñación f
  n aanmunting f; munting f
  d Prägung f

658 coinage
  f système m monétaire
  i sistema m monetario
  e sistema m monetario
  n muntsysteem n
  d Münzsystem n

659 coiner
  f monnayeur m
  i coniatore m
  e acuñador m
  n munter m
  d Präger m; Münzer m

660 collateral; collateral security
  f nantissement m; garantie f additionnelle
  i co-cauzione f; garanzia f supplementare
  e colateral m; garantía f; prenda f
  n additionele zekerheid f
  d Sicherheit f; Nebensicherheit f

661 collateral loan
  f prêt m garanti par des effets
  i prestito m garantito da effetti
  e préstamo m respaldado por efectos en garantía
  n lening f tegen onderpand van effecten
  d Darlehen n gegen Sicherheit

* **collateral security** → **660**

662 collect v
  f encaisser; percevoir; recouvrer
  i incassare; riscuotere
  e cobrar; recaudar
  n innen; incasseren
  d einkassieren; kassieren; eintreiben; einziehen; erheben

663 collectable
  f encaissable
  i riscotibile
  e cobrable
  n inbaar
  d einziehbar; einkassierbar

664 collecting bank
  f banque f d'encaissement
  i banca f che incassa
  e banco m de cobranzas; banco m de recaudaciones

  n incassobank f
  d Inkassobank f

665 collection
  f encaissement m; perception f; recouvrement m
  i incasso m; riscossione f
  e cobro m; cobranza f; recaudación f
  n incasso n; inning f
  d Inkasso n; Einkassierung f; Eintreibung f; Erhebung f

666 collection charges
  f frais mpl d'encaissement
  i spese fpl di riscossione
  e gastos mpl de cobranza
  n incassokosten mpl
  d Einzugskosten fpl

667 collection department
  f département m d'encaissement
  i sezione f incassi; ufficio m riscossioni
  e departamento m de cobranzas
  n incasso-afdeling f
  d Einkassierungsabteilung f

* **collection draft** → **1025**

668 collection fee
  f commission f d'encaissement
  i provvigione f d'incasso
  e comisión f de cobranza
  n incassocommissie f; incassokosten mpl
  d Einziehungsprovision f; Einzugsspesen fpl

669 collection teller
  f receveur m
  i cassiere m allo sportello
  e recibidor m; cajero m; encargado de cobrar
  n employé m belast met de inning van kwitanties
  d Schalterbeamter m für den Inkassoverkehr

670 collector
  f encaisseur m; receveur m
  i esattore m; ricevitore m
  e cobrador m; recaudador m
  n ontvanger m; inner m
  d Einkassierer m; Kassierer m; Einnehmer m

671 co-maker *(US)*
  f cogarant m
  i commallevadore m; controfirmatario m
  e cogarante m; cofirmante m; refuerzo m de garantía

n medeborg *m*
d Mitbürge *m*; Mitunterzeichner *m*

672 commerce
f commerce *m*
i commercio *m*
e comercio *m*
n handel *m*
d Handel *m*; Geschäft *n*; Handelsver-
kehr *m*

673 commercial
f commercial
i commerciale
e comercial
n commercieel; handels-
d kommerziell; kaufmännisch; Handels-;
Geschäfts-; geschäftlich; handelsüblich

674 commercial account
f compte *m* commercial
i conto *m* commerciale
e cuenta *f* de comercio; cuenta *f* comercial
n handelsrekening *f*; commerciële
rekening *f*
d Handelskonto *n*; Geschäftskonto *n*

675 commercial bank
f banque *f* pour le commerce
i banca *f* commerciale
e banco *m* comercial
n handelsbank *f*
d Handelsbank *f*

676 commercialize *v*
f commercialiser
i commercializzare
e comercializar
n in de handel brengen
d kommerzialisieren; in den Handel
bringen

677 commercial letter of credit
f lettre *f* de crédit commerciale
i lettera *f* di credito commerciale
e carta *f* de crédito comercial
n commerciële kredietbrief *m*
d Handelskreditbrief *m*; Warenkredit-
brief *m*; Akkreditiv *n*

678 commercial papers
f effets *mpl* de commerce; papiers *mpl* de
commerce
i effetti *mpl* di commercio
e papeles *mpl* de negocios
n handelspapier *n*
d Handelspapiere *npl*

679 commission
f commission *f*
i provvigione *f*; commissione *f*
e comisión *f*
n provisie *f*; commissie *f*
d Provision *f*; Kommission *f*

680 commission merchant
f commissionnaire *m*
i commissionario *m*
e comisionista *m*
n commissionair *m*
d Kommissionär *m*

681 commodity agreement
f accord *m* sur un produit de base
i accordo *m* circa un prodotto basilare
e acuerdo *m* sobre un producto básico
n basisgoederenovereenkomst *f*
d Abkommen *n* über Grundwaren

682 commodity loan
f prêt *m* en nature; prêt *m* en
marchandises
i prestito *m* in natura
e préstamo *m* en especie
n krediet *n* in goederen
d Warenkredit *m*

* **common stock** *(US)* → **1721**

683 company
f compagnie *f*; société *f*
i compagnia *f*; società *f*
e compañia *f*
n vennootschap *f*; maatschappij *f*
d Gesellschaft *f*

684 compensation
f compensation *f*; indemnité *f*
i compensazione *f*; rimunerazione *f*
e compensación *f*; retribución *f*
n schadeloosstelling *f*; vergoeding *f*
d Schadloshaltung *f*; Vergütung *f*

685 competitive bidding
f appel *m* d'offres
i licitazione *f* pubblica
e licitación *f* pública
n openbaar bod *n*
d öffentliche Preisausschreibung *f*

686 composition
f arrangement *m*; compromis *m*
i accomodamento *m*
e composición *f*; arreglo *m*
n vergelijk *n*; compromis *n*
d Vergleich *m*

687 composition with creditors
f arrangement *m* avec les créanciers
i accomodamento *m* con i creditori
e arreglo *m* con los acreedores
n overeenkomst *f* met de crediteuren
d Gläubigervergleich *m*

688 compound interest
f intérêt *m* composé
i interesse *m* composto
e interés *m* compuesto
n samengestelde interest *m*; interest *m* op
    interest; rente *f* op rente
d Zinseszins *m*

689 compromise
f compromis *m*
i compromesso *m*
e compromiso *m*
n minnelijke schikking *f*; compromis *n*
d Kompromiss *m/n*; Zugeständnis *n*

690 comptroller *(US)*
f directeur-inspecteur *m* d'une banque
i direttore *m* di banca con funzioni
    ispettive
e director *m* de banco con funciones
    inspectivas
n thesaurier-hoofdcontroleur *m*
d Bankdirektor *m* mit Aufsichtsfunktionen

691 comptroller of the currency
f contrôleur *m* de la monnaie
i direttore *m* dell'ufficio valute
e director *m* del departamento de divisas
n hoofd *n* van de valuta-afdeling
d Währungskommissar *m*

692 compulsory saving; forced saving
f épargne *f* forcée
i risparmio *m* forzato
e ahorro *m* forzoso
n gedwongen sparen *n*
d Zwangssparen *n*

693 computation
f computation *f*; calcul *m*
i computo *m*; calcolo *m*; calcolazione *f*
e cómputo *m*; cálculo *m*
n berekening *f*
d Berechnung *f*; Kalkulation *f*

694 compute *v*
f computer; calculer
i computare; calcolare
e computar; calcular
n berekenen
d berechnen; kalkulieren

695 concern
f entreprise *f*; société *f*
i impresa *f*; azienda *f*
e empresa *f*; sociedad *f*
n onderneming *f*; maatschappij *f*
d Unternehmen *n*; Betrieb *m*

696 conclude *v*
f conclure; terminer
i concludere
e concluir; cerrar
n besluiten; afsluiten
d abschliessen

697 conditional endorsement
f endossement *m* conditionnel
i girata *f* condizionale
e endoso *m* condicional
n voorwaardelijk endossement *n*
d bedingtes Indossament *n*

698 conditional order
f ordre *m* conditionnel; commande *f*
    conditionnelle
i ordine *m* condizionale; ordinazione *f*
    condizionale
e orden *f* condicional; pedido *m* a
    condición
n voorwaardelijke order *f*
d bedingter Auftrag *m*

699 condonation
f remise *f* d'une dette
i condono *m*
e condonación *f*
n kwijtschelding *f*
d Erlass *m*; Erlassung *f*

700 condone *v*
f remettre
i condonare
e condonar
n kwijtschelden
d erlassen

701 confirm *v*
f confirmer
i confermare
e confirmar
n bevestigen; bekrachtigen
d bestätigen; bekräftigen

702 confirmation
f confirmation *f*
i confermazione *f*; conferma *f*
e confirmación *f*
n bevestiging *f*; bekrachtiging *f*
d Bestätigung *f*; Bekräftigung *f*

703 confirmed credit
f crédit *m* confirmé
i credito *m* confermato
e crédito *m* confirmado
n bevestigd krediet *n*
d bestätigter Kredit *m*

704 confiscate v
f confisquer
i confiscare
e confiscar; decomisar; secuestrar;
incautarse de
n verbeurdverklaren; confisqueren; in
beslag nemen
d in Beschlag nehmen

705 consign v
f consigner; expédier; livrer
i consegnare
e consignar; entregar a consignación
n consigneren; in consignatie geven
d konsignieren; in Konsignation senden

706 consignee
f consignataire *m*
i consegnatario *m*
e consignatario *m*
n geconsigneerde *m*; consignataris *m*
d Konsignatar *m*; Empfänger *m*

707 consigner; consignor
f consignateur *m*; expéditeur *m*
i consegnante *m*
e consignador *m*; expedidor *m*
n consigneerder *m*; consignant *m*
d Konsignant *m*

708 consignment
f consignation *f*
i consegna *f*
e consignación *f*
n consignatie *f*
d Konsignation *f*

* **consignor** → 707

709 consolidate v
f consolider
i consolidare
e consolidar
n consolideren
d konsolidieren

710 consolidated balance sheet
f bilan *m* consolidé
i bilancio *m* generale consolidato
e balance *m* general consolidado
n geconsolideerde balans *f*
d konsolidierte Bilanz *f*

711 consolidated fund
f fonds *m* consolidé
i fondo *m* consolidato
e fondo *m* consolidado
n geconsolideerd fonds *n*
d konsolidierter Fonds *m*

712 consolidated loan
f emprunt *m* de consolidation
i prestito *m* consolidato
e empréstito *m* consolidado; empréstito *m*
unificado
n geconsolideerde lening *f*
d konsolidierte Anleihe *f*

713 consolidated mortgage
f hypothèque *f* consolidée
i ipoteca *f* consolidata
e hipoteca *f* consolidada
n geconsolideerde hypotheek *f*
d konsolidierte Hypothek *f*

714 consolidation
f consolidation *f*
i consolidazione *f*
e consolidación *f*
n consolidatie *f*
d Konsolidierung *f*

715 consols
f fonds *mpl* consolidés
i fondi *mpl* consolidati; cartelle *fpl* del
debito consolidato
e fondos *mpl* consolidados; títulos *mpl* de
deuda consolidados
n consols *mpl*
d Konsols *mpl*; konsolidierte Staatspapiere
npl

716 consortium
f consortium *m*; groupe *m*
i consorzio *m*
e consorcio *m*
n consortium *n*
d Konsortium *n*

717 consular fees
f droits *mpl* consulaires
i diritti *mpl* consolari
e derechos *mpl* consulares; gastos *mpl*
consulares
n consulaire leges *fpl*; consulaire rechten
npl
d Konsulargebühren *fpl*

718 consular invoice
f facture *f* consulaire
i fattura *f* consolare
e factura *f* consular

n consulaire factuur *f*
d Konsularfaktur *f*; Konsulatsfaktur *f*

719 consumer credit *(US)*
f crédit *m* au consommateur
i credito *m* al consumatore
e crédito *m* de consumidor; crédito *m*
pagadero en cuotas mensuales
n afbetalingskrediet *n*;
consumentenkrediet *n*
d Konsumentenkredit *m*

720 consumer goods
f biens *mpl* de consommation
i beni *mpl* di consumo
e bienes *mpl* de consumo
n consumptiegoederen *npl*;
verbruiksgoederen *npl*
d Verbrauchsgüter *npl*; Konsumgüter *npl*

721 consumer price
f prix *m* à la consommation
i prezzo *m* al consumo
e precio *m* al consumidor
n consumentenprijs *m*; consumptieprijs *m*
d Verbraucherpreis *m*

722 consumer surplus
f surplus *m* du consommateur
i eccedenza *f* del consumatore
e excedente *m* del consumidor
n consumentenoverschot *n*
d Konsumentenrente *f*

723 consumption economy
f économie *f* de consommation
i economia *f* di consumo
e economía *f* de consumo
n consumptie-economie *f*
d Konsumwirtschaft *f*

724 contango rate
f prix *m* du report; taux *m* du report
i tassa *f* di riporto
e precio *m* de la prolongación
n prolongatietarief *n*
d Reportsatz *m*; Reportkurs *m*; Report-
prämie *f*

725 contingency fund
f fonds *m* de réserve pour dépenses
imprévues
i fondo *m* di riserva per spese inpreviste
e fondo *m* para imprevistos
n extrareservefonds *n*
d ausserordentlicher Reservefonds *m*

726 contingent interest
f intérêt *m* conditionnel

i interesse *m* condizionale
e interés *m* condicional
n voorwaardelijke rente *f*
d bedingter Zins *m*

727 contingent liability
f obligation *f* éventuelle
i obbligazione *f* contingenziale
e obligación *f* contingente
n voorwaardelijke aansprakelijkheid *f*
d Eventualverpflichtung *f*; Eventual-
verbindlichkeit *f*

728 contingent reserve
cf. **contingency fund**
f provision *f* pour pertes
i riserva *f* per imprevisti
e reserva *f* para imprevistos
n reserve *f* voor onvoorziene uitgaven
d ausserordentliche Reserve *f*

729 continued bond
f obligation *f* renouvelée
i titolo *m* rinovato; titolo *m* con scadenza
prorogata
e título *m* de vencimiento aplazado
n geprolongeerde obligatie *f*
d prolongierte Obligation *f*

730 continuing guaranty *(US)*; **continuing
security**
f garantie *f* renouvelée automatiquement
i garanzia *f* permanente
e garantía *f* permanente
n permanente garantie *f*
d laufende Garantie *f*; Dauergarantie *f*

731 contract
f contrat *m*
i contratto *m*
e contrato *m*; contrata *f*
n contract *n*; verdrag *n*
d Vertrag *m*; Kontrakt *m*

732 contract *v*
f contracter
i contrattare; contrarre
e contratar; contraer
n contracteren
d einen Vertrag abschliessen; kontrahieren

733 contracting parties
f parties *fpl* contractantes
i parti *fpl* contraenti
e partes *fpl* contratantes
n contracterende partijen *fpl*
d vertragschliessende Parteien *fpl*;
Vertragsparteien *fpl*; vertragschliessende
Teile *mpl*

734 contractionary policy
f politique f d'austérité
i politica f restrittiva
e política f de austeridad; política f de contracción
n contractiepolitiek f; inkrimpingspolitiek f
d Kontraktionspolitik f

735 contract note
f bordereau m d'achat; bordereau m de vente
i fissato m di borsa; bollato m di borsa
e nota f de contrato; nota f de compraventa
n afsluitnota f
d Schlussschein m; Schlussnote f

736 contract price
f prix m contractuel
i prezzo m contrattuale
e precio m contractual
n contractuele prijs m
d Vertragspreis m; Kontraktpreis m

737 contribution
f contribution f
i contributo m; contribuzione f
e contribución f
n bijdrage f
d Beitrag m

738 contributories
f contribuants mpl
i contribuenti mpl
e contribuyentes mpl
n contribuanten mpl; bijdragers mpl
d Beitragenden mpl

739 control
f contrôle m
i controllo m
e control m; contralor m; fiscalización f
n controle f
d Kontrolle f; Aufsicht f

740 control account *(US)*; **controlling account**
f compte m de contrôle
i conto m di controllo
e cuenta f de control; cuenta f total
n controle-rekening f
d Kontrollkonto n; Hauptbuchsammel-konto n

741 control interest
f intérêt m de contrôle financier
i interesse m della parte maggioritaria
e interés m mayoritario
n meerderheidsbelang n; overheersend

belang n
d massgebendes Kapitalinteresse n; Mehrheitsbeteiligung f

742 controlled economy
f économie f dirigée
i economia f controllata; economia f diretta
e economía f dirigida
n geleide economie f
d Planwirtschaft f; geplante Wirtschaft f

* **controlling account** → **740**

743 conventional interest
f intérêt m conventionnel
i interesse m convenzionale
e interés m convencional
n gebruikelijke interest m
d konventionelle Zinsen mpl

744 conversion
f conversion f
i conversione f
e conversión f
n conversie f
d Konversion f

745 conversion at par
f conversion f à la parité
i conversione f alla pari
e conversión f a la par
n conversie f a pari
d Parikonversion f

746 convert v
f convertir
i convertire
e convertir
n converteren
d konvertieren

747 convertibility
f convertibilité f
i convertibilità f
e convertibilidad f
n convertibiliteit f
d Konvertierbarkeit f

748 convertible currency
f monnaie f convertible
i moneta f convertibile
e moneda f convertible
n converteerbare valuta f
d konvertierbare Währung f

749 convertible debenture
f obligation f convertible
i obbligazione f convertibile; obbligazione

f conversion
e obligación f convertible
n converteerbare obligatie f
d Wandelobligation f

750 convertible securities
  f effets *mpl* convertibles; valeurs *fpl*
    convertibles
  i effetti *mpl* convertibili; valori *mpl*
    convertibili
  e efectos *mpl* convertibles; valores *mpl*
    convertibles
  n converteerbare effecten *npl*
  d konvertierbare Effekten *pl*

751 convey *v*
  f transférer
  i trasferire
  e traspasar; transferir
  n overdragen
  d übertragen; abtreten

752 conveyance
  f transfert *m*; cession *f*
  i trapasso *m*; trasferimento *m*; cessione *f*
  e traspaso *m*; transferencia *f*; cesión *f*
  n overdracht *f*; cessie *f*
  d Übertragung *f*; Abtretung *f*

753 coparcener; parcener
  f cohéritier *m*
  i coerede *m*
  e coheredero *m*
  n mede-erfgenaam *m*
  d Miterbe *m*

* corporate body → 413

754 corporation
  f corporation *f*; société *f*
  i corporazione *f*; società *f*
  e corporación *f*; sociedad *f*
  n corporatie *f*; genootschap *n*;
    maatschappij *f*; vennootschap *f*
  d Korporation *f*; Gesellschaft *f*

755 corpus *(US)*
  f capital *m* d'un trust; propriétés *fpl* d'un
    trust
  i capitali *mpl* di un trust; proprietà *fpl* di
    un trust
  e capital *m* de un trust; propiedades *fpl*
    de un trust
  n vermogen *n* van een trust
  d Kapital *n* und Eigentum *n* eines Trusts

756 correspondent bank
  f banque *f* correspondante
  i banca *f* corrispondente

e banco *m* corresponsal
n correspondent *m*
d Korrespondenzbank *f*

757 cost
  f coût *m*; prix *m*
  i costo *m*
  e coste *m*; costo *m*
  n kosten *mpl*; prijs *m*
  d Kosten *fpl*; Preis *m*

758 cost *v*
  f coûter
  i costare
  e costar
  n kosten
  d kosten

759 cost accounting
  f comptabilité *f* analytique; calcul *m* des
    frais
  i calcolo *m* dei costi
  e contabilidad *f* de costos
  n kostenberekening *f*
  d Kostenkalkulation *f*; Kostenrechnung *f*

760 costing
  f établissement *m* du prix de revient
  i calcolo *m* di costo
  e cálculo *m* de costos
  n kostprijsberekening *f*; calculatie *f*
  d Kostenpreisberechnung *f*

761 cost of living
  f coût *m* de la vie
  i costo *m* della vita
  e costo *m* de vida
  n kosten *mpl* van levensonderhoud;
    levensonderhoud *n*
  d Lebenshaltungskosten *fpl*

762 cost price
  f prix *m* de revient; prix *m* coûtant
  i prezzo *m* di costo
  e precio *m* de costo
  n kostprijs *m*
  d Kostenpreis *m*; Einkaufspreis *m*

763 count *v*
  f compter
  i contare
  e contar
  n tellen
  d zählen

764 counter
  f comptoir *m*; guichet *m*
  i sportello *m*
  e mostrador *m*; ventanilla *f*

n loket *n*; kas *f*; toonbank *f*
d Schalter *m*

765 counter check *(US)*
f chèque *m* de guichet
i assegno *m* allo sportello
e cheque *m* de mostrador; cheque *m* contra la propia cuenta corriente
n kascheque *m*
d Schalterscheck *m*

766 counter clerk
f employé *m* au guichet
i impiegato *m* allo sportello
e empleado *m* que atiende al público; dependiente *m*
n loketbediende *m*; loketklerk *m*
d Schalterangestellter *m*

767 counter error
f erreur *f* compensatoire
i errore *m* compensatore
e error *m* compensatorio
n zich opheffende fout *f*
d Ausgleichsfehler *m*

768 counterfeit; forgery
f falsification *f*; contrefaçon *f*
i falsificazione *f*
e falsificación *f*
n vervalsing *f*
d Fälschung *f*; Verfälschung *f*

769 counterfeit *v*; **debase** *v*; **forge** *v*
f falsifier; contrefaire
i falsificare
e falsificar
n vervalsen; namaken
d fälschen; verfälschen

* **counterfeit coin** → **339**

770 counterfeiter; forger
f falsificateur *m*; contrefacteur *m*
i falsificatore *m*
e falsificador *m*
n vervalser *m*
d Fälscher *m*; Verfälscher *m*

771 counterfeit money
f fausse monnaie *f*
i moneta *f* falsa
e dinero *m* falso
n vals geld *n*
d Falschgeld *n*

772 countermand *v*
f contremander; décommander; révoquer
i revocare; annullare; cancellare

e revocar; cancelar; dejar sin efecto
n intrekken; herroepen
d widerrufen

773 countersign *v*
f contresigner
i controfirmare
e refrendar; contrafirmar
n contrasigneren; medeondertekenen
d gegenzeichnen; mitunterzeichnen

774 counting house
f bureau *m* de comptabilité; comptoir *m*
i ufficio *m* per la tenuta di contabilità
e oficina *f* de contabilidad; despacho *m*
n kantoor *n*
d Büro *n*; Kontor *n*

775 coupon
f coupon *m*
i cedola *f* d'interessi
e talón *m* de intereses; cupón *m* de intereses
n coupon *m*
d Zinsschein *m*; Kupon *m*

* **coupon bond** → **348**

776 coupon book
f registre *m* de coupons payables
i registro *m* delle cedole d'interessi
e registro *m* de cupones de intereses a pagar
n couponboek *n*
d Kuponkonto *n*

* **course of exchange** → **1937**

777 court of bankruptcy
f cour *f* de faillissements
i tribunale *m* per i fallimenti
e tribunal *m* de quiebras
n faillissementsrechtbank *f*
d Konkursgericht *n*

778 covenant
f convention *f*; contrat *m*
i convenzione *f*; patto *m*
e convenio *m*; pacto *m*
n overeenkomst *f*; verdrag *n*
d Vertrag *m*; Abkommen *n*

779 cover *v*
f couvrir
i coprire
e cubrir
n dekken
d decken

780 cover
f garantie f; couverture f; nantissement m
i garanzia f; copertura f
e garantía f; fianza f; cobertura f
n dekking f
d Deckung f

781 covering deed
f acte m de garantie
i certificato m di garanzia
e acta f de garantía
n dekkingsakte f
d Treuhandurkunde f

782 cover note
f contrat m provisoire d'assurance
i polizza f di assicurazione provvisoria
e póliza f provisional de seguro
n voorlopig verzekeringscontract n
d vorläufiger Versicherungsschein m

783 credit
f crédit m
i credito m
e crédito m
n krediet n
d Kredit m; Borg m

784 credit v
f créditer
i accreditare
e acreditar
n crediteren
d gutschreiben; kreditieren

785 credit agreement; credit arrangement
f accord m de crédit
i accordo m di credito
e convenio m de crédito
n kredietovereenkomst f
d Kreditabkommen n

786 credit balance
f solde m créditeur; avoir m
i saldo m creditore; saldo m avere;
    avere m
e saldo m acreedor; haber m
n creditsaldo n; batig saldo n
d Kreditsaldo m; Habensaldo m; Haben n;
    Guthaben n

787 credit bank
f banque f de crédit
i banca f di credito
e banco m de créditos
n kredietbank f
d Kreditbank f

788 credit basis
f base f de crédit
i base f di credito
e base f de crédito
n kredietbasis f
d Kreditbasis f

789 credit department; loan department
f service m des crédits
i ufficio m crediti
e departamento m de créditos; sección f
    de créditos
n kredietafdeling f
d Kreditabteilung f

790 credit facilities
f facilités fpl de crédit
i concessione f di credito; linea f di
    credito
e facilidades fpl de crédito
n kredietfaciliteiten fpl
d Kreditfazilitäten fpl

791 credit form *(US)*
f formulaire m de crédit (avec le bilan
    annexé); formule f de crédit (avec le
    bilan annexé)
i modulo m di credito (con bilancio
    aggiunto)
e formulario m de solicitud de crédito (con
    balance adjunto)
n kredietaanvraag f (vergezeld van balans)
d Kreditformular n (mit beiliegender
    Bilanz)

* **credit institution** → 1513

792 credit insurance
f assurance f de crédits
i assicurazione f sul credito
e seguro m sobre el crédito
n kredietverzekering f
d Kreditversicherung f

793 credit interest
f intérêts mpl créditeurs
i interessi mpl creditori
e intereses mpl acreedores
n creditrente f
d Habenzinsen mpl

794 credit ledger
f grand livre m des crédits
i registro m dei crediti
e registro m de créditos
n kredietregister n
d Kreditregister n

* **credit limit** → 1514

795 credit note
f note f de crédit
i nota f di credito
e nota f de crédito
n creditnota f
d Gutschriftsanzeige f

796 creditor
f créditeur m; créancier m
i creditore m
e acreedor m
n crediteur m; schuldeiser m
d Gläubiger m

797 creditor account
f compte m créditeur
i conto m creditore
e cuenta f acreedora
n rekening f die een creditsaldo aanwijst
d Guthabenkonto n

798 creditor country
f pays m créancier
i paese m creditore
e país m acreedor
n crediteurland n
d Gläubigerland n; Gläubigerstaat m

799 creditors' meeting; meeting of creditors
f assemblée f de créanciers
i assemblea f dei creditori
e reunión f de acreedores; asamblea f de acreedores
n verificatievergadering f; vergadering f van schuldeisers; crediteurenvergadering f
d Gläubigerversammlung f

800 credit policy
f politique f de crédit
i politica f creditizia
e política f crediticia
n kredietpolitiek f
d Kreditpolitik f

801 credit slip; paying-in slip
f fiche f de versement
i distinta f di pagamento; distinta f di versamento
e ficha f de pago; nota f de pago
n stortingsnota f
d Einzahlungsbeleg m; Einzahlungsschein m

802 credit society
f société f de crédit mutuel
i società f di credito
e sociedad f de créditos; sociedad f financiadora

n kredietvereniging f
d Kreditgesellschaft f

803 credit union
f coopérative f de crédit
i unione f di credito
e unión f de créditos; cooperativa f de créditos
n kredietvereniging f
d Kreditverein m; Kreditunion f; Kreditgenossenschaft f

804 creditworthiness; solvency
f capacité f d'emprunt; solvabilité f
i solvenza f; solvibilità f
e capacidad f crediticia; solvencia f
n kredietwaardigheid f; solventie f
d Kreditwürdigkeit f; Bonität f; Solvenz f; Zahlungsfähigkeit f

805 crisis
f crise f
i crisi f; crise f
e crisis f
n crisis f
d Krise f

806 crossed cheque
f chèque m barré
i assegno m sbarrato
e cheque m cruzado
n gekruiste cheque m
d gekreuzter Scheck m; Verrechnungsscheck m

807 crossover discount rate
f taux m d'indifférence; taux m d'actualisation critique
i tasso m di pareggiamento; tasso m di equilibrio
e tasa m de actualización de equilibrio
n kruiselings discontopercentage n
d Angleichungssatz m

808 cross rate
f cross rate m
i parità f indiretta
e tipo m cruzado; paridad f indirecta
n kruiselingse wisselkoers m
d Usance-Kurs m; indirekte Parität f

809 crown
f couronne f
i corona f
e corona f
n kroon f
d Krone f

810 cum dividend
 f avec dividende
 i con dividendo
 e con dividendo
 n met dividend; cum dividend
 d mit Dividende

811 cum drawing
 f tirage m compris
 i con tratta
 e con derecho a sorteo
 n met uitlotingsrecht
 d inklusive Ziehung

812 cum new
 f droit de souscription attaché; nouvelle
    émission comprise
 i con nuova emissione
 e incluso el derecho de compra de acciones
    a emitirse
 n cum claim; met recht op
    voorkeursaankoop van nieuwe aandelen
 d mit Bezugsrecht auf junge Aktien

813 cumulative dividend
 f dividende m cumulatif
 i dividendo m cumulativo
 e dividendo m acumulativo
 n cumulatief dividend n
 d kumulative Dividende f

814 currency
 f devises fpl
 i divise fpl; valuta f
 e divisas fpl
 n deviezen npl; valuta f
 d Devisen fpl; Valuta f

 * currency → 1613

815 currency bill
 f traite f en monnaie étrangère
 i cambiale f in valuta estera
 e letra f en dinero extranjero
 n wissel m luidende in vreemde valuta
 d Wechsel m in ausländischer Währung

816 currency bond
 f obligation f (payable) en monnaie
    étrangère
 i obbligazione f in moneta estera
 e título m (pagadero) en dinero extranjero
 n obligatie f luidende in vreemde valuta
 d Obligation f in ausländischer Valuta

817 currency certificate (US)
 f certificat m du Trésor; bon m du Trésor
 i certificato m del Tesoro; buono m del
    Tesoro

 e certificado m del Tesoro; bono m del
    Tesoro
 n schatkistbon m
 d Schatzanweisung f

818 currency liabilities
 f dettes fpl en monnaie
 i passività fpl in moneta nazionale
 e pasivos mpl en moneda nacional
 n valutaverplichtingen fpl
 d Passiva npl in einheimischer Währung;
    Verbindlichkeiten fpl in einheimischer
    Währung

819 currency of bill
 f terme m d'une lettre d'échange
 i validità f di una cambiale
 e período m de validez de una letra de
    cambio
 n looptijd m van een wissel
 d Lauffrist f eines Wechsels; Geltungs-
    dauer f eines Wechsels

**820 current account; account current;
    checking account (US); drawing account**
 f compte m courant
 i conto m corrente
 e cuenta f corriente
 n rekening-courant f; lopende rekening f
 d Kontokorrent n; laufende Rechnung f

821 current-account ledger
 f grand livre m des comptes courants
 i libro m mastro dei conti correnti
 e libro m de cuentas corrientes
 n register n van lopende rekeningen
 d Kontokorrentbuch n

822 current assets
 f actif m courant
 i capitali mpl di rotazione; capitali mpl
    d'esercizio
 e activo m realizable; activo m corriente
 n activa npl; lopend actief n
 d Umlaufvermögen n

823 current liabilities
 f passif m courant
 i passivo m circolante
 e pasivo m circulante; pasivo m corriente
 n lopende verplichtingen fpl
 d laufende Verbindlichkeiten fpl

824 current maturities
 f échéances fpl à moins d'un an
 i scadenze fpl a meno di un anno
 e vencimientos mpl a menos de un año
 n kortlopende verplichtingen fpl (met een
    looptijd van minder dan een jaar)

d kurzfristige Verbindlichkeiten *fpl* (mit
  einer Laufzeit von weniger als einem
  Jahr); kurze Papiere *npl*

825 current money
  f monnaie f en cours; monnaie f en
    circulation
  i moneta f corrente; moneta f in
    circolazione
  e moneda f corriente; moneda f de
    circulación general
  n in omloop zijnd geld n
  d kursierendes Geld n

826 current ratio
  f ratio m de liquidité générale
  i coefficiente m di liquidità generale
  e coeficiente m de liquidez general
  n liquiditeitsverhouding f
  d Liquiditätskennzahl f

827 current yield
  f produit m courant
  i prodotto m corrente; reddito m corrente
  e rendimiento m corriente; rédito m
    normal
  n huidig rendement n; huidige opbrengst f
  d laufende Rendite f; laufender Ertrag m

828 curtail v
  f réduire; diminuer
  i ridurre
  e reducir; disminuir; restringir
  n bekrimpen; besnoeien; korten; verkorten;
    beknotten
  d schmälern; einschränken; kürzen; ver-
    mindern

829 curtailment
  f réduction f; diminution f
  i riduzione f
  e reducción f; restricción f
  n vermindering f; reductie f; besnoeiing f
  d Schmälerung f; Einschränkung f;
    Abschöpfung f; Kürzung f; Verminde-
    rung f

830 custodianship *(US)*
  f garde f
  i custodia f
  e custodia f
  n bewaring f; hoede f
  d Aufbewahrung f; Verwahrung f

831 custodian trustee
  f curateur m tutélaire
  i fiduciario m custode
  e agente m fiduciaro
  n beheerder m belast met de bewaring van

waardepapieren
  d Treuhänder m

832 custody
  f garde f
  i custodia f
  e custodia f
  n bewaring f
  d Aufbewahrung f

833 custom
  f clientèle f
  i clientela f
  e clientela f
  n cliëntèle f
  d Kundschaft f

834 customary
  f habituel; ordinaire
  i usuale
  e corriente
  n gebruikelijk
  d gebräuchlich

835 customer
  f client m
  i cliente m
  e cliente m
  n cliënt m; klant m
  d Kunde m

836 customhouse
  f douane f; bureau m de douane
  i dogana f
  e aduana f; oficina de aduanas
  n douane f; douanekantoor n
  d Zoll m; Zollamt n

837 customized check *(US)*
  f chèque m avec en-tête
  i assegno m intestato
  e cheque m membretado
  d mit Überschrift versehener Scheck m

838 customs duty
  f droit m de douane
  i dazio m doganale
  e derecho m de aduana
  n in- en uitgaande rechten npl
  d Zoll m

839 cut *(US)*
  f total m d'un paquet de chèques
  i totale m di un fascio di assegni
  e total m de un fajo de cheques
  n totaal n van een bundel cheques
  d Summe f einer Partie Schecks

840 cut-off *(US)*
  f bilan *m* périodique de chèques aux fins
    de contrôle
  i bilancio *m* periodico di assegni a scopo
    di controllo
  e balance *m* periódico de cheques con
    fines de control
  n periodieke chequebalans *f*
  d periodische Scheckbilanz *f* für Kontroll-
    zwecke

841 cut-off rate of return
  f seuil *m* d'admissibilité; taux *m* limite de
    rentabilité
  i tasso *m* di redditibilità accetabile
  e tasa *f* de rentabilidad aceptable
  n beperkt rentepercentage *n*
  d begrenzter Rentabilitäts-Prozentsatz *m*

842 cut slip *(US)*
  f bande *f* de papier sur laquelle on écrit le
    total d'un "cut"
  i striscia *f* di carta sulla quale si annota il
    totale di un "cut"
  e faja *m* de papel en que se inscribe el
    total de un "cut"
  n notabriefje *n* van totaal
  d Papierstreifen *m* auf welchem die
    Summe eines "cut" aufgeschrieben wird

D

843 damage
 f dommage *m*; dégâts *mpl*
 i danno *m*; danneggiamento *m*
 e daño *m*; perjuicio *m*
 n schade *f*
 d Schaden *m*; Beschädigung *f*

844 damage *v*
 f nuire; endommager; détériorer
 i danneggiare
 e dañar; perjudicar
 n schaden; benadelen; beschadigen
 d beschädigen; schaden

845 data
 f données *fpl*; documentation *f*
 i dati *mpl*
 e datos *mpl*; información *f*
 n bijzonderheden *fpl*; gegevens *npl*
 d Einzelheiten *fpl*; Angaben *fpl*

846 date
 f date *f*
 i data *f*
 e fecha *f*
 n datum *m*
 d Datum *n*

847 date *v*
 f dater
 i datare
 e fechar; datar
 n dateren
 d datieren

848 date
 f échéance *f*
 i termine *m*
 e plazo *m*
 n dagtekening *f*
 d Termin *m*; Sicht *f*

* **date of maturity** → 1032

849 daybook
 f livre-journal *m*; journal *m*
 i libro *m* giornale
 e libro *m* de diario; libro *m* diario
 n dagkasboek *n*; journaal *n*
 d Journal *n*; Tagebuch *n*

850 day loan
 f emprunt *m* quotidien
 i prestito *m* giornaliero
 e préstamo *m* diario
 n daglening *f*; lening *f* voor een dag;

 daggeld *n*
 d täglich fälliges Geld *n*

851 days of grace
 f jours *mpl* de grâce
 i giorni *mpl* di grazia
 e días *mpl* de prórroga especial; días *mpl* de cortesía
 n respijtdagen *mpl*
 d Fristtage *mpl*

* **day-to-day money** → 501

852 dead account
 f compte *m* inactif; compte *m* paralysé
 i conto *m* inattivo
 e cuenta *f* sin movimiento; cuenta *f* inactiva
 n dode rekening *f*
 d totes Konto *n*; unbewegtes Konto *n*

853 deadline
 f terme *m* d'échéance
 i giorno *m* di scadenza
 e fecha *f* de vencimiento; vencimiento *m*; plazo *m*
 n vervaldag *m*; termijn *m*
 d Verfalltermin *m*; Frist *f*

854 dead loan
 f emprunt *m* non payé à échéance
 i prestito *m* non pagato alla scadenza
 e préstamo *m* no pagado en la fecha de vencimiento
 n lening *f* die op de vervaldag niet terugbetaald is
 d am Verfalltage nicht bezahlte Anleihe

855 dead loan
 f emprunt *m* sans date d'échéance
 i prestito *m* senza scadenza
 e préstamo *m* sin fecha de vencimiento
 n lening *f* zonder vastgestelde vervaldag
 d Anleihe *f* ohne Verfallfrist

856 deadlock
 f impasse *f*; arrêt *m*; situation *f* sans issue
 i ristagno *m*
 e estancamiento *m*; detención *f*; paralización *f*; callejón *m* sin salida
 n impasse *f*; slop *n*
 d Stockung *f*; Stillstand *m*

857 dead loss
 f perte *f* sèche
 i perdita *f* assoluta
 e pérdida *f* total

n totaalverlies *n*
d Gesamtverlust *m*; Totalverlust *m*

858 dead rent
f loyer *m* minimum
i affitto *m* minimo
e arrendamiento *m* mínimo fijo
n minimum huur *f*
d Minimalpacht *f*

859 dead stock
f capital *m* inactif; capital *m* improductif
i capitale *m* improduttivo
e capital *m* improductivo
n dood kapitaal *n*
d totes Kapital *n*

860 deal *v*
f négocier; faire une transaction
i negoziare; fare una transazione
e negociar; cerrar trato
n handelen; een zaak doen
d handeln

861 deal
f accord *m*; transaction *f*; affaire *f*
i affare *m*
e trato *m*; negocio *m*
n transactie *f*; zaak *f*
d Vertrag *m*; Geschäft *n*

862 dealer
f marchand *m*; négociant *m*
i commerciante *m*
e agente *m*; comerciante *m*
n handelaar *m*; koopman *m*
d Händler *m*; Kaufmann *m*

863 dear money
f argent *m* cher
i denaro *m* ad alto interesse
e dinero *m* que se presta a alto interés
n duur geld *n*
d teures Geld *n*

864 death benefit
f indemnité *f* en cas de décès
i somma *f* riscotibile in caso di morte
e beneficio *m* por muerte; suma *f* pagadera en caso de muerte
n uitkering *f* bij overlijden
d Sterbegeld *n*

* **death duties** → 1102

* **debase** *v* → 769

865 debenture; debenture bond
f obligation *f*; titre *m*; bon *m*

i obbligazione *f*; titolo *m*
e obligación *f*; título *m*; bono *m*
n obligatie *f*; schuldbrief *m*
d Obligation *f*; Schuldverschreibung *f*

866 debenture holder
f obligataire *m*; porteur *m* d'obligations
i portatore *m* di obbligazioni
e tenedor *m* de obligaciones
n obligatiehouder *m*
d Obligationsinhaber *m*

867 debenture stock
f obligation *f* transférable en sommes partielles
i obbligazione *f* trasferibile per somme parziali
e obligación *f* transferible en sumas parciales
n obligatie *f* die in delen overdraagbaar is
d Obligation *f* die man in Teilbeträgen überweisen kann

868 debit
f débit *m*
i debito *m*
e débito *m*
n debet *n*
d Soll *n*; Debet *n*; Lastschrift *f*

869 debit *v*
f débiter
i addebitare
e debitar; cargar en cuenta
n debiteren
d belasten; debitieren

870 debit interest
f intérêts *mpl* débiteurs
i interessi *mpl* debitori
e intereses *mpl* deudores
n debetrente *f*
d Sollzinsen *mpl*

871 debit ticket; charge ticket
f note *f* de débit
i nota *f* di addebito
e nota *f* de débito
n debetnota *f*
d Debetnote *f*; Belastungsanweisung *f*

872 debt
f dette *f*; créance *f*
i debito *m*
e deuda *f*; débito *m*
n schuld *f*
d Schuld *f*

873 debt consolidation
 f consolidation *f* de la dette
 i consolidazione *f* di debito
 e consolidación *f* de la deuda
 n consolidatie *f* van de schulden
 d Konsolidierung *f* der Schulden

874 debt-equity ratio
 f ratio *m* d'endettement; ratio *m* de
    solvabilité
 i coefficiente *m* di indebitamento
 e coeficiente *m* de endeudamiento
 n schuldverhoudingcoëfficiënt *m*
 d Verschuldungskoeffizient *m*

875 debtor
 f débiteur *m*
 i debitore *m*
 e deudor *m*
 n debiteur *m*; schuldenaar *m*
 d Schuldner *m*

876 debt rearrangement; debt reorganization
 f réaménagement *m* de la dette
 i riorganizzazione *f* di debito
 e reorganización *f* de la deuda
 n reorganisatie *f* van de schuld
 d Umschuldung *f*

877 debt refinancing
 f refinancement *m* de la dette
 i rifinanziamento *m* di debito
 e refinanciación *f* de la deuda
 n herfinanciering *f* van de schuld
 d Neufinanzierung *f* der Schuld

878 debt relief
 f allègement *m* de la dette
 i alleviamento *m* di debito
 e alivio *m* de la deuda
 n schuldvermindering *f*
 d Schulderleichterung *f*

* **debt reorganization** → 876

879 debt service
 f service *m* de la dette
 i servizio *m* del debito
 e servicio *m* de la deuda
 n schuldendienst *m*
 d Schuldendienst *m*

880 debt-service ratio
 f ratio *m* du service de la dette
 i coefficiente *m* del servizio del debito
 e coeficiente *m* del servicio de la deuda
 n schuldendienstverhouding *f*
 d Koeffizient *m* des Schuldendiensts

881 debt-service requirements
 f obligations *fpl* au titre du service de la
    dette
 i obbligazione *f* attinente al servizio del
    debito
 e obligaciones *fpl* relacionadas con el
    servicio de la deuda
 n schuldendienstverplichtingen *fpl*
 d Verschreibungen *fpl* des Schulden-
    diensts

882 debt servicing capacity
 f aptitude *f* à assurer le service de la dette
 i capacità *f* di attendere il servizio del
    debito
 e capacidad *f* para atender el servicio de la
    deuda
 n capaciteit *f* om de schuldendienst te
    betalen
 d Möglichkeit *f* die Schuldendienst zu
    bezahlen

883 declaration
 f déclaration *f*
 i dichiarazione *f*
 e declaración *f*
 n aanmelding *f*; verklaring *f*
 d Anmeldung *f*; Erklärung *f*

884 declaration of options
 f réponse *f* des primes
 i dichiarazione *f* di premi ,
 e declaración *f* de primas; respuesta *f* de
    primas
 n aanzegging *f* van een optie;
    premieaanzegging *f*
 d Prämienerklärung *f*

885 declare *v*
 f déclarer
 i dichiarare
 e declarar
 n aangeven; verklaren
 d anmelden; erklären

886 declare *v* **a dividend**
 f fixer le dividende
 i dichiarare un dividendo
 e declarar un dividendo
 n een dividend declareren
 d Dividende verteilen; Dividende festsetzen

887 decline
 f baisse *f*; chute *f*; fléchissement *m*
 i ribasso *m*; caduta *f*; declinazione *f*
 e baja *f*; descenso *m*
 n daling *f*
 d Fall *m*; Verfall *m*; Rückgang *m*; Baisse *f*

888 declining balance method
f amortissement *m* dégressif
i sistema *m* di ammortizzazione di saldo decrescente
e sistema *m* de amortización de saldo decreciente
n afnemende afschrijving *f*
d abnehmende Tilgung *f*

889 decrease v
f diminuer; réduire
i diminuire; ridurre
e disminuir; reducir
n verminderen; afnemen
d vermindern

890 decrease
f diminution *f*; réduction *f*
i diminuzione *f*; riduzione *f*
e disminución *f*; reducción *f*; decrecimiento *m*
n vermindering *f*; afname *f*
d Verminderung *f*; Abnahme *f*

891 deduct v
f déduire; décompter
i dedurre; detrarre
e deducir; descontar
n aftrekken
d in Abzug bringen; abziehen; abrechnen

892 deduction; discount; rebate
f déduction *f*; escompte *m*
i deduzione *f*; ribasso *m*; sconto *m*
e deducción *f*; descuento *m*
n korting *f*; aftrek *m*; disconto *n*
d Abzug *m*; Abschlag *m*; Diskont *m*; Skonto *m*

893 deed; act
f acte *m*; document *m*
i atto *m*; documento *m*
e escritura *f*; documento *m*; acto *m*
n akte *f*; document *n*
d Urkunde *f*; Dokument *n*; Akte *f*

894 deed v
f transférer par un acte
i trasferire mediante un atto
e transferir mediante escritura; hacer una escritura de traspaso
n overdragen bij akte
d überschreiben durch urkundliche Beglaubigung

895 deed of arrangement; letter of licence
f contrat *m* d'arrangement
i scrittura *f* di concordato; atto *m* di accomodamento

e escritura *f* de concordato
n akte *f* van overeenkomst
d Vergleichsurkunde *f*

896 deed of assignment
f acte *m* de cession
i atto *m* di cessione
e escritura *f* de cesión
n akte *f* van cessie
d Abtretungsurkunde *f*; Übertragungsurkunde *f*

897 deed of gift
f acte *m* de donation
i contratto *m* di donazione
e escritura *f* de donación
n schenkingsakte *f*
d Schenkungsbrief *m*; Stiftungsurkunde *f*

898 deed of partnership
f acte *m* de société
i contratto *m* sociale
e contrato *m* de sociedad
n akte *f* van vennootschap
d Gesellschaftsvertrag *m*; Gesellschaftsstatuten *npl*

899 deed poll
f acte *m* unilatéral
i scrittura *f* unilaterale
e escritura *f* unilateral
n eenzijdige verbintenis *f*
d einseitiger Vertrag *m*

900 defaced coin
f monnaie *f* défigurée
i moneta *f* sfigurata
e moneda *f* desfigurada
n beschadigde munt *f*
d lädierte Münze *f*

* **defalcate** v → **1064**

* **defalcation** → **1065**

901 default
f défaut *m*
i mora *f*
e mora *f*; incumplimiento *m*
n gebrek *n*; verstek *n*
d Verzug *m*

902 defaulted bond
f obligation *f* en souffrance
i obbligazione *f* in mora
e obligación *f* en mora
n noodlijdende obligatie *f*; obligatie *f* waarop couponbetaling gestaakt is
d notleidende Obligation *f*

903 default on obligations
f manquement m aux obligations
i mancanza f di complimento delle
obbligazioni
e incumplimiento m de obligaciones
n niet nakomen n van verplichtingen
d nicht Erfüllung f der Verbindlichkeiten

904 default on payment
f défaut m de paiement
i mancanza f di pagamento
e incumplimiento m de pago
n wanbetaling f
d Zahlungsverzug m; Zahlungseinstellung f

905 defeasance
f annulation f
i annullamento m
e anulación f
n annulering f
d Annullierung f

906 defer v
f différer; remettre; renvoyer; ajourner
i differire; rimandare
e diferir; prorrogar; postergar
n uitstellen
d verschieben; aufschieben; verzögern

907 deferred annuity
f annuité f différée; rente f à paiement
différé
i annualità f rinviata
e anualidad f diferida
n uitgestelde rente f
d hinausgeschobene Annuität f; hinausgeschobene Jahresrente f

908 deferred bond
f obligation f d'intérêt différé
i obbligazione f rinviata
e título m de interés diferido
n obligatie f met uitgestelde rente
d Obligation f mit ausgeschobener Verzinsung

909 deferred credit
f crédit m différé; crédit m ajourné
i credito m differito
e crédito m diferido; crédito m demorado
n uitgesteld krediet n
d aufgeschobener Kredit m

910 deferred debit
f débit m différé
i debito m differito
e débito m diferido

n uitgesteld debet n
d aufgeschobene Schuld f

911 deferred shares
f actions fpl différées
i azioni fpl differite
e acciones fpl diferidas
n uitgestelde aandelen npl
d Nachzugsaktien fpl

912 deferred stock
f capital m en actions différées
i capitale m in azioni differite
e capital m en acciones diferidas
n kapitaal n in uitgestelde aandelen
d Aktienkapital n mit aufgeschobenen
Zinsen

913 deficiency advances
f avances fpl (de la Bank of England au
gouvernement) pour couvrir des déficits
temporaires
i anticipi mpl (della Bank of England al
governo) per coprire passività tempo-
ranee
e anticipos mpl (del Bank of England al
gobierno) para cubrir déficits pasajeros
n voorschotten npl (door de Bank of
England aan de regering verstrekt) tot
dekking van een tijdelijk deficit
d Vorschüsse mpl (der Bank of England
an die Regierung) zur Deckung vorüber-
gehender Defizite

914 deficiency bill
f emprunt m à courte échéance de la Bank
of England au gouvernement
i prestito m a breve scadenza della Bank
of England al governo
e empréstito m a corto plazo del Bank of
England al gobierno
n kortlopende rekening f door de Bank of
England verstrekt aan de regering
d kurzfristige Anleihe f der Bank of
England an die Regierung

915 deficit
f déficit m
i deficit m; ammanco m
e déficit m
n deficit n; tekort n
d Defizit n; Manko n

916 deficit country
f pays m déficitaire
i paese m deficitario
e país m deficitario
n deficitland n; land n met balanstekort
d Defizitland n

917 deficit financing
f financement *m* par le déficit budgétaire
i finanziamento *m* mediante deficit di bilancio
e financiación *f* mediante déficit presupuestal
n begrotingsfinanciering *f*
d Defizitfinanzierung *f*

918 deficit spending
f dépenses *fpl* par le déficit budgétaire
i spese *fpl* mediante deficit di bilancio
e gastos *mpl* mediante déficit presupuestal
n deficituitgaven *fpl*
d Defizitausgaben *fpl*

919 deflate *v*
f provoquer déflation
i defalzionare
e deflactar
n deflateren
d Deflation durchführen

920 deflation; disinflation
f déflation *f*
i deflazione *f*
e deflación *f*
n deflatie *f*
d Deflation *f*

921 deflator
f déflateur *m*
i deflatore *m*
e deflactor *m*
n deflator *m*
d Deflationsmittel *n*

922 defraud *v*
f frauder
i defraudare
e defraudar
n frauderen; bedriegen; ontvreemden
d betrügen; hinterziehen

923 delay *v*
f retarder
i ritardare
e demorar; retrasar
n uitstellen; vertragen
d verzögern; aufschieben

924 delay
f retard *m*; demeure *f*; délai *m*
i ritardo *m*; dilazione *f*
e demora *f*; retardo *m*
n uitstel *n*; vertraging *f*
d Verzögerung *f*; Verzug *m*

925 delegate *v*
f déléguer
i delegare
e delegar
n delegeren; afvaardigen
d beauftragen; abordnen; Vollmacht erteilen

926 delete *v*
f annuler; effacer
i annullare; cancellare
e anular; tachar; borrar
n doorhalen; uitwissen
d streichen; tilgen

927 deliver *v*
f livrer; délivrer
i consegnare
e entregar
n leveren; afleveren; uitleveren
d liefern; abliefern; ausliefern

928 delivery
f livraison *f*; délivrance *f*
i consegna *f*
e entrega *f*
n levering *f*; aflevering *f*; leverantie *f*; uitlevering *f*
d Lieferung *f*; Ablieferung *f*; Auslieferung *f*

929 delivery bond
f engagement *m* de livraison
i impegno *m* di consegna
e compromiso *m* de entrega
n verbintenis *f* tot levering; leveringsverplichting *f*
d Lieferungsverbindung *f*

930 delivery note
f récépissé *m* de livraison
i nota *f* di consegna
e nota *f* de entrega
n leveringsnota *f*; leveringsbriefje *n*
d Lieferschein *m*

931 delivery order
f ordre *m* de livraison; bulletin *m* de livraison
i ordine *m* di consegna
e orden *f* de entrega
n opdracht *f* tot (uit)levering
d Lieferungsschein *m*; Lieferungsanweisung *f*

932 demand
f demande *f*
i domanda *f*; richiesta *f*
e demanda *f*

n vraag *f*; navraag *f*; vordering *f*
d Nachfrage *f*; Forderung *f*; Bedarf *m*

933 demand bill
f lettre *f* de change à vue
i cambiale *f* a vista
e letra *f* a la vista
n zichtwissel *m*; zichtwisselbrief *m*
d Sichtwechsel *m*

934 demand deposit
f dépôt *m* à vue
i deposito *m* a vista
e depósito *m* a la vista
n zichtdeposito *n*; direct opvraagbaar
deposito *n*
d Sichteinlage *f*

935 demand draft; stock draft; stock cheque
f traite *f* à vue
i tratta *f* a vista
e giro *m* a la vista
n zichtwissel *m*
d Sichttratte *f*

* demand loan → 501

936 demise
f transfert *m*; cession *f*; legs *m* par
testament
i cessione *f*; legato *m*
e traspaso *m*; cesión *f*; legado *m*
n overdracht *f*; testamentaire vermaking *f*;
legatering *f*; legaat *n*
d Abtretung *f*; Zession *f*; Vermächtnis *n*;
Legat *n*

937 demise *v*
f céder; léguer
i cedere; legare
e ceder; legar
n overdragen; vermaken; legateren
d übertragen; vermachen

938 demonetize *v*
f démonétiser
i demonetare
e desmonetizar
n ontmunten; ontwaarden
d ausser Kurs setzen; entwerten

939 denomination
f coupure *f*; valeur *f* nominale
i pezzatura *f*; valore *m* nominale
e denominación *f*; valor *m* nominal
n coupure *f*; nominale waarde *f*
d Stückelung *f*; Abschnitt *m*; Nennwert *m*

940 depleted
f épuisé
i esaurito
e agotado
n uitgeput
d erschöpft

941 deponent
f déposant *m*
i deponente *m*; esponente *m*;
dichiarante *m*
e deponente *m*; declarante *m*
n deponent *m*; getuige *m*
d Aussagender *m*

942 deposit *v*
f déposer; mettre en dépôt
i depositare
e depositar
n deponeren
d deponieren; hinterlegen

943 deposit
f dépôt *m*
i deposito *m*
e depósito *m*
n deposito *n*
d Einlage *f*; Depot *n*

944 deposit accounts
f dépôts *mpl* à intérêt
i depositi *mpl* ad interesse
e depósitos *mpl* a interés
n rentedragende deposito's *npl*
d verzinsliche Einlagen *fpl*

945 deposit bank; bank of deposit
f banque *f* de dépôts
i banca *f* di depositi
e banco *m* de depósitos
n depositobank *f*
d Depositenbank *f*

946 deposit in escrow
f dépôt *m* conditionnel
i deposito *m* condizionato
e depósito *m* sujeto a condiciones
n deposito *n* onder voorwaarde
d bedingte Einlage *f*

947 deposit ledger
f livre *m* des dépôts
i registro *m* dei depositi
e registro *m* de depósitos
n stortingsregister *n*
d Depositenregister *n*; Depositenkonto *n*

948 depository bank
f banque *f* dépositaire

i banca *f* depositaria
e banco *m* depositario
n depositobank *f*
d Depotbank *f*

949 deposit passbook
f livret *m* de dépôt
i libretto *m* di depositi
e libreta *f* de depósitos
n stortingsboekje *n*
d Bankbuch *n*; Einlageheft *n*

950 deposit receipt
f récépissé *m* de dépôt
i certificato *m* di deposito
e recibo *m* de depósito
n depositoreçu *n*
d Depositenschein *m*

951 deposit slip *(US)*
f fiche *f* de versement
i modulo *m* di dichiarazioni dei depositi;
modulo *m* di deposito
e formulario *m* de declaración de depósito;
formulario *m* de déposito
n stortingsopgave *f*
d Einzahlungszettel *m*

952 depreciate *v*
f déprécier; se déprécier
i deprezzare; deprezzarsi; perdere il valore
e depreciar; depreciarse; desvalorizar;
desvalorizarse; perder el valor
n depreciëren; verminderen in waarde;
ontwaarden
d entwerten; sinken im Wert

953 depreciated currency
f devises *fpl* dépréciées
i divise *fpl* deprezzate; denaro *m*
deprezzato
e divisas *fpl* depreciadas; dinero *m*
depreciado
n ontwaarde valuta *f*
d entwertetes Geld *n*

954 depreciation
f dépréciation *f*
i deprezzamento *m*; svalorizzazione *f*
e depreciación *f*; desvalorización *f*
n depreciatie *f*; waardevermindering *f*;
ontwaarding *f*
d Entwertung *f*

955 depreciation allowance
f provision *f* pour dépréciation
i riserva *f* per deprezzamento
e reserva *f* para depreciación
n depreciatiereserve *f*

d Entwertungsbetrag *m*; Abwertungsbetrag *m*

956 depreciation of currency
f dépréciation *f* de la monnaie
i svalutazione *f* monetaria
e depreciación *f* de la moneda
n geldontwaarding *f*
d Währungsabwertung *f*; Währungsent-
wertung *f*

957 depression
f dépression *f*
i depressione *f*
e depresión *f*
n depressie *f*
d Depression *f*

958 devaluate *v*; **devalue** *v*
f dévaluer
i svalutare
e devaluar; depreciar
n devalueren; ontwaarden
d abwerten; entwerten

959 devaluation
f dévaluation *f*
i svalutazione *f*
e devaluación *f*
n devaluatie *f*; waardevermindering *f*
d Abwertung *f*; Entwertung *f*; Deval-
vation *f*

* **devalue** *v* → **958**

960 development bank
f banque *f* de développement
i banca *f* di sviluppo
e banco *m* de desarrollo; banco *m* de
fomento
n ontwikkelingsbank *f*
d Entwicklungsbank *f*

961 development credit agreement
f accord *m* de crédit de développement
i convenio *m* di credito di sviluppo
e convenio *m* de crédito de fomento
n ontwikkelingskredietovereenkomst *f*
d Entwicklungskreditabkommen *n*

962 development finance company
f société *f* financière de développement
i istituzione *f* finanziaraia di sviluppo
e institución *f* financiera de desarrollo
n ontwikkelingsfinancierings-
maatschappij *f*
d Finanzierungsgesellschaft *f* für Entwicklungszwecke

963 devise v
f léguer
i legare
e legar
n vermaken
d vermachen

964 devise
f legs m immobilier
i legato m di immobili
e legado m de inmuebles
n nalatenschap f van grondbezit
d Vermächtnis n von Grundbesitz

965 devisee
f légataire m; héritier m
i legatario m; erede m
e legatario m; heredero m
n legataris m; erfgenaam m
d Legatar m; Erbe m

966 difference account *(US)*
f compte m des différences
i conto m delle differenze
e cuenta f de diferencias
n verschillenrekening f
d Differenzenkonto n

967 digested bonds *(US)*
f obligations fpl bien placées
i obbligazioni fpl ben collocate
e obligaciones fpl bien colocadas
n goed geplaatste obligaties fpl
d gut plazierte Obligationen fpl; fest untergebrachte Obligationen fpl

968 diminishing returns
f rendements mpl décroissants
i rendimento m descrescente
e rendimientos mpl decrecientes
n afnemende provenuen npl
d abnehmende Grenzerträge mpl

969 direct reduction; mortgage *(US)*
f hypothèque f à réduction directe
i ipoteca f a riduzione diretta
e hipoteca f de reducción directa
n hypotheek f met lineaire aflossing
d Hypothek f mit direkter Tilgung f

970 disburse v
f débourser; payer
i sborsare; pagare
e desembolsar; pagar
n uitbetalen; voorschieten
d auszahlen

971 disbursement
f déboursement m; avance f

i sborso m; pagamento m
e desembolso m; pago m
n uitbetaling f; voorschot n
d Auszahlung f; Ausgabe f

972 disbursing account
f compte m des paiements
i conto m dei pagamenti
e cuenta f de pagos
n betalingsrekening f
d Auszahlungskonto n

973 discharge v
f acquitter
i scaricare
e exonerar; dar recibo; dar finiquito
n ontlasten; ontheffen; kwijting verlenen
d entlasten; quittieren

974 discharge; remission
f décharge f; acquit m; quittance f
i scarico m; ricevuta f; quietanza f
e exoneración f; recibo m; finiquito m;
quitanza f
n ontlasting f; ontheffing f; kwijting f
d Entlastung f; Quittung f

975 discharged bill
f lettre f de change payée
i cambiale f pagata
e letra f de cambio pagado
n betaalde wissel m
d eingelöster Wechsel m

976 discharge of bankrupt
f réhabilitation f d'un failli
i riabilitazione f del fallito
e rehabilitación f de un fallido
n rehabilitatie f van een gefailleerde
d Rehabilitierung f eines Konkurs-
schuldners

977 discount v
f escompter
i scontare
e descontar; hacer (un) descuento
n disconteren; aftrekken
d diskontieren; skontieren

978 discount v
f payer
i pagare
e pagar
n betalen
d abrechnen; bezahlen

* **discount** → 892

979 discountability
f escomptabilité f
i scontabilità f
e descontabilidad f
n disconteerbaarheid f
d Diskontierbarkeit f

980 discountable bill
f effet m bancable
i cambiale f negoziabile
e letra f negociable
n verhandelbare wissel m
d bankfähiger Wechsel m

981 discount bank
f banque f d'escompte
i banca f di sconto
e banco m de descuentos
n discontobank f
d Diskontbank f

982 discount department
f service m d'escomptes
i sezione f sconti
e sección f de descuentos
n disconto-afdeling f
d Diskontabteilung f

983 discounted cash flow method
f méthode f d'actualisation des flux
  financiers
i metodo m di aggiornamento del flusso di
  fondi
e método m de actualización de flujos de
  fondos
n verdisconteerde cashflow-methode f
d Barwertrechnung f

984 discount ledger
f livre m de lettres escomptées
i libro m delle cambiali scontate
e libro m de letras descontadas
n discontoboek n
d Diskontwechselbuch n

985 discount rate
f taux m d'escompte
i tasso m di sconto
e tasa f de descuento
n discontotarief n; disconto n
d Diskontsatz m

* **discount register** → 387

986 discredit v
f discréditer; décréditer
i screditare
e desacreditar

n in diskrediet brengen
d diskreditieren

987 diseconomies
f déséconomies fpl
i diseconomie fpl
e deseconomías fpl
n negatieve economieën fpl; ontsparingen
  fpl
d Entsparungen fpl

988 dishonour
f non-acceptation f; non-paiement m
i mancata accettazione f; mancato
  pagamento m
e no aceptación f; falta f de pago
n non-acceptatie f; nonbetaling f; niet
  honoreren n
d Nichtannahme f; Nichteinlösung f; Nicht-
  zahlung f; Nichtbezahlung f

989 dishonour v
f ne pas accepter; ne pas payer
i non accettare; non pagare
e no aceptar; no pagar
n niet accepteren; niet honoreren; niet
  betalen
d nicht akzeptieren; nicht honorieren; nicht
  bezahlen

* **disinflation** → 920

990 disinflationary
f déflationniste
i deflazionario
e deflacionario; deflacionista
n desinflationistisch
d deflationistisch

991 disinvestment
f désinvestissement m
i disinvestimento m
e desinversión f
n desinvestering f
d Desinvestition f

992 dissaving
f désépargne f
i risparmio m negativo
e desahorro m; ahorro m negativo
n ontsparing f
d negative Ersparnis f; Entsparung f

993 dissolution
f dissolution f; liquidation f
i scioglimento m; liquidazione f
e disolución f; liquidación f
n ontbinding f
d Auflösung f; Liquidation f

994 dissolve *v*
f dissoudre; liquider
i sciogliere; liquidare
e disolver; liquidar
n ontbinden
d auflösen; liquidieren

995 distribution
f distribution *f*
i distribuzione *f*
e distribución *f*
n verdeling *f*; uitkering *f*
d Verteilung *f*; Ausschüttung *f*

996 dividend
f dividende *m*
i dividendo *m*
e dividendo *m*
n dividend *n*; uitkering *f*; winstaandeel *n*
d Dividende *f*; Gewinnanteil *m*

997 dividend check *(US)*
f chèque *m* pour le paiement de
dividendes; chèque *m* de dividendes
i assegno *m* per pagare dividendi; assegno
m dei dividendi
e cheque *m* en pago de dividendos; cheque
m de dividendos
n dividendcheque *m*
d Dividendenscheck *m*

998 dividend counterfoil; dividend coupon
f talon *m* de dividende; coupon *m* de
dividende
i talloncino *m* dei dividendi
e talón *m* de dividendo; cupón *m* de
dividendo
n dividendtalon *m*
d Dividendenbogen *m*; Dividenden-
schein *m*

999 dividend warrant; dividend mandate
f ordonnance *f* de paiement de dividendes
i ordine *m* di pagamento di dividendi
e orden *f* de pago de dividendos
n opdracht *f* tot uitbetaling van dividend
d Dividendenauszahlungsschein *m*

1000 dock dues; dock charges
f droits *mpl* de bassin
i diritti *mpl* di darsena; spese *fpl* di
darsena
e derechos *mpl* de dársena
n dokgeld *n*
d Dockgebühren *fpl*; Dockgeld *n*

* **dock warrant** → 2421

1001 document
f document *m*
i documento *m*
e documento *m*
n document *n*; akte *f*
d Dokument *n*; Urkunde *f*

1002 documentary bill; documentary draft
f lettre *f* documentaire; traite *f*
documentaire
i tratta *f* documentaria; cambiale *f*
documentaria
e letra *f* documentaria
n documentaire wissel *m*
d Dokumentenwechsel *m*; Dokumenten-
tratte *f*

1003 documentary credit
f crédit *m* documentaire
i credito *m* documentario
e crédito *m* documentario
n documentair krediet *n*
d Dokumentenkredit *m*; Dokumentenakkreditiv *n*

* **documentary draft** → 1002

1004 documentary letter of credit
f lettre *f* de crédit documentaire
i lettera *f* di credito documentaria
e carta *f* de crédito documentaria
n documentaire kredietbrief *m*
d Dokumentenakkreditiv *n*

1005 documentary proof
f pièce *f* justificative
i prova *f* documentata
e prueba *f* documentada
n bewijs *n*; gestaafd met documenten;
bewijsstuk *n*
d Beweisstück *n*

1006 dollar area
f zone *f* dollar
i zona *f* del dollaro; area *f* del dollaro
e área *m* del dólar
n dollargebied *n*; dollarzone *f*
d Dollarraum *m*; Dollarblock *m*

1007 dollar gap
f insuffisance *f* de dollars
i deficit *m* del dollaro
e déficit *m* del dólar
n dollargebrek *n*; gebrek *n* aan dollars
d Dollarlücke *f*

1008 domestic currency
f monnaie *f* nationale
i moneta *f* nazionale

e moneda *f* nacional
n nationale valuta *f*
d Landeswährung *f*; einheimische
  Währung *f*

1009 domestic economy
f économie *f* nationale
i economia *f* interna; economia *f*
  nazionale
e economía *f* interna; economía *f* nacional
n nationale economie *f*
d Landeswirtschaft *f*

1010 domestic savings
f épargne *f* intérieure
i risparmio *m* interno; risparmio *m*
  nazionale
e ahorro *m* interno
n nationale besparingen *fpl*
d Landesersparnis *f*; Nationalersparnis *f*;
  Staatsersparnisse *fpl*

1011 domestic trade
f commerce *m* intérieur
i commercio *m* interno
e comercio *m* interno
n binnenlandse handel *m*
d Binnenhandel *m*

1012 domiciled bill
f lettre *f* de change domiciliée
i cambiale *f* domiciliata
e letra *f* de cambio domiciliada
n gedomicilieerde wissel *m*
d Domizilwechsel *m*

1013 donate *v*
f faire (une) donation
i donare
e donar
n schenken
d schenken

1014 donation
f donation *f*
i donazione *f*
e donación *f*; donativo *m*
n schenking *f*
d Schenkung *f*; Spende *f*

1015 donor
f bailleur *m* de fonds
i provveditore *m* di fondi
e donante *m/f*
n schenker *m*
d Stifter *m*; Schenker *m*

1016 dormant account
f compte *m* sans mouvement

i conto *m* inattivo
e cuenta *f* sin movimiento
n slapende rekening *f*; dode rekening *f*
d umsatzloses Konto *n*

1017 dormant balance; unclaimed balance
f solde *m* dormant
i saldo *m* inattivo
e saldo *m* inactivo
n ongebruikt liggend saldo *n*
d umsatzloses Guthaben *n*

1018 double creditor
f créditeur *m* de deux charges; créditeur
  m double
i creditore *m* per doppio addebitamento
e acreedor *m* de dos gravámenes; doble
  acreedor *m*
n dubbele crediteur *m*
d zweifacher Gläubiger *m*

1019 double entry accounting
f comptabilité *f* en partie double
i contabilità *f* in partita doppia
e contabilidad *f* por partida doble
n dubbel-boekhouden *n*
d doppelte Buchführung *f*

1020 downturn *(economic)*
f passage *m* à la phase descendante
i inizio *m* della fase discendente
e iniciación *f* de la fase descendente
n inzinking *f* (in de economie)
d Konjunkturabschwung *f*

1021 downward trend
f tendance *f* à la baisse
i tendenza *f* al ribasso
e tendencia *f* descendente
n neergaande tendens *f*
d fallende Tendenz *f*

1022 draft
f lettre *f* de change; traite *f*
i tratta *f*; cambiale *f*
e letra *f*; libranza *f*
n traite *f*; wissel *m*
d Tratte *f*; Wechsel *m*

1023 draft
f virement *m*
i mandato *m* di pagamento
e giro *m*
n mandaat *n*
d Zahlungsanweisung *f*

1024 draft
f chèque *m*
i assegno *m*

e cheque *m*
n cheque *m*
d Scheck *m*

1025 draft for collection; collection draft
f lettre *f* à l'encaissement
i cambiale *f* per l'incasso
e letra *f* al cobro
n incassowissel *m*
d Inkassowechsel *m*

* **drain of bullion** → 516

1026 draw *v* a bill
f tirer une lettre
i emettere una cambiale
e emitir una letra; librar una letra
n een wissel trekken
d einen Wechsel ziehen; einen Wechsel trassieren

1027 drawee
f tiré *m*
i trassato *m*; trattario *m*
e librado *m*
n betrokkene *m*
d Trassat *m*; Bezogener *m*

1028 drawer
f tireur *m*
i traente *m*
e librador *m*
n trekker *m*
d Trassant *m*; Aussteller *m*

* **drawing account** → 820

1029 drop
f baisse *f*; chute *f*
i declinazione *f*; caduta *f*
e caída *f*; baja *f*
n daling *f*
d Fall *m*

1030 dual system *(US)*
f système *m* de double comptabilité
i sistema *m* di doppia contabilità
e sistema *m* de doble contabilización
n dubbele boekhouding *f*
d doppeltes Buchhaltungssystem *n*

1031 due
f venu à échéance
i scaduto
e vencido
n vervallen
d verfallen; überfällig

1032 due date; date of maturity
f échéance *f*; jour *m* d'échéance
i scadenza *f*
e fecha *f* de vencimiento
n vervaldag *m*
d Verfalltag *m*

1033 due on demand
f payable sur demande
i pagabile dietro domanda
e pagadero a solicitud
n betaalbaar op zicht
d zahlbar auf Verlangen

1034 dull market
f marché *m* calme
i mercato *m* fiacco
e mercado *m* flojo
n lusteloze markt *f*
d flauer Markt *m*

1035 dullness
f dépression *f*; recul *m*; ralentissement *m*
i rilassamento *m*
e depresión *f*; estancamiento *m*; inactividad *f*
n slapte *f*; lusteloosheid *f*
d Flaute *f*

1036 dummy transaction
f affaire *f* simulée
i affare *m* fittizio
e negocio *m* ficticio
n schijntransactie *f*
d Scheingeschäft *n*

1037 dump *v*
f vendre un produit à un prix inférieur à sa valeur normale
i vendere sotto costo
e vender a precios inferiores a los normales
n verkopen tegen lagere dan normale prijzen
d verkaufen zu Schleuderpreisen

1038 dumping
f "dumping" *m*
i "dumping" *m*
e "dumping" *m*
n dumping *f*
d "Dumping" *m*; Schleuderausfuhr *f*

1039 dunning letter
f lettre *f* d'avertissement
i lettera *f* sollecitatoria; lettera *f* per esigere pagamento
e carta *f* de solicitud de pago

    n maanbrief *m*
    d Mahnbrief *m*

1040 duplicate cheque
    f double *m* de chèque; chèque *m* en
       double
    i assegno *m* bancario duplicato
    e duplicado *m* de cheque
    n cheque *m* in duplo; duplikaat-cheque *m*
    d Scheckduplikat *n*

1041 dutiable
    f taxable
    i soggetto a tasse
    e sujeto a impuestos
    n belastbaar
    d steuerpflichtig; steuerbar; abgabepflichtig

1042 duty
    f droit *m*; taxe *f*
    i diritti *mpl*; tassa *f*; imposta *f*; dazio *m*
    e derecho *m*; impuesto *m*
    n rechten *npl*; belasting *f*
    d Gebühren *fpl*; Zoll *m*

1043 duty-free
    f exempt de droit
    i esente da imposta
    e libre de derechos; libre de impuestos
    n belastingvrij
    d steuerfrei

E

1044 early warning system
f système *m* d'alerte
i tempestivo sistema *m* di allarme
e sistema *m* de alarma
n waarschuwingssysteem *n*
d Alarm-System *n*

1045 earmarked *(cheque)*
f réservé pour le paiement de certains comptes
i riservato al pagamento di determinati conti
e destinado para el pago de determinadas cuentas
n bestemd voor het betalen van bepaalde rekeningen
d zurückgestellt zur Bezahlung bestimmter Rechnungen

1046 earn *v*
f gagner
i guadagnare
e ganar
n verdienen
d verdienen

1047 earned surplus
f bénéfices *mpl* non distribués
i utili *mpl* non distribuiti
e utilidades *fpl* no distribuidas
n ingehouden winsten *fpl*
d einbehaltene Gewinne *mpl*

* **earning power** → 1883

1048 earnings
f gains *mpl*; profits *mpl*
i guadagno *m*; benefici *mpl*
e ganancias *fpl*; beneficios *mpl*
n winsten *fpl*; verdiensten *fpl*
d Verdienst *m*; Gewinne *mpl*

1049 economic benefits
f avantages *mpl* économiques
i benefici *mpl* economici
e beneficios *mpl* económicos
n economische voorzieningen *fpl*
d Wirtschaftsrendite *f*; Wirtschaftsgewinne *mpl*

1050 economic indicator
f indicateur *m* économique
i indicatore *m* economico
e indicador *m* económico
n conjunctuurindicator *m*
d Konjunkturindikator *m*

1051 economic management
f gestion *f* de l'économie
i gestione *f* economica
e gestión *f* económica
n economisch beleid *n*
d Konjunkturlenkung *f*

1052 economic rate of return
f taux *m* de rentabilité économique
i tasso *m* di rendimento economico
e tasa *f* de rendimiento económico
n economisch rendementspercentage *n*
d wirtschaftliche Verzinsungssatz *m*

1053 economies of scale
f économies *fpl* d'échelle
i economie *fpl* scalari
e economías *fpl* de escala
n schaaleconomieën *fpl*
d Einsparungen *fpl* durch Erhöhung der Produktionskapazität

1054 effective date
f date *f* d'entrée en vigueur
i data *f* d'entrata in vigore
e fecha *f* de entrada en vigor
n datum *m* van van kracht worden
d Zeitpunkt *m* des Inkrafttretens

1055 effective exchange rate
f taux *m* de change effectif
i tasso *m* di cambio effettivo
e tipo *m* de cambio efectivo
n effectieve wisselkoers *m*
d Effektivwechselkurs *m*

1056 effective interest rate
f taux *m* d'intérêt réel
i tasso *m* d'interesse effettivo
e tipo *m* de interés efectivo
n effectieve rentevoet *m*
d effektiver Zinssatz *m*

1057 effects
f effets *mpl*; biens *mpl* personnels
i effetti *mpl*; beni *mpl*
e efectos *mpl*; bienes *mpl*
n goederen *npl*; bezittingen *fpl*
d Habe *f*; Güter *npl*

1058 elasticity of demand
f élasticité *f* de la demande
i elasticità *f* della domanda
e elasticidad *f* de la demanda
n elasticiteit *f* van de vraag
d Nachfrageelastizität *f*

1059 elastic limit
f limite *m* élastique

i limite *m* variabile
e límite *m* variable
n rekbare grens *f*
d dehnbare Grenze *f*

1060 eligible currency
f monnaie *f* agréée
i moneta *f* scelta
e moneda *f* admisible
n verkiesbare munteenheid *f*
d qualifizierte Währung *f*

1061 eligible paper
f effets *mpl* bancables
i effetti *mpl* bancari; valori *mpl*
  negoziabili
e efectos *mpl* negociables
n bankabel papier *n*
d erstklassiges Wertpapier *n*

1062 embargo
f embargo *m*; séquestre *m*
i sequestro *m*; embargo *m*
e embargo *m*
n beslag *n*; embargo *n*
d Beschlagnahme *f*

1063 embargo *v*
f mettre l'embargo sur
i mettere il sequestro sopra
e embargar
n beslag leggen op; embargo leggen op
d beschlagnahmen; in Beschlag nehmen

1064 embezzle *v*; **defalcate** *v*
f détourner; s'approprier des fonds
i appropriarsi indebitamente sottrarre
e desfalcar; cometer un desfalco
n verduisteren
d unterschlagen; veruntreuen

1065 embezzlement; defalcation; peculation
f détournement *m* de fonds
i appropriazione *f* indebita
e desfalco *m*
n verduistering *f*
d Unterschlagung *f*; Veruntreuung *f*

1066 emergency money
f papier-monnaie *m* à circulation forcée
i banconota *f* a corso forzoso
e papel *m* moneda de circulación forzosa
n noodgeld *n*
d Notgeld *n*

1067 employer
f employeur *m*; patron *m*
i dattore *m* di lavoro
e empleador *m*

n werkgever *m*
d Arbeitgeber *m*

1068 employment
f emploi *m*; poste *m*; place *f*
i impiego *m*
e empleo *m*
n betrekking *f*; baan *f*
d Anstellung *f*; Stellung *f*

1069 empower *v*
f autoriser; donner pouvoir
i autorizzare; facoltare
e autorizar; facultar
n machtigen
d bevollmächtigen; Vollmacht erteilen

1070 enact *v*
f décréter; ordonner
i decretare
e decretar; ordenar
n bepalen; gelasten
d verordnen

1071 enactment
f décret *m*
i decreto *m*; disposizione *f*
e decreto *m*; ordenanza *f*
n bepaling *f*; verordening *f*
d Verordnung *f*

1072 encash *v*
f encaisser
i incassare; riscuotere
e cobrar
n incasseren
d einkassieren

1073 enclosure
f annexe *f*; pièce *f* annexée
i allegato *m*; annesso *m*
e adjunto *m*
n bijlage *f*
d Beilage *f*

1074 encumbrance; incumbrance
f charge *f*
i gravame *m*
e gravamen *m*; carga *f*
n bezwaring *f*; schuldenlast *m*; last *m*
d Last *f*; Belastung *f*

1075 endogenous factor
f facteur *m* endogène
i fattore *m* endogeno
e factor *m* endógeno
n endogene factor *m*
d Endogenfaktor *m*; endogener Faktor *m*

1076 endorse *v*; **indorse** *v*
f endosser
i girare
e endosar
n endosseren
d indossieren; girieren

1077 endorsed bond; indorsed bond
f titre *m* endossé par une autre firme
i titolo *m* garantito con altra firma
e título *m* respaldado por otra firma
n obligatie *f* door een tweede firma gegarandeerd
d Schuldverschreibung *f* garantiert durch eine zweite Firma

1078 endorsee; indorsee
f endossé *m*
i giratario *m*
e endosatario *m*
n geëndosseerde *m*
d Indossatar *m*; Indossat *m*

1079 endorsement; indorsement; indorsation
f endossement *m*; endos *m*
i girata *f*
e endoso *m*
n endossement *n*
d Indossament *n*; Indossierung *f*; Giro *n*

1080 endorser; indorser
f endosseur *m*
i girante *m*
e endosador *m*; endosante *m*
n endossant *m*
d Indossant *m*; Girant *m*

1081 endow *v*
f doter; douer
i dotare
e dotar
n doteren
d dotieren

1082 endowment insurance policy
f police *f* d'assurance en dotation
i polizza *f* di assicurazione dotale
e póliza *f* de seguro dotal
n doteringspolis *f*
d Police *f* einer Aussteuerversicherung

1083 enforce *v* **payment**
f exiger le paiement
i esigere il pagamento
e exigir el pago
n manen tot betaling
d die Zahlung mahnen

1084 entrust *v*
f confier; charger
i affidare; incaricare
e confiar; encargar
n toevertrouwen
d anvertrauen

1085 equalization fund
f fonds *m* de péréquation
i fondo *m* di perequazione
e fondo *m* de equiparación
n egalisatiefonds *n*
d Ausgleichsfonds *m*

1086 equilibrating capital flow
f flux *m* de capitaux compensateurs
i flusso *m* equilibratore di capitali
e corriente *f* equilibradora de capital
n kapitaalevenwichtsstroom *m*
d ausgleichender Kapitalfluss *m*

1087 equipment bonds
f bons *mpl* d'équipement
i buoni *mpl* per l'acquisto di equipaggiamento
e títulos *mpl* para compra de equipos
n schuldbekentenis *f* dienende tot de aanschaf van uitrusting
d Schuldverschreibung *f* zum Ankauf von Ausrüstungsmaterial

1088 equitable assets
f biens *mpl* de succession assignés par un tribunal judiciaire
i beni *mpl* di successione assegnati da boni viri
e bienes *mpl* de sucesión asignados por un tribunal de equidad
n gerechtelijk omschreven boedel *m*
d Nachlassvermögen *n* übertragen durch Billigkeitsgericht

1089 equitable mortgage
f lettre *f* d'hypothèque donnant garantie
i ipoteca *f* in cui il mutuatario cede i titoli di una proprietà in garanzia
e hipoteca *f* en que el prestatario cede los títulos de una propiedad como garantía
n tot zekerheid gedeponeerde hypotheekakte *f*
d Verpfändung *f* des Besitztitels (an einem Grundstück)

1090 equities
f obligations *fpl*; titres *mpl*; actions *fpl*
i obbligazioni *fpl*; titoli *mpl*; azioni *fpl*
e obligaciones *fpl*; títulos *mpl*; acciones *fpl*

n obligaties *fpl*; aandelen *npl*
d Obligationen *fpl*; Aktien *fpl*

1091 equity
 f valeur *f* réelle; différence *f* entre la
   valeur nette et la charge hypothécaire
   d'une propriété
 i valore *m* reale; differenza *f* fra il valore
   netto ed il gravame ipotecario di una
   proprietà
 e valor *m* real; diferencia *f* entre el valor
   neto y el gravamen hipotecario de una
   propiedad
 n reële waarde *f*; actief *n* na aftrek van
   hypotheek
 d Realwert *m*; Differenz *f* zwischen Nettowert und hypothekarische Belastung
   eines Grundstücks

* **equity capital** → 2160

1092 equity financing; equity investment
 f participation *f* au capital
 i partecipazione *f* al capitale sociale
 e participación *f* en el capital social
 n deelname *f* in het aandelenkapitaal
 d Investition *f* in Gesellschaftskapital

1093 equity of redemption
 f droit *m* hypothécaire de rachat
 i diritto *m* ipotecario di riscato
 e derecho *m* hipotecario de rescate
 n recht *n* om een hypotheek af te lossen
 d Hypothekenablösungsrecht *n*

1094 equity securities
 f titres *mpl* de spéculation; titres *mpl*
   jouissant de dividends
 i valori *mpl* di speculazione; titoli *mpl* a
   dividendo
 e valores *mpl* de especulación; valores
   mpl que arrojan dividendos
 n speculatieve waarden *fpl*
 d Spekulationspapiere *npl*; Dividenden-
   papiere *npl*

1095 escalation clause *(prices)*
 f clause *f* de révision
 i clausola *f* di revisione
 e cláusula *f* de reajuste
 n waarde-aanpassingsclausule *f*
 d Wertsteigerungsklausel *f*; Gleitklausel *f*

1096 escalator clause *(wages)*
 f clause *f* d'indexation; clause *f* d'échelle
   mobile
 i clausola *f* di scala mobile
 e cláusula *f* de escala móvil

n indexeringsclausule *f*
d Indexklausel *f*

1097 escheat
 f déshérence *f*; dévolution *f* de biens à
   l'État
 i eredità *f* devoluta allo Stato
 e reversión *f* de bienes abintestatos al
   estado
 n vervallen *n* van goederen aan de Staat
 d Heimfall *m* an den Staat

1098 escrow
 f document *m* déposé en garantie
 i documento *m* depositato in garanzia
 e plica *f*; documento *m* depositado en
   garantía
 n als garantie gedeponeerde schriftelijke
   verbintenis *f*
 d als Sicherheit hinterlegtes Dokument *n*

1099 escrow account
 f compte *m* de garantie bloqué
 i conto *m* di garanzia bloccato
 e cuenta *f* de garantía bloqueada
 n garantierekening *f*
 d Garantiekonto *n*

1100 escrow agent
 f dépositaire *m* légal d'un document
 i depositario *m* legale di documenti
 e depositario *m* legal de documentos
 n bewaarder *m* van documenten
 d Treuhänder *m* von hinterlegten
   Dokumenten

1101 escrow funds
 f fonds *mpl* mis en dépôt légal
 i fondi *mpl* in consegna legale
 e fondos *mpl* en plica
 n in bewaring gegeven gelden *npl*
 d beim Treuhänder hinterlegte Gelder *npl*

1102 estate duties; death duties
 f taxes *fpl* successorales; droit *m* de
   succession
 i tasse *fpl* di successione
 e impuestos *mpl* de sucesión; impuesto *m*
   sobre la herencia
 n successierecht *n*
 d Erbschaftssteuer *f*; Nachlasssteuer *f*

1103 Euro-currency market
 f marché *m* des euro-monnaies
 i mercato *m* delle Euro-divise
 e mercado *m* de eurodivisas
 n Euro-deviezenmarkt *f*
 d Euro-Währungsmarkt *m*

1104 Eurodollars
f euro-dollars *mpl*
i Euro-dollari *mpl*
e eurodólares *mpl*
n Eurodollars *mpl*
d Eurodollars *mpl*

1105 European flotations
f émissions *fpl* lancées en Europe
i emissione *f* di obbligazioni in Europa
e emisiones *fpl* de obligaciones en Europa
n Europese emissies *fpl*
d Euro-Emissionen *fpl*

1106 excess reserve
f réserve *f* extraordinaire
i riserva *f* in eccedenza
e reserva *f* en exceso
n extrareserve *f*
d überschüssige Reserve *f*

1107 exchange
f échange *m*
i cambio *m*
e cambio *m*
n wisselkoers *m*
d Wechsel *m*

1108 exchange
f devises *fpl*
i divise *fpl*; valuta *f*
e divisas *fpl*
n deviezen *npl*; valuta *f*
d Devisen *fpl*; Valuta *f*; Währung *f*

1109 exchange adjustment
f ajustement *m* de change
i aggiornamento *m* dei cambi
e ajuste *m* cambiario
n aanpassing *f* van de wisselkoers
d Wechselkurs-Berichtigung *f*

1110 exchange allocation
f allocation *f* de change
i assegnazione *f* di divise
e otorgamiento *m* de divisas
n deviezentoewijzing *f*
d Devisenzuteilung *f*

* exchange arbitration → 180

1111 exchange broker
f agent *m* de change
i agente *m* di cambio; sensale *m* di cambio
e agente *m* de cambios; corredor *m* de cambios
n wisselmakelaar *m*

d Wechselagent *m*; Wechselmakler *m*; Devisenmakler *m*

1112 exchange budget
f budget *m* de devises
i bilancio *m* di divise; calcolo *m* di divise
e presupuesto *m* de divisas
n deviezenbegroting *f*
d Devisenberechnung *f*

1113 exchange control
f contrôle *m* des changes
i controllo *m* degli scambi
e control *m* de cambios
n deviezencontrole *f*
d Devisenkontrolle *f*; Devisenbewirtschaftung *f*

1114 exchange cost
f coût *m* en devises
i costo *m* in divise
e costo *m* en divisas
n deviezenkosten *mpl*
d Devisenkosten *fpl*

1115 exchange cover; foreign exchange reserves
f réserves *fpl* de devises; réserves *fpl* de change
i disponibilità *f* di divise; riserva *f* di divise
e reservas *fpl* de divisas
n deviezenreserve *f*
d Devisendecke *f*; Währungsreserven *fpl*

1116 exchange permit
f autorisation *f* de change
i permesso *m* di cambio
e permiso *m* de cambio
n deviezenvergunning *f*
d Devisengenehmigung *f*

* exchange rate → 1937

1117 exchange rate flexibility
f flexibilité *f* des changes
i flessibilità *f* dei tipi di cambio
e flexibilidad *f* de los tipos de cambio
n flexibiliteit *f* van de wisselkoersen
d Flexibilität *f* der Kurse

1118 exchange restrictions
f restrictions *fpl* de change
i restrizioni *fpl* di cambio
e restricciones *fpl* cambiarias
n deviezenbeperkingen *fpl*
d Devisenbeschränkungen *fpl*

1119 exchange risk
f risque m de change
i rischio m cambiario
e riesgo m cambiario
n koersrisico n
d Kursrisiko m

1120 exchanges
f paiement m entre banques par liquidation de différences
i pagamenti mpl fra banche a mezzo compensazione delle differenze
e pagos mpl entre bancos mediante compensación de diferencias
n betalingen fpl tussen banken via de clearingskas
d zwischen Banken vorgenommener Zahlungsausgleich m

1121 exchange stability
f stabilité f des changes
i stabilità f dei cambi
e estabilidad f de los tipos de cambio
n stabiliteit f van de wisselkoersen
d Stabilität f der Wechselkurse

1122 exchange transactions
f transactions fpl de change; opérations fpl de change
i transazioni fpl cambiarie
e transacciones fpl cambiarias; operaciones fpl cambiarias
n deviezentransacties fpl
d Devisengeschäfte npl

1123 exchanging cheques
f chèques mpl sur une banque encaissés dans une autre banque
i assegni mpl emessi su una banca e cambiati in denaro da un'altra banca
e cheques mpl sobre un banco cambiados por dinero en efectivo en otro banco
n cheques mpl op een bank geïncasseerd bij een andere bank
d auf eine Bank ausgestellte Schecks, die durch eine andere Bank eingelöst werden

1124 exchequer account
f compte m du trésor
i conto m del tesoro
e cuenta f del tesoro
n schatkistrekening f
d Schatzkonto m

1125 exchequer bill
f bon m du Trésor
i buono m del Tesoro
e bono m del Tesoro

n schatkistobligatie f; schatkistpapier n
d Schatzanweisung f

1126 excise tax
f impôt m indirect; droit m de consommation
i imposta f al consumo
e impuesto m al consumo
n verbruiksbelasting f
d Verbrauchsabgabe f

1127 ex-dividend
f ex-dividende; sans dividende
i senza dividendo; senza diritto a dividendo
e ex dividendo; sin derecho a dividendo
n ex-dividend; zonder recht op vervallen dividend
d ex Dividende; ausschliesslich Dividende; ohne Dividende

1128 execute v
f exécuter
i eseguire
e ejecutar
n voltrekken
d vollstrecken; durchführen; ausführen

1129 execute v a deed
f signer un acte
i rilasciare una scrittura
e otorgar una escritura
n een akte passeren
d eine Urkunde ausfertigen

1130 execution creditor
f créditeur m avec droit à saisie
i creditore m esecutore
e acreedor m ejecutante
n crediteur m met recht van executie
d Vollstreckungsgläubiger m

1131 executive
f exécutif
i esecutivo
e ejecutivo
n leidende; directie-
d leitender; führender; Vorstand-

1132 executor
f exécuteur m testamentaire
i esecutore m testamentario
e albacea m
n executeur-testamentair m; boedelredder m
d Testamentsvollstrecker m

1133 exemption
f remise f; exemption f

i esonero *m*; esenzione *f*
e condonación *f*; exoneración *f*
n kwijtschelding *f*
d Erlass *m*

1134 ex factory price
f prix *m* sortie; prix *m* de fabrique
i prezzo *m* di fabbrica
e precio *m* en fábrica
n fabrieksprijs *m*
d Fabrikpreis *m*

1135 exogenous factor
f facteur *m* exogène
i fattore *m* esogeno
e factor *m* exógeno
n exogene factor *m*
d Ausseneinflüsse *mpl*; exogener
Faktor *m*

1136 expansionary policy
f politique *f* d'expansion
i politica *f* espansionista
e política *f* expansionista
n expansiepolitiek *f*
d Expansionspolitik *f*

* **expend** *v* → **2210**

* **expense account** → **30**

1137 expenses; expenditures
f dépenses *fpl*; frais *mpl*
i spese *fpl*
e gastos *mpl*; erogaciones *fpl*
n uitgaven *fpl*; onkosten *mpl*
d Ausgaben *fpl*; Unkosten *fpl*; Aufwendungen *fpl*

1138 expensive
f cher
i caro
e caro; costoso
n duur; kostbaar
d teuer

1139 expert appraisal
f expertise *f*; rapport *m* d'expertise
i tassazione *f* peritale
e tasación *f*; avalúo *m* pericial
n expertise *f*; expertiserapport *n*
d Begutachtung *f* durch Sachverständige;
Gutachten *n*

1140 expire *v*; **mature** *v*
f échoir; expirer
i scadere
e vencer; expirar

n vervallen; aflopen
d verfallen; erlöschen

**1141 expiry date; maturity (of a bill of
exchange)**
f date *f* d'échéance
i giorno *m* di scadenza
e fecha *f* de vencimiento
n vervaldatum *m*; vervaldag *m*
d Verfalldatum *n*; Verfalltag *m*

1142 export *v*
f exporter
i esportare
e exportar
n uitvoeren; exporteren
d ausführen; exportieren

1143 export; exportation
f exportation *f*
i esportazione *f*
e exportación *f*
n export *m*; uitvoer *m*
d Export *m*; Ausfuhr *f*

1144 export certificate
f certificat *m* d'exportation
i certificato *m* di esportazione
e certificado *m* de exportación
n certificaat *n* van uitvoer
d Exportbescheinigung *f*; Ausfuhrberechtigungsschein *m*

1145 export credit
f crédit *m* pour l'exportation
i credito *m* di esportazione
e crédito *m* de exportación
n exportkrediet *n*
d Ausfuhrkredit *m*

1146 export duties
f droits *mpl* d'exportation
i diritti *mpl* di esportazione
e derechos *mpl* de exportación
n uitvoerrechten *npl*
d Ausfuhrzoll *m*

1147 exporter
f exportateur *m*
i esportatore
e exportador *m*
n exporteur *m*
d Exporteur *m*; Ausfuhrhändler *m*

1148 export firm
f maison *f* d'exportation
i ditta *f* esportatrice
e firma *f* exportadora; casa *f* exportadora

n exportfirma *f*; exporthuis *n*
d Exportfirma *f*; Exporthaus *n*

1149 export licence; export permit
f licence *f* d'exportation
i licenza *f* di esportazione
e licencia *f* de exportación
n uitvoervergunning *f*
d Ausfuhrbewilligung *f*

1150 export quota
f quote-part *f* d'exportation
i quota *f* di esportazione
e cuota *f* de exportación; cupo *m* de
  exportación
n uitvoerquota *f*
d Exportkontingent *n*

1151 export trade
f commerce *m* d'exportation
i commercio *m* di esportazione
e comercio *m* de exportación
n uitvoerhandel *m*
d Ausfuhrhandel *m*

1152 expropriate *v*
f exproprier
i espropriare
e expropiar
n onteigenen
d enteignen; expropriieren

1153 expropriation
f expropriation *f*
i espropriazione *f*
e expropiación *f*
n onteigening *f*
d Enteignung *f*; Expropriation *f*

1154 extend *v*
f proroger
i prorogare
e prorrogar; prolongar
n verlengen
d verlängern

1155 extension
f prorogation *f*
i proroga *f*
e prórroga *f*; ampliación *f*
n verlenging *f*
d Verlängerung *f*; Prolongation *f*

1156 extra
f supplémentaire
i extra; supplementare
e extra; suplementario
n extra-
d Extra-; Sonder-

1157 extracharges
f frais *mpl* supplémentaires
i spese *fpl* extra; spese *fpl* accessorie
e gastos *mpl* suplementarios
n extrakosten *mpl*
d Extraspesen *fpl*; Kostenzuschlag *m*

* **extract of account** → 7

* **extra-interest** → 1424

F

1158 face amount
f montant *m* nominal
i importo *m* nominale
e importe *m* nominal
n nominaal bedrag *n*
d Nennbetrag *m*

1159 face capital
f capital *m* nominal
i capitale *m* nominale
e capital *m* nominal
n nominaal kapitaal *n*
d Nennkapital *n*

1160 face value; nominal value
f valeur *f* nominale
i valore *m* nominale
e valor *m* nominal
n nominale waarde *f*
d Nennwert *m*; Nominalwert *m*

1161 factor
f agent *m*; représentant *m*
i agente *m*
e agente *m* mercantil
n agent *m*; vertegenwoordiger *m*
d Agent *m*; Handlungsagent *m*

1162 factor income
f revenu *m*; rémunération *f* des facteurs
i reddito *m*; rimunerazione *f* dei fattori
e ingresos *mpl* de los factores
n factorinkomen *n*
d Faktoreinkommen *n*

1163 fail v
f faire faillite
i fallire
e quebrar
n failliet gaan; failleren; bankroet gaan
d Bank(e)rott *m* machen

1164 failure
f faillite *f*
i fallimento *m*
e quiebra *f*
n faillissement *n*; bankroet *n*
d Bank(e)rott *m*

1165 fall v due
f échoir; venir à échéance
i scadere
e vencer; caducar
n vervallen
d verfallen; fällig sein

1166 falsification
f falsification *f*
i falsificazione *f*
e falsificación *f*
n vervalsing *f*
d Fälschung *f*

1167 falsify v
f falsifier
i falsificare
e falsificar
n vervalsen
d fälschen

1168 farm credit
f crédit *m* agricole
i credito *m* agricolo
e crédito *m* agrícola
n landbouwkrediet *n*
d Agrarkredit *m*

1169 farm loan
f emprunt *m* agricole
i prestito *m* agricolo
e préstamo *m* agrario
n landbouwlening *f*
d Landeskulturanleihe *f*

* **fas → 1265**

1170 federals (US)
f documents *mpl* émis par une banque d'une ville dans laquelle se trouve une banque de la Réserve Fédérale
i documenti *mpl* emessi da banche di città nelle quali v'è una banca della Riserva Federale
e documentos *mpl* librados en bancos de ciudades donde hay un banco de la Reserva Federal
n documenten *npl* afgegeven door banken in een stad waar een Nationale Reserve-bank is
d Dokumente *npl* ausgestellt in Banken von solchen Städten, in denen es eine Filiale der Landeszentralbank gibt

1171 fees
f honoraires *mpl*
i onorario *m*
e honorarios *mpl*
n honorarium *n*
d Honorar *n*; Gebühren *fpl*

1172 fidelity insurance; fidelity bond
f assurance *f* contre soustraction par des employés
i assicurazione *f* contro le truffe
e seguro *m* contra estafas de empleados

n verzekering *f* tegen verduistering door
employés
d Veruntreuungsgarantie *f*; Garantieversicherung *f*

1173 fiduciary
f fiduciaire
i fiduciario
e fiduciario
n fiduciair
d treuhänderisch; fiduziär

1174 fiduciary loan
f prêt *m* fiduciaire
i prestito *m* fiduciario
e préstamo *m* fiduciario
n ongedekte lening *f*
d ungedeckte Anleihe *f*

1175 fiduciary service
f service *m* fiduciaire
i servizio *m* fiduciario
e servicio *m* fiduciario
n dienst *m* als fideïcommissaris
d Treuhänderdienst *m*

1176 figure
f chiffre *m*
i cifra *f*
e cifra *f*
n cijfer *n*
d Zahl *f*; Ziffer *f*

1177 finance
f finance(s) *f(pl)*
i finanze *fpl*; finanza *f*
e finanza(s) *f(pl)*
n financiën *fpl*; geldwezen *n*
d Finanzen *fpl*; Finanz *f*

1178 finance *v*
f financer
i finanziare
e financiar
n financieren
d finanzieren

1179 finance charges
f frais *mpl* de financement
i spese *fpl* finanziarie
e gastos *mpl* de financiación
n financieringskosten *mpl*
d Finanzierungskosten *fpl*

1180 finance company
f société *f* de financement
i compagnia *f* financiatrice
e compañia *f* financiadora

n financieringsmaatschappij *f*
d Finanzierungsgesellschaft *f*

* **finance market** → 1186

1181 financial
f financier
i finanziario
e financiero
n financieel
d finanziell

1182 financial claim
f créance *f* financière
i credito *m* finanziario; titolo *m* di credito
e título *m* de crédito; acreencia *f*
n financiële schuldvordering *f*
d Schuldtitel *m*

1183 financial credit
f crédit *m* financier; crédit *m* acheteur
i credito *m* finanziario
e crédito *m* de financiación
n financieringskrediet *n*
d Finanzierungskredit *m*

1184 financial embarrassment
f difficultés *fpl* financières
i difficoltà *fpl* finanziarie
e dificultades *fpl* financieras
n financiële moeilijkheden *fpl*
d finanzielle Schwierigkeiten *fpl*

1185 financial incomes
f revenus *mpl* financiers
i entrate *fpl* finanziarie
e ingresos *mpl* financieros
n geldelijke inkomsten *fpl*
d Finanzerträge *mpl*

1186 financial market; finance market
f marché *m* financier; marché *m* des
capitaux
i mercato *m* finanziario
e mercado *m* financiero
n kapitaalmarkt *f*
d Kapitalmarkt *m*

1187 financial operations
f opérations *fpl* financières
i operazioni *fpl* finanziarie
e operaciones *fpl* financieras
n financiële transacties *fpl*
d Finanzgeschäfte *npl*

1188 financial papers
f effets *mpl* financiers
i effetti *mpl* finanziari; valor *mpl*
finanziari

e efectos *mpl* financieros; valores *mpl*
  financieros
n waardepapieren *npl*
d Wertpapiere *npl*

1189 financial plan
f plan *m* de financement
i piano *m* di finanziamento
e plan *m* financiero
n financieringsplan *n*
d Finanzierungsplan *m*

1190 financial rate of return
f taux *m* de rentabilité financière
i tasso *m* di rendimento finanziario
e tasa *f* de rendimiento financiero
n financieel rendementspercentage *n*
d Verzinsungssatz *m*; Ertragsrate *f*

1191 financial responsibility
f responsabilité *f* financière
i responsabilità *f* finanziaria
e responsabilidad *f* financiera
n financiële verantwoordelijkheid *f*
d finanzielle Haftung *f*

1192 financial restraint; stringency
f resserrement *m* du crédit; compression *f*
i restringimento *m* del credito
e restricción *f* del crédito
n kredietbeperking *f*
d Kreditbeschränkung *f*

1193 financial world
f monde *m* financier
i mondo *m* finanziario
e mundo *m* financiero
n financiële wereld *f*; geldwereld *f*
d Finanzwelt *f*

1194 financial year
f année *f* comptable; année *f* financière;
  exercice *m*; exercice *m* budgétaire;
  année *f* budgétaire
i anno *m* finanziario
e año *m* financiero; ejercicio *m* económico
n financieel jaar *n*; boekjaar *n*
d Rechnungsjahr *n*; Geschäftsjahr *n*;
  Betriebsjahr *n*; Wirtschaftsjahr *n*;
  Finanzjahr *n*

1195 financier
f financier *m*
i finanziere *m*
e financista *m*
n financier *m*
d Finanzmann *m*

1196 fine
f amende *f*
i multa *f*
e multa *f*
n boete *f*
d Geldstrafe *f*; Busse *f*

1197 fine *v*
f mettre à l'amende
i multare
e multar
n beboeten
d strafen; bestrafen; eine Geldstrafe
  verhängen

1198 fine gold
f or *m* fin
i oro *m* fino
e oro *m* fino
n fijn goud *n*
d Feingold *n*

1199 fineness *(of a noble metal)*
f titre *m*
i titolo *m*; lega *f*
e ley *f*
n gehalte *n*
d Feingehalt *m*

1200 fire insurance
f assurance *f* contre l'incendie
i assicurazione *f* contro l'incendio
e seguro *m* contra incendios
n brandverzekering *f*
d Feuerversicherung *f*

1201 fire underwriters
f compagnie *f* d'assurance contre
  l'incendie
i società *f* d'assicurazione contro gli
  incendi
e compañia *f* de seguros contra incendios
n brandassuradeuren *mpl*;
  brandverzekeringsmaatschappij *f*;
  brandwaarborgmaatschappij *f*; brand-
  assurantiemaatschappij *f*
d Feuerversicherungsgesellschaft *f*

1202 firm
f établissement *m*; entreprise *f*
i ditta *f*
e firma *f*
n firma *f*
d Firma *f*; Unternehmung *f*

1203 first lien
f premier droit *m* de rétention
i primo gravame *m*; gravame *m*
  privilegiato

e primer gravamen *m*; gravamen *m*
  privilegiado
n eerste recht *n* van retentie
d erstes Zurückhaltungsrecht *n*

1204 first mortgage
f première hypothèque *f*
i prima ipoteca *f*
e primera hipoteca *f*
n eerste hypotheek *f*
d Ersthypothek *f*; erststellige Hypothek *f*

1205 first mortgage bond
f obligation *f* de première hypothèque
i obbligazione *f* di prima ipoteca
e obligación *f* de primera hipoteca
n obligatie *f* van eerste hypotheek
d Pfandbrief *m* der ersten Hypothek

1206 fiscal revenue
f recettes *fpl* financières; recettes *fpl*
  fiscales
i entrate *fpl* fiscali
e ingresos *mpl* fiscales
n belastingopbrengst *f*
d Staatseinkünfte *fpl*

1207 fiscal year
f année *f* budgétaire; année *f* fiscale;
  exercice *m*
i anno *m* d'esercizio
e año *m* fiscal; ejercicio *m*
n fiscaal jaar *n*; begrotingsjaar *n*
d Rechnungsjahr *n*; Betriebsjahr *n*

1208 fixed assets
f capitaux *mpl* fixes; valeurs *fpl*
  immobilisées
i attivi *mpl* fissi
e activo *m* fijo
n vaste activa *npl*
d Anlagevermögen *n*; feste Aktiven *npl*

1209 fixed capital
f capital *m* immobilisé; capital *m* placé en
  biens immeubles
i capitale *m* fisso; capitale *m*
  immobilizzato
e capital *m* fijo; capital *m* en inmuebles
n vastgelegd kapitaal *n*
d festes Kapital *n*; feste Kapitalanlagen
  fpl

1210 fixed charges
f frais *mpl* fixes
i spese *fpl* fisse
e gastos *mpl* fijos
n vaste kosten *mpl*
d feste Spesen *fpl*

1211 fixed debt
f dette *f* fixe
i debito *m* fisso
e deuda *f* fija
n vaste schuld *f*
d feste Schuld *f*

1212 fixed deposit
f dépôt *m* à terme
i deposito *m* a scadenza fissa
e depósito *m* a plazo fijo
n deposito *n* op vaste termijn
d feste Einlage *f*

1213 fixed income
f revenu *m* fixe
i entrate *fpl* fisse
e entradas *fpl* fijas
n vast inkomen *n*
d festes Einkommen *n*

1214 fixed income securities
f titres *mpl* à revenu fixe
i valori *mpl* di rendite fisse
e valores *mpl* de rentas fijas
n vastrentende waardepapieren *npl*
d festverzinsliche Wertpapiere *npl*

1215 fixed investment
f investissement *m* fixe; investissement *m*
  dans l'équipement
i investimento *m* in capitale fisso
e inversión *f* en capital fijo
n vaste investering *f*
d Anlageinvestitionen *fpl*; Sachinvesti-
  tionen *fpl*

1216 fixed rate financing
f financement *m* à taux fixe
i finanziamento *m* con tasso d'interesse
  fisso
e financiamiento *m* con tipo de interés fijo
n financiering *f* met vaste rente
d festverzinsliche Finanzierung *f*

1217 fixed term
f terme *m* fixe; échéance *f* fixe
i scadenza *f* fissa
e plazo *m* fijo
n vaste termijn *m*
d fester Termin *m*; terminiert

1218 fixtures
f biens *mpl* meubles d'une entreprise
i beni *mpl* mobiliari di una società
e bienes *mpl* muebles de una empresa
n roerende goederen *npl* van een
  onderneming
d Mobiliar *n* eines Unternehmens

1219 float v
 f mettre en circulation
 i porre in circolazione
 e poner en circulación
 n in omloop brengen; in circulatie brengen
 d in Umlauf setzen

1220 float
 f somme f des chèques pas encore crédités
 i ammontare m degli assegni non ancora accreditati
 e suma f de los cheques todavía no acreditados
 d Summe f der noch nicht gutgeschriebenen Schecks

1221 floatation; flotation
 f libération f du cours de change
 i liberazione f del tipo di cambio
 e liberación f del tipo de cambio
 n vrijgave f van de wisselkoers
 d Freigabe f des Wechselkurses

1222 floaters
 f titres mpl au porteur de premier ordre
 i titoli mpl di prim'ordine al portatore
 e títulos mpl de primera clase al portador
 n eersteklas-waarden fpl aan toonder
 d erstklassige Inhaberpapiere npl

1223 floating assets
 f actif m flottant; actif m roulant
 i attivo m fluttuante; attivo m circolante
 e activo m flotante; activo m circulante
 n vlottende activa npl
 d flüssige Anlagen fpl; Umlaufsvermögen n

1224 floating capital
 f capital m circulant; fonds m de roulement
 i capitale m circolante
 e capital m circulante
 n vlottend kapitaal n
 d Umlaufskapital n

1225 floating cash reserve
 f volant m de trésorerie
 i riserva f di cassa fluttuante
 e reserva f flotante en efectivo; encaje m flotante; encaje m circulante
 n vlottende kasreserve f
 d Umlaufkassenreserve f; schwebende Kassenreserve f

1226 floating charge
 f frais mpl flottants; charges fpl flottantes
 i gravame m fluttuante

 e gravamen m flotante
 n vlottende lasten mpl
 d schwebende Belastung f

1227 floating debt; unfunded debt
 f dette f flottante
 i debito m fluttuante
 e deuda f flotante
 n vlottende schuld f
 d schwebende Schuld f

1228 floating policy
 f police f flottante
 i polizza f fluttuante
 e póliza f flotante
 n vlottende polis f; lopende polis f
 d laufende Police f

1229 float v **the exchange rate**
 f libérer le cours de change
 i liberare il tipo di cambio
 e liberar el tipo de cambio
 n de wisselkoers vrijgeven
 d den Wechselkurs freigeben

1230 florin
 f florin m
 i fiorino m
 e florín m
 n gulden m
 d Gulden m

* **flotation** → **1221**

* **flotation** *(bonds)* → **1464**

1231 flotation costs
 f frais mpl d'émission
 i spese fpl di emissione
 e gastos mpl de emisión
 n emissiekosten mpl; uitgiftekosten mpl
 d Ausgabekosten fpl

* **fob** → **1273**

1232 follow-up financing
 f financement m complémentaire
 i finanziamento m complementario
 e financiamiento m complementario
 n aanvullende financiering f
 d Anschlussfinanzierung f

1233 forbearance
 f jours mpl de grâce
 i giorni mpl di favore
 e días mpl de gracia; indulgencia f de morosidad
 n uitstel n; respijtdagen mpl
 d Nachsichttage mpl; Stundung f

1234 forced loan
f emprunt m forcé
i prestito m forzoso
e empréstito m forzoso
n gedwongen lening f
d Zwangsanleihe f

1235 forced sale
f vente f forcée
i vendita f forzosa
e venta f forzosa
n gedwongen verkoop m
d Zwangsverkauf m

* **forced saving** → 692

1236 force majeure
f force f majeure
i forza f maggiore
e fuerza f mayor
n force f majeure; overmacht m
d höhere Gewalt f

1237 foreclose v
f entamer un jugement hypothécaire
i intavolare giudizio ipotecario
e entablar juicio hipotecario
n hypothecair beslag leggen
d die Zwangsvollstreckung betreiben aus einer Hypothek

1238 foreclosure
f jugement m hypothécaire
i giudizio m ipotecario
e juicio m hipotecario
n executie f van hypotheek
d Zwangsvollstreckung f einer Hypothek

1239 foreclosure sale
f vente f par jugement hypothécaire
i vendita f per giudizio ipotecario
e venta f por juicio hipotecario
n verkoop m ingevolge hypothecair beslag
d Zwangsverkauf m auf Grund einer verfallenen Hypothek

1240 foreign assets
f avoirs mpl à l'étranger; avoirs mpl extérieurs
i crediti mpl sull'estero; averi mpl esteri
e activos mpl en el exterior; activos mpl sobre el exterior
n vreemd actief n; vreemde waarden fpl
d Fremdwerte mpl

1241 foreign bill
f lettre f de change sur l'étranger
i cambiale f sull'estero
e letra f sobre el exterior
n wissel m op het buitenland
d Auslandswechsel m

1242 foreign borrowing
f emprunt m à l'étranger
i prestiti mpl all'estero
e empréstitos mpl en el exterior
n buitenlandse lening f; geldleningen fpl in het buitenland
d ausländische Geldanleihen fpl; Geldanleihen fpl im Ausland

1243 foreign currency; foreign exchange
f monnaie f étrangère; devises fpl étrangères; devises fpl
i moneta f estera; divise fpl estere
e dinero m extranjero; divisas fpl extranjeras; divisas fpl
n vreemd geld n; buitenlands geld n; deviezen npl
d Fremdwährung f; ausländische Währung f; Devisen fpl

1244 foreign exchange cost
f coût m en devises
i costo m in divise
e costo m en divisas
n deviezenkosten mpl
d Währungskosten fpl

1245 foreign exchange market
f marché m des changes
i mercato m delle divise; mercato m dei cambi
e mercado m de divisas; mercado m de cambios
n deviezenmarkt m
d Devisenmarkt m

* **foreign exchange reserves** → 1115

1246 foreign securities
f valeurs fpl étrangères
i valori mpl stranieri
e valores mpl extranjeros
n buitenlandse waarden fpl
d Auslandswertpapiere npl

1247 foreign trade
f commerce m extérieur
i commercio m estero
e comercio m exterior
n buitenlandse handel m
d Aussenhandel m

1248 forfeit
f perte f de droits
i perdita f di diritti
e pérdida f de derechos

n verlies n; verbeuring f
d Verwirkung f; Einbusse f

1249 forfeit v
f perdre par confiscation
i perdere per confisca
e perder por confiscación
n verbeuren
d verwirken; einbüssen

1250 forfeit
f amende f
i multa f; ammenda f
e multa f
n boete f
d Busse f

* **forge** v → 769

1251 forged cheque
f chèque m falsifié; chèque m faux
i assegno m falsificato; assegno m falso
e cheque m falsificado; cheque m falso
n vervalste cheque m; valse cheque m
d gefälschter Scheck m; falscher Scheck m

1252 forged transfer
f virement m faux
i trasferimento m falso
e transferencia f falsa
n vervalste overmaking f
d falsche Überweisung f

* **forger** → 770

* **forgery** → 768

1253 form
f bulletin m; formulaire m; formule f
i modulo m
e formulario m
n formulier n
d Formular n

1254 formalities
f formalités fpl
i formalità fpl
e formalidades fpl
n formaliteiten fpl
d Formalitäten fpl

1255 forward v
f expédier; envoyer
i spedire
e expedir; enviar
n verzenden; toezenden; doen toekomen
d expedieren; absenden; übersenden

1256 forward cover
f couverture f à terme
i copertura f a termine
e cobertura f a término; cobertura f a plazo
n termijndekking f
d Termindeckung f

1257 forward price *(of silver)*
f cotation f à terme
i quotazione f per consegna e pagamento a termine
e cotización f de precios por entrega y pago a término
n termijnprijs m; termijnnotering f
d Terminpreis m; Terminnotierung f

1258 forward transactions; futures
f opérations fpl à terme; opérations fpl à découvert
i operazioni fpl a termine; operazioni fpl allo scoperto
e operaciones fpl a término; futuros mpl
n termijntransactie f
d Termingeschäfte npl

1259 founders' shares
f actions fpl de fondateur
i azioni fpl di fondazione
e acciones fpl de fundador
n oprichtersaandelen npl
d Gründeraktien fpl

1260 franc area
f zone f franc
i zona f del franco; area f del franco
e área f del franco; zona f del franco
n franczone f
d Franczone f; Francraum m

1261 franchise
f franchise f; privilège m
i franchigia f; privilegio m
e franquicia f; privilegio m
n vrijdom m; franchise f; privilege n
d Franchise f; Vorrecht n

1262 fraud
f fraude f
i frode f
e fraude m
n bedrog n; fraude f
d Betrug m; Schwindel m

1263 fraudulent bankruptcy
f banqueroute f frauduleuse
i bancarotta f fraudolenta
e quiebra f fraudulenta
n bedrieglijke bankbreuk f; frauduleus

bankroet *n*
d betrügerischer Bankrott *m*

1264 free
f franco
i franco; libero
e franco; libre
n franco
d franko; frei

1265 free alongside ship; fas
f franco le long du bord; fas
i franco lungobordo; fas
e franco al costado del buque; fas
n vrij langszij; fas
d frei Schiffseite; fas

* **free-enterprise economy** → **1271**

1266 free foreign exchange
f monnaies *fpl* librement convertibles; change *m* libre
i cambi *mpl* liberi
e divisas *fpl* de libre convertibilidad; divisas *fpl* libres
n vrij converteerbare deviezen *npl*
d frei konvertierbare Devisen *fpl*

1267 freehold
f propriété *f* foncière exempte d'impôts
i proprietà *f* fondiaria esente da imposta
e propiedad *f* absoluta libre de impuestos
n onbezwaard grondbezit *n*
d freier Grundbesitz *m*; freies Grundeigentum *n*

1268 freeholder
f propriétaire *m* foncier
i proprietario *m* assoluto
e propietario *m* absoluto
n onbeperkt eigenaar *m*; volledig eigenaar *m*
d uneingeschränkter Eigentümer *m*

1269 free-limit loan
f prêt *m* librement accordé
i prestito *m* accordato liberamente
e préstamo *m* de aprobación autónoma
n open-limiet lening *f*
d frei gewährtes Darlehen *n*

1270 free market
f marché *m* libre
i mercato *m* libero
e mercado *m* libre
n vrije markt *f*
d freier Markt *m*

1271 free-market economy; free-enterprise economy
f économie *f* du marché libre
i economia *f* del mercato libero; economia *f* libera
e economía *f* de mercado libre; economía *f* de libre empresa
n vrije-markteconomie *f*
d freie Marktwirtschaft *f*

1272 free of charge
f sans frais; gratuit
i franco (di) spese
e libre de gastos; gratis
n kosteloos; gratis; zonder kosten
d spesenfrei; kostenfrei

1273 free on board; fob
f franco à bord; fob
i franco a bordo; fob
e franco a bordo; fob
n vrij aan boord; fob
d frei an Bord; fob

1274 free reserves
f réserves *fpl* disponibles
i riserve *fpl* disponibili
e reservas *fpl* disponibles
n vrije reserves *fpl*
d freie Rücklagen *fpl*

1275 frozen account
f compte *m* immobilisé; compte *m* gelé
i conto *m* bloccato; conto *m* congelato
e cuenta *f* bloqueada; cuenta *f* congelada
n geblokkeerde rekening *f*
d blockiertes Konto *n*

1276 frozen capital
f capitaux *mpl* gelés; capitaux *mpl* bloqués
i capitale *m* congelato; capitale *m* bloccato
e capital *m* congelado; capital *m* bloqueado
n bevroren kapitaal *n*; geblokkeerd kapitaal *n*
d gesperrte Guthaben *npl*; festliegende Gelder *npl*

1277 fulfil(l) *v*
f remplir; exécuter
i adempiere; eseguire
e cumplir; ejecutar
n vervullen; verwezenlijken
d erfüllen; vollziehen

1278 fulfil(l)ment
f accomplissement *m*; exécution *f*; réalisation *f*

i adempimento *m*; esecuzione *f*
e cumplimiento *m*; ejecución *f*
n vervulling *f*; voltrekking *f*;
   verwezenlijking *f*
d Erfüllung *f*; Vollziehung *f*

1279 full amount
f montant *m* total
i importo *m* totale
e monto *m* total
n totaalbedrag *n*
d Gesamtbetrag *m*; voller Betrag *m*

1280 full bill of lading
f connaissement *m* complet
i polizza *f* di carico a piena responsabilità
e conocimiento *m* de embarque de
   responsabilidad total
n vol connossement *n*
d volles Konnossement *n*

1281 full endorsement
f endossement *m* complet
i girata *f* in pieno
e endoso *m* completo
n volledig endossement *n*
d vollständiges Indossament *n*

* **full-paid shares** → **1756**

1282 full payment
f paiement *m* intégral
i pagamento *m* totale; pagamento *m*
   integrale
e pago *m* total
n volledige betaling *f*
d Vollzahlung *f*; Vollbezahlung *f*

1283 full settlement
f règlement *m* de tout le compte
i liquidazione *f* completa
e liquidación *f* total
n volledige kwijting *f*
d vollständige Abrechnung *f*

1284 fully paid-up capital
f capital *m* entièrement versé
i capitale *m* interamente versato
e capital *m* totalmente integrado
n volgestort kapitaal *n*; volledig gestort
   kapitaal *n*
d voll eingezahltes Kapital *n*

1285 funded debt
f dette *f* consolidée
i debito *m* consolidato
e deuda *f* consolidada
n geconsolideerde schuld *f*
d fundierte Schuld *f*

1286 funds
f fonds *mpl*
i fondi *mpl*
e fondos *mpl*
n fondsen *npl*; gelden *npl*
d Fonds *mpl*; Gelder *npl*

* **futures** → **1258**

G

1287 galloping inflation
 f inflation f galopante
 i inflazione f galoppante
 e inflación f galopante
 n galopperende inflatie f
 d galoppierende Inflation f

1288 gambling policy
 f police f de spéculation
 i polizza f di speculazione
 e póliza f de especulación
 n hazardpolis f
 d Spekulationspolice f

1289 gap
 f déficit m; écart m
 i deficit m; breccia f
 e déficit m; brecha f
 n deficit n; tekort n
 d Defizit n; Lücke f

1290 garbling
 f fusion f de monnaies d'or et d'argent
   pour la fabrication de joyaux
 i fusione f di monete di oro o argento per
   la fabbricazione di gioielli
 e fundición f de monedas de oro o plata
   para fabricar joyas
 n versmelten n van gouden en zilveren
   muntstukken ter vervaardiging van
   juwelen
 d Einschmelzen n von Gold- oder Silber-
   münzen zur Schmuckherstellung

 * **GDP** → **1306**

1291 general creditor
 f créditeur m non privilégié
 i creditore m ordinario
 e acreedor m ordinario; acreedor m
   solidario
 n schuldeiser m zonder bevoorrechting
 d Gesamtgläubiger m

1292 general guaranty
 f garantie f générale
 i garanzia f generale
 e garantía f sin restricciones
 n onbeperkte borgstelling f
 d uneingeschränkte Garantie f

1293 general ledger
 f journal m général
 i libro m mastro generale
 e libro m diario central

 n algemeen grootboek n
 d allgemeines Hauptbuch n

1294 general mortgage
 f hypothèque f générale
 i ipoteca f generale
 e hipoteca f general
 n algemene hypotheek f
 d Gesamthypothek f

 * **gilt-edged securities** → **411**

 * **GNP** → **1308**

1295 gold bonds *(US)*
 f obligations fpl payables en or
 i obbligazioni fpl il cui interesse si paga
   in monete d'oro
 e obligaciones fpl cuyo interés se paga en
   monedas de oro
 n goudobligaties fpl
 d Goldobligationen fpl

1296 gold coin
 f monnaie f d'or
 i moneta f d'oro
 e moneda f de oro
 n gouden munt f
 d Goldmünze f

 * **gold holdings** → **1298**

1297 gold points; bullion points; specie points
 f points mpl de l'or
 i punti mpl dell'oro
 e puntos mpl del oro
 n goudpunten mpl
 d Goldpunkte mpl

1298 gold reserves; gold holdings
 f réserves fpl d'or
 i riserve fpl in oro
 e reservas fpl en oro
 n goudreserves fpl
 d Goldbestand m

1299 gold standard
 f étalon m d'or
 i tipo m d'oro
 e patrón m oro
 n gouden standaard m
 d Goldstandard m

1300 gold value
 f valeur f or
 i valore m oro
 e valor m oro
 n goudwaarde f
 d Goldwert m

1301 goodwill *(of a firm)*
f achalandage *m*; clientèle *f*
i buonuscita *f*
e llave *f*
n goodwill *f*; cliëntèle *f*
d Goodwill *n*; Geschäftswert *m*; ideeller
Wert *m*; Kundschaft *f*

1302 government bonds; government papers
f titres *mpl* de l'État; effets *mpl* publics
i titoli *mpl* di Stato; valori *mpl* pubblici
e títulos *mpl* del Estado; efectos *mpl*
públicos; efectos *mpl* del Estado
n staatsobligaties *fpl*; staatsfondsen *npl*
d Staatspapiere *npl*

1303 grace period
f différé *m* d'amortissement
i periodo *m* di grazia
e período *m* de gracia
n respijttermijn *m*
d Nachfrist *f*; Frist *f*; Respekttage *mpl*

1304 graft
f subornation *f*; pots-de-vin *mpl*
i concussione *f*; subornazione *f*;
commissione *f* illegale
e cohecho *m*; concusión *f*; coima *f (SA)*;
comisión *f* ilegal
n steekpenningen *mpl*
d Bestechung *f*; Schmiergeld *n*

1305 greenbacks *(US)*
f billets *mpl* de banque
i banconote *fpl*; biglietti *mpl* di banca
e billetes *mpl* de banco
n bankbiljetten *npl*
d Banknoten *fpl*

1306 gross domestic product; GDP
f produit *m* intérieur brut; PIB
i prodotto *m* interno brutto; PIB
e producto *m* interno bruto; PIB
n bruto binnenlands product *n*; BBP
d Bruttoinlandsprodukt *n*; BIP

1307 gross fixed investment
f investissement *m* brut en capital fixe
i investimento *m* lordo in capitale fisso
e inversión *f* bruta en capital fijo
n bruto vaste investering *f*
d Bruttoanlageinvestition *f*

1308 gross national product; GNP
f produit *m* national brut; PNB
i prodotto *m* nazionale lordo; PNL
e producto *m* nacional bruto; PNB
n bruto nationaal product *n*; BNP
d Bruttosozialprodukt *n*; BSP

1309 gross profit
f bénéfice *m* brut
i beneficio *m* lordo
e beneficio *m* bruto
n brutowinst *f*
d Rohgewinn *m*; Bruttogewinn *m*

1310 group banking
f syndicat *m* de banques
i consorzio *m* bancario; banche *fpl*
consorziali
e consorcio *m* bancario
n bankconsortium *n*; banksyndicaat *n*
d Bankenkonsortium *n*; Konsortialbanken
fpl

1311 guarantee; guaranty
f garantie *f*
i garanzia *f*
e garantía *f*; fianza *f*
n borg *m*; borgstelling *f*
d Garantie *f*; Gewähr *f*; Bürgschaft *f*

1312 guarantee *v*
f garantir; avaliser
i garantire
e garantir; garantizar
n garanderen
d garantieren; Gewähr leisten

1313 guaranteed stock
f actions *fpl* garanties
i azioni *fpl* con interessi garantiti
e acciones *fpl* con intereses garantidos
n aandelen *npl* met gegarandeerd dividend
d Aktien *fpl* mit garantierter Dividendenzahlung

1314 guarantor; surety
f garant *m*
i garante *m*; mallevadore *m*
e garante *m*; fiador *m*
n garant *m*; borg *m*
d Garant *m*; Bürge *m*; Gewährsmann *m*

* **guaranty → 1311**

1315 guaranty deposit
f dépôt *m* en garantie
i deposito *m* di garanzia
e depósito *m* de garantía
n garantiedeposito *n*
d Garantiehinterlegung *f*

1316 guaranty funds
f fonds *mpl* de garantie; moyens *mpl* de
garantie
i fondi *mpl* di garanzia
e fondos *mpl* de garantía

n garantiefondsen *npl*
d Garantiefonds *mpl*; Garantiemittel *npl*

H

1317 handling charges
f frais *mpl* de manutention
i spese *fpl* di manutenzione; spese *fpl* di
manipulazione
e gastos *mpl* de manipulación; gastos *mpl*
de tramitación
n behandelingskosten *mpl*
d Manipulationsgebühr *f*

1318 hand notes
f billets *mpl* de banque coupés en deux et
envoyés séparément par la poste
i banconote *fpl* tagliate a meta e inviate
separatamente per posta
e billetes *mpl* de banco cortados al medio
y enviados separadamente por correo
n bankbiljetten *npl* doormidden gesneden
en separaat per post verzonden
d Banknoten *fpl* in der Mitte zerschnitten
und getrennt per Post verschickt

1319 hard currency; strong currency
f monnaie *f* forte; devise *f* forte
i moneta *f* forte
e moneda *f* fuerte; moneda *f* dura
n harde valuta *f*
d harte Währung *f*

1320 hardening of loan terms
f durcissement *m* des conditions de prêt
i appesantimento *m* delle condizioni dei
prestiti
e empeoramiento *m* de las condiciones de
préstamo
n verzwaring *f* van de leningsvoorwaarden;
verharding *f* van de leningsvoorwaarden
d Erschwerung *f* der Anleihebedingungen

1321 hard loan
f prêt *m* aux conditions commerciales;
prêt *m* aux conditions du marché
i prestito *m* a condizioni ordinarie
e préstamo *m* en condiciones ordinarias
d Kredit *m* der zu den Marktsätzen
verzinst wird

1322 head teller
f caissier *m* en chef
i cassiere *m* principale
e cajero *m* jefe; cajero *m* principal
n hoofdkassier *m*
d Hauptkassierer *m*

1323 hedging
f couverture *f* (des opérations à terme)
i copertura *f* (delle operazioni a termine)

e cobertura *f* (de operaciones a plazo)
n dekkingen *fpl* (van termijntransacties)
d Deckungen *fpl* (der Termingeschäfte)

1324 heir
f héritier *m*
i erede *m*
e heredero *m*
n erfgenaam *m*
d Erbe *m*

1325 heritable
f héritable
i ereditabile
e heredable
n erfelijk; vererfbaar
d erblich; erbbar

1326 heritable bond *(Sc.)*
f titre *m* en garantie
i titolo *m* di garanzia
e título *m* de garantia
n garantiebewijs *n*
d Garantieschein *m*

1327 heritage
f héritage *m*
i eredità *f*
e herencia *f*
n erfgoed *n*; erfenis *f*
d Erbschaft *f*

1328 high income countries
f pays *mpl* à revenu élevé
i paesi *mpl* a entrate elevate
e países *mpl* de altos ingresos
n landen *npl* met hoge inkomsten
d Länder *npl* die hohe Einkünfte haben

* hock *v* → **1786**

1329 holder
f porteur *m*; titulaire *m*
i portatore *m*; possessore *m*
e portador *m*; tenedor *m*
n houder *m*; bezitter *m*
d Inhaber *m*; Besitzer *m*

* holder for value → **414**

* holder in due course → **414**

1330 holding company; holding
f société *f* holding; holding *f*; trust *m* de
valeurs
i società *f* holding
e compañia *f* holding; trust *m* de valores;
compañia *f* tenedora de acciones de otras
sociedades

   n holding company *f*; holding-
       maatschappij *f*; houdstermaatschappij *f*
   d Holdinggesellschaft *f*; Holding *f*; Dach-
       gesellschaft *f*

1331 hold-overs *(US)*
   f travail *m* par équipe en dehors des
       heures normales
   i lavori *mpl* a turno fuori orario
   e trabajos *mpl* en turnos fuera de hora
   n ploegenarbeid *f* verricht buiten de
       normale werktijd
   d Schichtarbeit *f* ausserhalb der normalen
       Arbeitszeit

1332 honour *v*; **take** *v* **up; retire** *v*
   f payer (une lettre); accepter (une lettre);
       honorer (une lettre)
   i pagare (una cambiale); accettare (una
       cambiale)
   e pagar (una letra); aceptar (una letra);
       descontar (una letra)
   n betalen (een wissel); honoreren (een
       wissel)
   d bezahlen (einen Wechsel); honorieren
       (einen Wechsel); akzeptieren (einen
       Wechsel); einlösen (einen Wechsel)

1333 hot money
   f capitaux *mpl* spéculatifs
   i capitali *mpl* speculativi
   e capital *m* especulativo
   n speculatief geld *n*
   d heisses Geld *n*

1334 hypothec *(sea)*
   f nantissement *m*; hypothèque *f*
   i ipoteca *f*
   e hipoteca *f*
   n kusting *f*
   d Hypothek *f*

1335 hypothecary
   f hypothécaire
   i ipotecario
   e hipotecario
   n hypothecair
   d hypothekarisch

   * **hypothecate** *v* → **1628**

I

1336 idle capital
f capital *m* oisif
i capitale *m* inattivo
e capital *m* inactivo
n dood kapitaal *n*
d unbenutztes Kapital *n*; unbeschäftigtes
Kapital *n*

1337 idle cash
f argent *m* oisif
i denaro *m* inattivo
e dinero *m* inactivo
n braakliggend geld *n*
d brachliegende Gelder *npl*

1338 idle liquidities
f liquidités *fpl* oisives
i fondi *mpl* liquidi inattivi
e fondos *mpl* liquidos inactivos
n braakliggende liquide middelen *npl*
d brachliegende Liquiditätsmittel *npl*

1339 illegal interest
f intérêt *m* illégal
i interesse *m* illegale
e interés *m* ilegal
n onwettige interest *m*
d ungesetzlicher Zins *m*

1340 imbalance in international payments
f déséquilibre *m* des paiements
internationaux
i squilibrio *m* nei pagamenti
internazionali
e desequilibrio *m* de los pagos
internacionales
n onevenwicht *n* in internationale
betalingen
d Ungleichgewicht *n* der internationalen
Zahlungen

1341 immediate annuity
f annuité *f* entrant en vigueur
immédiatement
i annualità *f* con effetto immediato;
annualità *f* anticipata
e anualidad *f* con efecto inmediato
n onmiddellijk ingaande rente *f*
d sofort beginnende Rente *f*

1342 immovable property; immovables
f biens *mpl* immeubles
i beni *mpl* immobili
e bienes *mpl* inmuebles; bienes *mpl*
raíces
n onroerende goederen *npl*

d Immobilien *fpl*; unbewegliches Eigentum *n*

1343 immunity from taxation
f immunité *f* fiscale
i immunità *f* fiscale
e inmunidad *f* tributaria
n belastingvrijdom *m*
d Abgabenfreiheit *f*

1344 impawn v
f mettre en gage
i impegnare
e empeñar; pignorar
n verpanden
d verpfänden

1345 impeachment of waste
f responsabilité *f* pour endommagement
d'un objet loué
i responsabilità *f* per danni causati alla
proprietà presa in affitto
e responsabilidad *f* por daños causados a
la propiedad alquilada
n aansprakelijkheid *f* voor schade aan een
gehuurd object
d Haftung *f* für Schäden am Mietgegen-
stand

1346 impeachment of waste
f inculpation *f* pour détérioration
i denuncia *f* per deterioramento
e acusación *f* por deterioro
n aanklacht *f* wegens veroorzaakte schade
d Mängelklage *f*

1347 impersonal account; nominal account
f compte *m* impersonnel; compte *m* à
numéro
i conto *m* impersonale
e cuenta *f* impersonal
n onpersoonlijke rekening *f*;
nummerrekening *f*
d Firmenkonto *n*

1348 implict export rate
f taux *m* d'exportation calculé
i tipo *m* di cambio di esportazione
implicito
e tipo *m* de cambio de exportación
implícito
n onvoorwaardelijke exportwisselkoers *m*
d ausgerechnete Exportkurs *m*

1349 import v
f importer
i importare
e importar

n importeren; invoeren
d importieren; einführen

* **import → 1351**

1350 import arrears
  f arriérés *mpl* d'importation
  i ritardi *mpl* nei pagamenti di
    importazioni
  e retrasos *mpl* en los pagos por
    importaciones
  n vertragingen *fpl* in de importbetalingen
  d rückständige Einfuhrzahlungen *fpl*

1351 importation; import
  f importation *f*
  i importazione *f*
  e importación *f*
  n invoer *m*; import *m*
  d Einfuhr *f*; Import *m*

1352 import credit
  f crédit *m* pour l'importation
  i credito *m* d'importazione
  e crédito *m* de importación
  n importkrediet *n*; invoerkrediet *n*
  d Importkredit *m*

1353 import duty
  f droits *mpl* d'importation; droits *mpl*
    d'entrée
  i diritti *mpl* d'importazione; dazio *m*
    d'importazione
  e derechos *mpl* de importación
  n invoerrechten *npl*; ingaande rechten *npl*
  d Einfuhrzoll *m*

1354 import permit; import licence
  f permis *m* d'importation
  i permesso *m* d'importazione
  e permiso *m* de importación
  n invoervergunning *f*
  d Einfuhrerlaubnis *f*

1355 import quota
  f contingent *m* d'importation
  i contingente *m* di importazione; quota *f*
    di importazione
  e cuota *f* de importación; cupo *m* de
    importación
  n invoerquotum *n*; invoerquota *f*
  d Einfuhrkontingent *n*

1356 import surcharge
  f surtaxe *f* à l'importation
  i sopratassa *f* di importazione
  e recargo *m* a la importación
  n invoertoeslag *m*
  d Importzuschlag *m*; Einfuhrzuschlag *m*

1357 imprest account
  f compte *m* d'avances de caisse
  i conto *m* anticipi
  e cuenta *f* de anticipos
  n voorschotrekening *f*
  d Vorschusskonto *n*

1358 inadequacy of reserves
  f insuffisance *f* des réserves
  i riserve *fpl* insufficienti
  e insuficiencia *f* de reservas
  n ontoereikendheid *f* van reserves
  d ungenügende Reserven *fpl*

1359 incentive payment
  f subvention *f*; prime *f*
  i premio *m* stimolo
  e prima *f*; incentivo *m*
  n premieloon *n*
  d Leistungslohn *m*

1360 inchoate instrument
  f document *m* incomplet
  i documento *m* incompleto
  e documento *m* incompleto
  n onvolledig document *n*
  d unvollständiges Dokument *n*

1361 income; revenue
  f revenu(s) *m(pl)*
  i entrata *f*; entrate *fpl*; reddito *m*
  e ingreso(s) *m(pl)*; renta *f*
  n inkomen *n*; inkomsten *fpl*
  d Einkommen *n*; Einkünfte *fpl*; Ertrag *m*

1362 income account
  f compte *m* de revenus
  i conto *m* delle entrate
  e cuenta *f* de ingresos
  n inkomstenrekening *f*
  d Ertragskonto *n*; Ertragsrechnung *f*

1363 income bond
  f bond *m* de revenus
  i buono *m* delle entrate
  e bono *m* de ingresos
  n inkomstenobligatie *f*
  d Gewinnschuldverschreibung *f*

1364 income bracket
  f tranche *f* de revenu; classe *f* de revenu
  i livello *m* di entrate; gruppo *m* di entrate
  e nivel *m* de ingresos; grupo *m* de
    ingresos
  n inkomensgroep *f*
  d Einkommensgruppe *f*

1365 income effect
  f effet *m* de revenu

i effetto *m* di rendita
e efecto *m* de ingreso
n income effect *n*
d Ertragswirkung *f*

1366 income elasticity
f élasticité *f* par rapport au revenu;
élasticité-revenu *f*
i elasticità *f* delle entrate; entrate *fpl*
elastiche
e elasticidad *f* de ingreso; elasticidad *f* con
respecto al ingreso
n elasticiteit *f* van de inkomsten
d Elastizität *f* des Einkommens; Ein-
kommenselastizität *f*

1367 income statement
f déclaration *f* de revenus
i dichiarazione *f* delle entrate
e declaración *f* de ingresos
n inkomstenbelastingaangifte *f*; opgave *f*
van inkomsten
d Einkommensteuererklärung *f*

1368 income tax
f impôt *m* sur le revenu
i imposta *f* sul reddito
e impuesto *m* a los ingresos; impuesto *m* a
la renta
n inkomstenbelasting *f*
d Einkommensteuer *f*

1369 income velocity of money
f vitesse *f* de transformation de la
monnaie en revenu
i velocità *f* di trasformazione del denaro in
rendite
e velocidad-ingreso *f* del dinero
n omloopsnelheid *f* van het geld
d Umlaufsgeschwindigkeit *f* des Einkommens

1370 inconvertible currency
f monnaie *f* non convertible
i denaro *m* non convertibile
e dinero *m* no convertible
n niet converteerbare valuta *f*
d nicht konvertierbare Währung *f*

1371 increasing returns
f rendements *mpl* croissants
i rendimento *m* crescente
e rendimientos *mpl* crecientes
n toenemende rendementen *npl*
d steigende Erträge *mpl*; zunehmende Erträge *mpl*

1372 incremental benefits
f avantages *mpl* supplémentaires

i utilità *fpl* suppletive
e beneficios *mpl* adicionales
n supplementaire winsten *fpl*
d Extragewinn *m*

1373 incremental rate of return
f taux *m* différentiel de rentabilité
i tasso *m* differenziale di redditibilità
e tasa *f* diferencial de rentabilidad
n differentiële rentabiliteitsverhouding *f*
d Differentialverzinsung *f*

* **incumbrance → 1074**

1374 indebted
f endetté
i indebitato
e endeudado
n diep in de schulden zittend; in schulden
gestoken
d verschuldet; schuldenbelastet

1375 indebtedness
f endettement *m*
i indebitamento *m*; addebito *m*
e endeudamiento *m*; adeudo *m*
n schuldenlast *m*
d Verschuldung *f*

1376 indebtedness
f dette *f*; créance *f*
i debito *m*
e deuda *f*
n schuld *f*
d Schuld *f*

* **indemnification → 1380**

1377 indemnify *v*
f indemniser; dédommager
i indennizzare
e indemnizar
n schadeloosstellen; vergoeden
d entschädigen; schadlos halten

1378 indemnitee
f indemnitaire *m*
i indennizzato *m*
e indemnizado *m*
n ontvanger *m* van een schadevergoeding
d Entschädigungsempfänger *m*; Entschädi-
gungsnehmer *m*

1379 indemnitor
f payeur *m* d'une indemnité
i indennizzatore *m*
e indemnizador *m*
n schadevergoeder *m*
d Entschädigender *m*

1380 indemnity; indemnification
f indemnité f; dédommagement m;
   compensation f
i indennità f; indennizzo m; risarcimento
   m danni
e indemnización f
n schadevergoeding f; schadeloosstelling f
d Entschädigung f; Schadenersatz m

1381 indemnity benefits
f profits mpl d'indemnité
i utili mpl d'indennità
e beneficios mpl de indemnización
n schadevergoedingsuitkering f
d Entschädigungsgewinn m; Entschä-
   digungsvorteil m

* **indemnity bond** → 423

1382 indemnity contract
f contrat m de compensation
i contratto m d'indennizzo
e contrato m de indemnización
n contract n tot schadevergoeding
d Entschädigungsvertrag m

1383 indemnity insurance
f assurance f de compensation
i assicurazione f d'indennità
e seguro m de indemnización
n verzekering f tegen schadevergoeding
d Schadenersatzversicherung f

1384 index-tied loan
f prêt m indexé
i prestito m con una clausola di valore
   stabile
e préstamo m reajustable
n indexgebonden lening f
d Indexanleihe f; indexgebundene Anleihe f

* **indorsation** → 1079

* **indorse** v → 1076

* **indorsed bond** → 1077

* **indorsee** → 1078

* **indorsement** → 1079

* **indorser** → 1080

1385 industrial accident
f accident m industriel
i accidente m industriale
e accidente m industrial

n bedrijfsongeval n
d Betriebsunfall m

* **industrials** → 1387

1386 industrial securities
f papiers mpl d'industrie
i titoli mpl industriali
e títulos mpl industriales
n industriële waarden fpl
d Industriepapiere npl

1387 industrial shares; industrials
f actions fpl industrielles
i azioni fpl industriali
e acciones fpl industriales
n industriële aandelen npl
d Industrieaktien fpl

1388 industry
f industrie f
i industria f
e industria f
n industrie f; nijverheid f
d Industrie f; Gewerbe n

1389 ineligible papers *(US)*
f valeurs fpl non bancables
i valori mpl non negoziabili
e efectos mpl no negociables
n waardepapieren npl die niet voor
   disconto in aanmerking komen
d nicht bankfähige Wertpapiere npl

1390 inflation
f inflation f
i inflazione f
e inflación f
n inflatie f
d Inflation f

1391 inflationary period
f période f d'inflation
i periodo m di inflazione
e período m de inflación
n inflatieperiode f
d Inflationszeit f

1392 inflationary pressures
f pressions fpl inflationnistes
i pressione f inflazionistica
e presiones fpl inflacionarias
n inflatoire krachten fpl; inflatoire druk m
d Inflationsdruck m; inflationistische
   Kräfte fpl; inflatorische Kräfte fpl

1393 inflow of capital; capital inflow
f entrée f de capitaux
i affluenza f di capitali

e entrada *f* de capitales; afluencia *f* de
  capitales
n kapitaaltoevloed *m*
d Kapitalzufuhr *f*; Kapitalzufluss *m*

1394 information
f information *f*
i informazione *f*
e información *f*
n informatie *f*; inlichting *f*
d Auskunft *f*; Information *f*

1395 ingot
f lingot *m*
i barra *f*
e lingote *m*; barra *f*
n baar *f*; staaf *f*
d Barren *m*

1396 inherit *v*
f hériter
i ereditare
e heredar
n erven; beërven
d erben

1397 input-output coefficient
f coefficient *m* technique; coefficient *m* de
  production
i coefficiente *m* di produzione
e coeficiente *m* de insumo-producto
n productiecoëfficiënt *m*
d Produktionskoeffizient *m*

1398 insolvency
f insolvabilité *f*
i insolvenza *f*; insolvabilità *f*
e insolvencia *f*
n insolventie *f*
d Insolvenz *f*; Zahlungsunfähigkeit *f*

1399 insolvent
f insolvable
i insolvente
e insolvente
n insolvent
d insolvent; zahlungsunfähig

1400 inspect *v*
f inspecter; contrôler; examiner
i ispezionare; controllare
e inspeccionar; fiscalizar; revisar
n inspecteren; nazien; controleren
d besichtigen; beaufsichtigen; kontrollieren;
  prüfen

1401 inspection
f inspection *f*
i ispezione *f*

e inspección *f*
n inspectie *f*; onderzoek *n*
d Besichtigung *f*; Aufsicht *f*

1402 instal(l)ment
f acompte *m*
i rata *f*
e cuota *f*; mensualidad *f*
n termijn *m*
d Rate *f*

1403 instruct *v*
f instruire
i istruire
e instruir
n opdragen; voorschrijven
d anweisen

1404 instrument
f instrument *m*; document *m*
i strumento *m*; istrumento *m*;
  documento *m*
e instrumento *m*; documento *m*
n document *n*
d Dokument *n*; Urkunde *f*

1405 instrument of acceptance
f instrument *m* d'acceptation
i strumento *m* di accettazione
e instrumento *m* de aceptación
n acceptatie-instrument *n*
d Akzeptsurkunde *f*

1406 insurable
f assurable
i assicurabile
e asegurable
n verzekerbaar
d versicherbar; versicherungsfähig

1407 insurable interest
f intérêt *m* assurable
i interesse *m* assicurabile
e interés *m* asegurable
n verzekerbaar interest *m*
d versicherbarer Zins *m*

1408 insurable risk
f risque *m* assurable
i rischio *m* assicurabile
e riesgo *m* asegurable
n voor verzekering vatbaar risico *n*; te
  verzekeren risico *n*
d Versicherungsrisiko *n*

1409 insurable value
f valeur *f* assurable
i valore *m* assicurabile
e valor *m* asegurable

n verzekerbare waarde *f*
d versicherbarer Wert *m*

1410 insurance; assurance
f assurance *f*
i assicurazione *f*
e seguro *m*
n verzekering *f*; assurantie *f*
d Versicherung *f*

1411 insurance broker
f courtier *m* d'assurances
i agente *m* d'assicurazione
e corredor *m* de seguros
n assurantiemakelaar *m*
d Versicherungsmakler *m*

1412 insurance company
f compagnie *f* d'assurances; société *f*
d'assurances
i compagnia *f* d'assicurazione
e compañía *f* de seguros
n verzekeringsmaatschappij *f*
d Versicherungsgesellschaft *f*

1413 insurance funds
f fonds *mpl* d'assurance
i fondi *mpl* d'assicurazione
e fondos *mpl* de seguro
n verzekeringsfondsen *npl*
d Versicherungsfonds *mpl*

1414 insurance policy; policy of insurance
f police *f* d'assurance
i polizza *f* d'assicurazione
e póliza *f* de seguros
n verzekeringspolis *f*; polis *f* van
assurantie
d Versicherungsschein *m*; Versicherungs-
police *f*

1415 insurance premium
f prime *f* d'assurance
i premio *m* d'assicurazione
e prima *f* de seguros
n verzekeringspremie *f*
d Versicherungsprämie *f*

1416 insure *v*; assure *v*
f assurer
i assicurare
e asegurar
n verzekeren
d versichern

1417 insuree
f assuré *m*
i assicurato *m*
e asegurado *m*

n verzekerde *m*
d Versicherter *m*

1418 insurer
f assureur *m*
i assicuratore *m*
e asegurador *m*
n assuradeur *m*; verzekeraar *m*
d Versicherer *m*

1419 intangible assets
f valeurs *fpl* intangibles; valeurs *fpl*
immatérielles
i attivi *mpl* intangibili
e activos *mpl* intangibles
n onaantastbare activa *npl*; immateriële
activa *npl*
d nicht greifbare Aktiva *npl*; immaterielle
Aktiva *npl*; unantastbare Vermögenswerte *mpl*

1420 interest
f intérêt *m*
i interesse *m*
e interés *m*; rédito *m*
n interest *m*; rente *f*
d Zins *m*; Zinsen *mpl*

1421 interest coupon
f coupon *m* d'intérêt
i cedola *f* d'interessi
e cupón *m* de intereses
n rentecoupon *m*
d Zinsschein *m*

1422 interest coverage
f couverture *f* de l'intérêt
i copertura *f* degli interessi
e cobertura *f* de los intereses
n rentedekking *f*
d Zinsdeckung *f*

1423 interest equalization tax
f taxe *f* de péréquation d'intérêts
i tassa *f* di perequazione d'interessi
e impuesto *m* de igualación de intereses
n rentevereffeningsbelasting *f*
d Zinsausgleichsteuer *f*

1424 interest fine; extra-interest
f intérêts *mpl* de retard
i interessi *mpl* di mora
e intereses *mpl* moratorios
n achterstallige interest *m*
d Verzugszinsen *mpl*

1425 interest policy
f police *f* d'assurance payant intérêts
i polizza *f* d'assicurazione con interessi

e póliza f de seguros con interés
n interestdragende polis f
d verzinslicher Versicherungsschein m

1426 interest rate
f taux m d'intérêt
i tasso m d'interessi
e tasa f de interés; tipo m de interés
n rentevoet m; rentetype n; rentestand m
d Zinssatz m; Zinsfuss m

1427 interest-rate differential
f écart m entre les taux d'intérêt
i margine m tra i tassi di interesse
e margen m entre las tasas de interés
n rentemarge f
d Zinsgefälle n

1428 interest revenue
f revenu m d'intérêts
i reddito m d'interessi
e rédito m de intereses
n renteopbrengst f
d Zinsertrag m

1429 interest subsidy
f bonification f d'intérêts
i sovvenzione f degli interessi
e subvención f de intereses
n rentesubsidie f
d Zinszuschuss m

1430 interest warrant
f ordonnance f de paiement d'intérêts
i ordine m di pagamento di interessi
e orden f de pago de intereses
n rentewarrant m
d Zinsenauszahlungsschein m

1431 interim dividend
f dividende m provisoire
i dividendo m provvisorio
e dividendo m provisional
n interimdividend n
d Interimsdividende f; Zwischen-
    dividende f

1432 internal cash generation
f création f de liquidités
i creazione f di liquidità
e recursos mpl provenientes de
    operaciones
n interne liquiditeitverschaffing f
d Liquiditätsgewinnung f

1433 internal loan
f emprunt m interne
i prestito m interno
e empréstito m interno

n binnenlandse lening f
d Inlandanleihe f

1434 internal rate of return
f taux m de rentabilité interne
i tasso m di reddito interno
e tasa f de rentabilidad interna
n interne rentevoet m
d interner Zinssatz m

**1435 International Bank for Reconstruction
    and Development**
f Banque f internationale pour la
    reconstruction et le développement
i Banca f Internazionale per la
    Ricostruzione e lo Sviluppo
e Banco m Internacional de
    Reconstrucción y Fomento
n Internationale Bank f voor Wederopbouw
    en Ontwikkeling
d Internationale Bank f für Wiederaufbau
    und Wirtschaftsförderung

1436 international liquidity
f liquidité f internationale
i liquidità f internazionale
e liquidez f internacional
n internationale liquiditeit f
d internationale Liquidität f

1437 International Monetary Fund
f Fonds m monétaire international
i Fondo m Monetario Internazionale
e Fondo m Monetario Internacional
n Internationaal Monetair Fonds n
d Internationaler Währungsfonds m

1438 international reserves
f réserves fpl internationales
i riserve fpl internazionali
e reservas fpl internacionales
n internationale reserves fpl
d Auslandsreserven fpl

1439 intestate
f intestat
i intestato
e intestado
n zonder achterlating van testament
d ohne Testament

1440 invalid
f nul; sans valeur; sans effet
i nullo; non valido
e nulo; sin valor
n ongeldig; krachteloos; waardeloos; niet
    van kracht
d ungültig; kraftlos; nichtig

1441 invalidate *v*
  f annuler; invalider; rendre nul
  i annullare; invalidare; rendere invalido
  e anular; invalidar
  n annuleren; ongeldig verklaren
  d annullieren; für ungültig erklären

1442 inventory
  f inventaire *m*
  i inventario *m*
  e inventario *m*
  n inventaris *m*
  d Inventar *n*; Bestand *m*; Bestandsverzeichnis *n*

1443 invest *v*
  f placer; investir
  i investire
  e colocar; invertir
  n beleggen; investeren
  d anlegen; investieren

1444 investment
  f placement *m*; investissement *m*
  i investimento *m*
  e inversión *f*
  n belegging *f*; investering *f*
  d Anlage *f*; Investition *f*

1445 investment bank
  f banque *f* d'affaires
  i banca *f* per investimenti
  e banco *m* de inversiones
  n investeringsbank *f*
  d Emissionshaus *n*

1446 investment company
  f société *f* d'investissement
  i società *f* d'investimento
  e compañia *f* inversora
  n beleggingsmaatschappij *f*
  d Investitionsgesellschaft *f*

1447 investment ledger
  f livre *m* de placements
  i libro *m* degli investimenti
  e libro *m* de inversiones
  n beleggingsregister *n*
  d Investitionshauptbuch *n*; Anlagekonto *n*

1448 investment paper
  f valeur *f* de placement
  i titolo *m* d'investimento
  e título *m* de inversión
  n beleggingspapier *n*
  d Anlagetitel *m*; Anlagepapier *n*

1449 investment revenue
  f revenu *m* des fonds placés

  i reddito *m* degli investimenti
  e rédito *m* de (las) inversiones
  n inkomsten *fpl* uit beleggingen
  d Ertrag *m* der Kapitalanlagen

1450 investment trust
  f coopérative *f* de placements; société *f* de placements de capitaux
  i cooperativa *f* d'investimenti
  e cooperativa *f* de inversiones
  n beleggingstrust *f*
  d Kapitalanlagegesellschaft *f*

1451 investor
  f bailleur *m* de fonds; investisseur *m*
  i persona *f* che fornisce capitali
  e inversor *m*; inversionista *m*
  n belegger *m*
  d Kapitalanleger *m*; Investor *m*

1452 invisible transactions
  f opérations *fpl* invisibles
  i transazioni *fpl* invisibili
  e operaciones *fpl* invisibles
  n onzichtbare transacties *fpl*
  d unsichtbare Geschäfte *npl*

1453 invoice
  f facture *f*
  i fattura *f*
  e factura *f*
  n factuur *f*
  d Faktur(a) *f*; Warenrechnung *f*

1454 involuntary bailment
  f dépôt *m* involontaire
  i deposito *m* involontario
  e depósito *m* involuntario
  n onvrijwillige deponering *f*
  d unfreiwillige Hinterlegung *f*

1455 involuntary bankruptcy
  f faillite *f* involontaire
  i fallimento *m* involontario
  e quiebra *f* involuntaria
  n onvrijwillig faillissement *n*
  d unfreiwilliger Konkurs *m*

* **iou** → **1890**

1456 irrecoverable
  f irrécouvrable; non récupérable
  i irrecuperabile; inesigibile
  e irrecuperable; inexigible
  n oninbaar
  d uneinbringlich

1457 irredeemable debenture
  f obligation *f* non amortissable

i obbligazione *f* non ammortizzabile
e obligación *f* no amortizable
n niet aflosbare obligatie *f*
d untilgbare Schuldverschreibung *f*

1458 irredeemable stock
f titres *mpl* non rachetables
i titoli *mpl* non riscattabili
e títulos *mpl* no rescatables
n niet aflosbare effecten *npl*
d unkündbare Wertpapiere *npl*; Wertpapiere *npl* ohne Rückkaufrecht

1459 irregular deposit
f dépôt *m* irrégulier
i deposito *m* irregolare
e depósito *m* irregular
n onregelmatig deposito *n*
d regelwidrige Einlage *f*; regelwidriges Depot *n*

1460 irregular endorsement
f endossement *m* irrégulier
i girata *f* irregolare
e endoso *m* irregular
n onregelmatig endossement *n*
d regelwidriges Indossament *n*

1461 irrevocable documentary credit
f crédit *m* documentaire irrévocable
i credito *m* documentario irrevocabile
e crédito *m* documentario irrevocable
n onherroepelijk documentair krediet *n*
d unwiderrufliches Dokumentenakkreditiv *n*

1462 irrevocable letter of credit
f lettre *f* de crédit irrévocable
i lettera *f* di credito irrevocabile
e carta *f* de crédito irrevocable
n onherroepelijke kredietbrief *m*
d unwiderrufliches Akkreditiv *n*

1463 irrevocable trust fund
f fonds *m* de fidéicommis irrévocable
i fondo *m* fiduciario irrevocabile
e fondo *m* fiduciario irrevocable
n onherroepelijke fondsbelegging *f*
d unwiderruflicher Treuhandfonds *m*

1464 issue; flotation *(bonds)*
f émission *f*
i emissione *f*
e emisión *f*
n emissie *f*; uitgifte *f*
d Emission *f*; Ausgabe *f*; Ausstellung *f*

1465 issue *v*
f émettre

i emettere
e emitir
n emitteren; uitgeven
d emittieren; ausgeben; ausstellen

1466 issued capital
f capital *m* émis
i capitale *m* emesso
e capital *m* emitido
n geëmitteerd kapitaal *n*
d ausgegebenes Kapital *n*

1467 issues on tap
f émissions *fpl* à guichets ouverts
i emissioni *fpl* aperte
e emisiones *fpl* abiertas
n open emissies *fpl*
d laufende Emission *f*

* **issuing bank** → 307

J

1468 job *v*
f spéculer (à la bourse)
i speculare (in borsa)
e especular (en la bolsa)
n speculeren (op de beurs)
d spekulieren (an der Börse)

* **jobber** → 2247

1469 jobber's turn
f profit *m* de l'intermédiaire (Bourse)
i profitto *m* del intermediario (Borsa)
e ganancia *f* del intermediario (bolsa)
n bemiddelingswinst *f*;
makelaarscourtage *f*
d Gewinn *m* des Börsenjobbers

1470 jobbery
f agio *m*; agiotage *m*
i aggio *m*; aggiotaggio *m*
e agio *m*; agiotaje *m*
n agio *n*; agiotage *f*
d Agio *n*; Aufgeld *n*; Agiotage *f*

1471 joint account
f compte *m* conjoint
i conto *m* congiunto
e cuenta *f* conjunta
n gemeenschappelijke rekening *f*
d Gemeinschaftskonto *n*; gemeinschaft-
liche Rechnung *f*

1472 joint and several liability
f responsabilité *f* solidaire
i responsabilità *f* solidale
e responsabilidad *f* solidaria
n gemeenschappelijke aansprakelijkheid *f*;
hoofdelijke aansprakelijkheid *f*
d Gesamtschuldnerschaft *f*

1473 joint contract
f contrat *m* en commun
i contratto *m* collettivo
e contrato *m* colectivo
n gemeenschappelijk contract *n*
d Gemeinschaftsvertrag *m*

1474 joint creditor; cocreditor
f co-créancier *m*
i creditore *m* in partecipazione;
concreditore *m*
e coacreedor *m*
n medeschuldeiser *m*; medecrediteur *m*
d Mitgläubiger *m*

1475 joint current account
f compte *m* courant conjoint
i conto *m* corrente sociale
e cuenta *f* corriente social
n gemeenschappelijke bankrekening *f*
d gemeinschaftliches Kontokorrent *n*

1476 joint debtor
f débiteur *m* solidaire
i condebitore *m*; debitore *m* in
partecipazione
e deudor *m* solidario
n medeschuldenaar *m*
d Mitschuldner *m*; Solidarschuldner *m*

1477 joint financing
f financement *m* conjoint
i finanziamento *m* congiunto
e financiamiento *m* conjunto
n gemeenschappelijke financiering *f*
d Gemeinfinanzierung *f*; gemeinsame
Finanzierung *f*

1478 joint policy
f police *f* conjointe
i polizza *f* collettiva
e póliza *f* conjunta
n gemeenschappelijke polis *f*
d Gesamtpolice *f*

1479 joint proprietor
f copropriétaire *m*
i comproprietario *m*
e copropietario *m*
n mede-eigenaar *m*
d Mitbesitzer *m*; Mitinhaber *m*

1480 joint stock
f capital *m* social
i capitale *m* sociale
e capital *m* social
n maatschappelijk kapitaal *n*
d Gesellschaftskapital *n*

1481 joint stock bank
f banque *f* par actions
i banca *f* per azioni
e banco *m* de accionistas
n bank *f* met een statutair
aandelenkapitaal
d Aktienbank *f*

1482 joint stock company
f société *f* par actions; société *f* anonyme
i società *f* per azioni; società *f* anonima
e sociedad *f* por acciones; sociedad *f*
anónima
n vennootschap *f* op aandelen; naamloze

vennootschap *f*
d Aktiengesellschaft *f*

1483 joint surety
 f garant *m* solidaire
 i commallevadore *m*
 e garante *m* solidario; fiador *m* solidario
 n medeborg *m*
 d Mitbürge *m*

1484 judgement creditor
 f créancier *m* en vertu d'un jugement
 i creditore *m* per giudizio
 e acreedor *m* por juicio
 n crediteur *m* volgens gerechtelijk vonnis
 d Vollstreckungsgläubiger *m*; gerichtlich
   anerkannter Gläubiger *m*

1485 judgement debt
 f dette *f* résultant d'un jugement
 i debito *m* per giudizio
 e deuda *f* por juicio
 n schuld *f* ingevolge gerechtelijke
   uitspraak
 d gerichtlich anerkannte Schuld *f*

1486 junior creditor
 f créditeur *m* secondaire
 i creditore *m* secondario
 e acreedor *m* en segunda instancia
 n secundaire schuldeiser *m*
 d nachstelliger Gläubiger *m*

1487 junior debt
 f dette *f* de rang inférieure
 i debito *m* secondario
 e deuda *f* subordinada
 n secundaire schuld *f*
 d nachstellige Schuld *f*

* **junior mortgage** → **2129**

K

1488 key currency
f monnaie f clé
i moneta f base; moneta f di riferimento
e moneda f clave
n sleutelvaluta f
d Leitwährung f

* **kite → 20**

1489 kite cheque; rubber check *(US)*
f chèque m sans provision
i assegno m scoperto; assegno m a vuoto
e cheque m sin fondos; cheque m en descubierto
n ongedekte cheque m
d Scheck m ohne Deckung; ungedeckter Scheck m

1490 kite flying
f émission f d'effets de complaisance
i emissione f di cambiali tra due persone per ottenere denaro mediante sconto di detti documenti in una banca
e libranza f de letras de cortesía
n wisselruiterij f
d Wechselreiterei f

1491 kiting *(cheques)*
f circulation f de chèques sans provision
i circolazione f di assegni scoperti
e circulación f de cheques sin fondos
n omloop m van ongedekte cheques
d Umlauf m von ungedeckten Schecks

L

1492 labor costs
f coûts *mpl* de main-d'oeuvre
i costo *m* della mano d'opera
e costos *mpl* de mano de obra
n arbeidskosten *mpl*
d Arbeitskosten *fpl*; Lohnkosten *fpl*

1493 lame duck
f spéculateur *m* insolvable
i speculatore *m* insolvente
e especulador *m* insolvente
n insolvente speculant *m*
d ruinierter Spekulant *m*

1494 land charges; land tax
f impôt *m* foncier; taxes *fpl* territoriales
i imposta *f* fondiaria
e impuesto *m* a las tierras; contribución *f* territorial
n grondbelasting *f*
d Grundsteuer *f*

1495 landing certificate
f certificat *m* de mise à terre
i certificato *m* di scarico
e certificado *m* de descarga
n certificaat *n* van lossing
d Löschungsschein *m*

1496 landing charges
f frais *mpl* de déchargement
i spese *fpl* di scarico
e gastos *mpl* de descarga
n loskosten *mpl*
d Löschungsgebühr *f*

* **land tax** → 1494

* **lawful money** → 1511

1497 law merchant
f code *m* mercantile
i diritto *m* mercantile
e derecho *m* mercantil
n wetboek *n* van koophandel
d Handelsrecht *n*

1498 leads and lags
f avances *fpl* et retards *mpl*
i anticipazioni *fpl* e ritardi *mpl* nei pagamenti
e adelantos *mpl* y atrasos *mpl*
n vooruitbetalingen *fpl* en vertragingen *fpl*
d Verkürzung *f* und Verlängerung *f* der Zahlungstermine

1499 lease
f bail *m*
i affitto *m*
e arriendo *m*; arrendamiento *m*
n pacht *f*; huur *f*
d Pacht *f*; Miete *f*

1500 leasehold *(property)*
f (propriété) louée à bail
i (proprietà) tenuta in affitto
e (propiedad) tenida en arriendo
n gehuurd (eigendom)
d Pacht(besitz)

1501 leasing
f crédit-bail *m*
i affitto *m*; appalto *m*
e arrendamiento *m*; arriendo *m*; alquiler *m*
n pacht *f*; huur *f*
d Verpachtung *f*; Vermietung *f*

1502 ledger
f grand livre *m*
i libro *m* mastro
e libro *m* mayor; mayor *m*
n grootboek *n*; legger *m*
d Hauptbuch *n*

1503 legacy
f legs *m*
i legato *m*
e legado *m*
n legaat *n*
d Vermächtnis *n*

1504 legal adviser
f conseiller *m* juridique
i consulente *m* legale
e asesor *m* letrado
n juridisch raadsman *m*; rechtskundig adviseur *m*
d Rechtsberater *m*

* **legal interest** → 1509

1505 legal investment
f placement *m* légal
i investimento *m* legale
e inversión *f* legal
n wettelijke belegging *f*
d gesetzliche Investition *f*; gesetzliche Anlage *f*

1506 legalization
f légalisation *f*
i legalizzazione *f*
e legalización *f*

n legalisatie *f*
d Legalisierung *f*

1507 legalize v
f légaliser
i legalizzare
e legalizar
n legaliseren
d legalisieren

1508 legal mortgage; statutory mortgage
f hypothèque *f* légale
i ipoteca *f* legale
e hipoteca *f* legal
n rechtsgeldige hypotheek *f*
d gesetzliche Hypothek *f*; rechtsgültige Hypothek *f*

1509 legal rate of interest; legal interest
f taux *m* d'intérêt légal
i tasso *m* d'interessi legale
e tipo *m* de interés legal
n wettelijk voorgeschreven rentevoet *m*
d gesetzlicher Zinsfuss *m*

1510 legal reserve
f réserve *f* légale
i riserva *f* legale
e reserva *f* legal
n wettelijk voorgeschreven reserve *f*
d gesetzlich vorgeschriebene Reserve *f*

1511 legal tender; lawful money
f monnaie *f* légale
i moneta *f* legale; moneta *f* di corso legale
e moneda *f* legal; moneda *f* de curso legal
n wettig betaalmiddel *n*
d gesetzliches Zahlungsmittel *n*

1512 lend v
f prêter
i prestare
e prestar
n lenen
d leihen; ausleihen; darleihen

1513 lending agency; credit institution
f institution *f* de crédit; établissement *m* de crédit
i istituzione *f* di credito
e institución *f* de crédito; organismo *m* crediticio
n kredietinstelling *f*
d Kreditinstitut *n*; Kreditanstalt *f*

1514 lending limit; credit limit
f plafond *m* de crédit
i limite *m* massimo dei prestiti; limite *m* di credito

e límite *m* de(l) crédito; límite *m* de(l) préstamo
n kredietplafond *n*; kredietlimiet *n*
d Beleihungsgrenze *f*; Kreditplafond *m*; Kreditgrenze *f*

1515 letter of allotment; allotment letter
f lettre *f* d'assignation
i lettera *f* di assegnazione
e carta *f* de adjudicación
n toewijzingsbiljet *n*
d Zuweisungsbrief *m*

1516 letter of credit; bill of credit
f lettre *f* de crédit; accréditif *m*
i lettera *f* di credito
e carta *f* de crédito
n kredietbrief *m*
d Kreditbrief *m*; Akkreditiv *n*

1517 letter of deposit
f lettre *f* de dépôt
i lettera *f* di deposito
e carta *f* de depósito
n depositoverklaring *f*
d Hinterlegungsurkunde *f*

1518 letter of guaranty
f lettre *f* d'aval
i lettera *f* di garanzia
e carta *f* de garantía
n garantieschrijven *n*
d Garantiebrief *m*

1519 letter of hypothecation
f lettre *f* hypothécaire
i lettera *f* di ipoteca
e carta *f* de hipoteca
n verklaring *f* van verhypothekering
d Verpfändungsurkunde *f*

1520 letter of indemnity
f lettre *f* d'indemnité
i lettera *f* d'indennità
e carta *f* de indemnización
n schadevergoedingsverklaring *f*
d Schadenersatzerklärung *f*

* **letter of licence** → 895

1521 letter of respite
f lettre *f* de répit
i lettera *f* di moratoria
e carta *f* de gracia; carta *f* de moratoria
n bericht *n* van uitstel van betaling
d Moratorium *n*

1522 letter of undertaking
f lettre *f* d'engagement

i lettera *f* di compromesso
e carta *f* de compromiso
n verbintenisverklaring *f*
d Verpflichtungserklärung *f*

1523 leveling-off
f plafonnement *m*
i livellamento *m*
e nivelación *f*; estabilización *f*
n nivellering *f*
d Nivellierung *f*

1524 level-line repayment
f amortissement *m* linéaire
i rimborso *m* in quote uguali
e amortización *f* en cuotas iguales
n lineaire amortisatie *f*
d Tilgung *f* in gleichen Raten

1525 leverage
f pouvoir *m* multiplicateur
i potere *m* moltiplicatore
e poder *m* multiplicador
n hefboomwerking *f*
d Multiplikationskraft *f*; Vergrösserungs-kraft *f*

1526 levy
f prélèvement *m*; levée *f*
i prelevamento *m*; gravame *m* tributario
e recaudación *f*; exacción *f*; gravamen *m* tributario
n belasting *f*; heffing *f*
d Erhebung *f*; Abgabe *f*

1527 liabilities
f passif *m*; dettes *fpl*; engagements *mpl*
i passività *fpl*; passivi *mpl*; debiti *mpl*; impegni *mpl*
e pasivo *m*; deudas *fpl*; obligaciones *fpl*
n passief *n*; schulden *fpl*; verplichtingen *fpl*
d Passiva *npl*; Schulden *fpl*; Verbindlich-keiten *fpl*

1528 liability
f responsabilité *f*
i responsabilità *f*
e responsabilidad *f*
n aansprakelijkheid *f*
d Verpflichtung *f*

1529 liability
f dette *f*
i debito *m*
e deuda *f*
n verantwoordelijkheid *f*; schuld *f*
d Schuld *f*

1530 licence
f licence *f*; permis *m*
i licenza *f*; permesso *m*
e licencia *f*; permiso *m*
n vergunning *f*; verlof *n*; toestemming *f*
d Erlaubnis *f*; Lizenz *f*; Genehmigung *f*

1531 lien
f droit *m* de rétention
i diritto *m* di ritenzione
e derecho *m* de retención
n recht *n* van retentie; retentierecht *n*; recht *n* van terughouding
d Zurückbehaltungsrecht *n*; Pfandrecht *n*

1532 life annuity; perpetual annuity
f rente *f* viagère
i rendita *f* vitalizia
e renta *f* vitalicia; anualidad *f* vitalicia
n lijfrente *f*
d Lebensrente *f*

1533 life assurance; life insurance
f assurance *f* sur la vie
i assicurazione *f* sulla vita
e seguro *m* de vida
n levensverzekering *f*
d Lebensversicherung *f*

1534 life interest
f rente *f* viagère
i rendita *f* vitalizia
e renta *f* vitalicia
n levenslang vruchtgebruik *n*
d lebenslängliche Nutzniessung *f*

1535 limited cheque
f chèque *m* limité
i assegno *m* bancario limitato
e cheque *m* limitado; cheque *m* con límite de importe
n gelimiteerde cheque *m*
d limitierter Scheck *m*

1536 limited liability company
f société *f* à responsabilité limitée
i società *f* a responsabilità limitata
e compañia *f* de responsabilidad limitada
n vennootschap *f* met beperkte aansprakelijkheid
d Gesellschaft *f* mit beschränkter Haftung (GmbH)

1537 line of credit
f montant *m* du crédit accordé par une banque
i ammontare *m* del credito concesso da una banca
e monto *m* del crédito otorgado por un

banco
n krediet n toegestaan door een bank
d gesamter, von einer Bank eingeräumter
  Kreditbetrag m

1538 liquid assets
  f avoirs *mpl* liquides; actif *m* disponible;
    disponibilités *fpl*
  i attivi *mpl* liquidi; mezzi *mpl* disponibili
  e activo *m* líquido; disponibilidades *fpl*
  n liquide middelen *npl*
  d flüssige Aktiva *npl*; flüssige Mittel *npl*;
    flüssige Anlagen *fpl*

1539 liquidate v
  f liquider; payer; solder
  i liquidare; pagare; saldare
  e liquidar; pagar; saldar
  n liquideren; vereffenen; betalen;
    afwikkelen
  d liquidieren; bezahlen

1540 liquidated debt
  f dette f soldée
  i debito m saldato
  e deuda f saldada
  n vereffende schuld f
  d liquidierte Schuld f

1541 liquidating dividend
  f dividende m de liquidation
  i dividendo m di liquidazione
  e dividendo m de liquidación
  n liquidatie-uitkering f
  d Liquidationsanteil m; Liquidationsrate f

1542 liquidating value
  f valeur f en liquidation
  i valore m di liquidazione
  e valor m de liquidación
  n waarde f bij liquidatie
  d Liquidationswert m

1543 liquidation
  f liquidation f; paiement m
  i liquidazione f; pagamento m
  e liquidación f; pago m
  n liquidatie f; vereffening f; betaling f;
    afwikkeling f
  d Liquidation f; Abrechnung f; Zahlung f

1544 liquidator
  f liquidateur m
  i liquidatore m
  e liquidador m
  n liquidateur m; vereffenaar m;
    boedelscheider m
  d Liquidator m; Masseverwalter m

1545 liquidity
  f liquidité f; disponibilités *fpl*
  i liquidità f; disponibilità f
  e liquidez f; disponibilidad f en dinero
  n liquiditeit f
  d Liquidität f; Geldflüssigkeit f

1546 liquidity position
  f position f de liquidité
  i stato f di liquidità
  e situación f de liquidez
  n liquiditeitspositie f
  d Liquiditätslage f

* **liquidity ratio** → 40

1547 liquidity shortage; liquidity squeeze
  f crise f de liquidité; pénurie f
  i insufficienza f di liquidità; crise f di
    liquidità
  e insuficiencia f de liquidez; iliquidez f
  n liquiditeitskrapte f
  d Liquiditätsmangel m

1548 listed securities
  f valeurs *fpl* admises à la cote officielle
  i valori *mpl* di borsa
  e valores *mpl* registrados en la bolsa
  n ter beurze genoteerde waarden *fpl*
  d an der Börse notierte Wertpapiere *npl*

1549 loan
  f prêt m; emprunt m
  i prestito m; mutuo m
  e empréstito m; préstamo m
  n lening f
  d Anleihe f; Darlehen n; Borg m

1550 loan account
  f compte m des prêts
  i conto m dei prestiti
  e cuenta f de empréstitos
  n leningrekening f
  d Anleihekonto n; Darlehenskonto n

1551 loan application
  f demande f de prêt
  i domanda f di prestito
  e solicitud f de préstamo
  n kredietaanvraag f
  d Kreditantrag m

1552 loan bank
  f établissement m de prêts
  i banca f di prestiti
  e banco m de préstamos
  n voorschotbank f
  d Darlehensbank f

1553 loan capital
 f emprunts *mpl*
 i capitale *m* preso a prestito
 e capital *m* en préstamo
 n leenkapitaal *n*
 d Anleihekapital *n*

1554 loan certificate
 f certificat *m* de prêt; titre *m* de prêt
 i certificato *m* di prestito
 e certificado *m* de préstamo
 n schuldbewijs *n*
 d Anleiheschein *m*

* loan department → 789

1555 loan portfolio
 f portefeuille *m* de prêts
 i portafolio *m* dei prestiti
 e cartera *f* de préstamo
 n leningportefeuille *f*
 d Anleiheportefeuille *f*

1556 loan recovery
 f recouvrement *m* du prêt
 i ricupero *m* di un prestito
 e recuperación *f* de un préstamo
 n terugkrijgen *n* van een lening
 d Krediteinbringung *f*

1557 loan teller
 f employé *m* au service des crédits
 i impiegato *m* del ufficio crediti
 e empleado *m* de la sección créditos
 n employé *m* van de kredietafdeling
 d Sachbearbeiter *m* der Kreditabteilung

1558 local draft
 f lettre *f* sur place
 i cambiale *f* sulla piazza
 e letra *f* sobre la plaza
 n loco-wissel *m*
 d Platzwechsel *m*

1559 lock *v* up capital
 f immobiliser des capitaux
 i immobilizzare capitale
 e inmovilizar capital
 n kapitaal vastleggen
 d Kapital festlegen

1560 lock-up of capital
 f immobilisation *f* de capitaux
 i immobilizzazione *f* di capitale
 e inmovilización *f* de capital
 n vastleggen *n* van kapitaal
 d Festlegung *f* von Kapitalien

1561 long term
 f à long terme
 i a lungo termine; a lunga scadenza
 e a largo plazo
 n langlopend; op lange termijn
 d langfristig

1562 long-term bill
 f billet *m* à longue échéance
 i cambiale *f* a lunga scadenza
 e letra *f* a largo plazo
 n langlopende wissel *m*; wissel *m* op lange termijn
 d langfristiger Wechsel *m*

1563 long-term credit
 f crédit *m* à long terme
 i credito *m* a lungo termine
 e crédito *m* a largo plazo
 n langlopend krediet *n*
 d langfristiger Kredit *m*

1564 lose *v*
 f perdre
 i perdere
 e perder
 n verliezen
 d verlieren

1565 loss
 f perte *f*
 i perdita *f*
 e pérdida *f*
 n verlies *n*
 d Verlust *m*

1566 lucrative
 f lucratif
 i lucrativo
 e lucrativo
 n winstgevend
 d gewinnbringend; lukrativ

1567 lump-sum contract
 f contrat *m* par somme globale
 i contratto *m* per prezzo globale
 e contrato *m* por precio global
 n contract *n* voor een globaal bedrag
 d Vertrag *m* über einen Pauschalbetrag

M

1568 made bill
f lettre f endossée
i cambiale f girata
e letra f endosada
n geëndosseerde wissel m
d indossierter Wechsel m; Auslandswechsel m

1569 mail transfer
f virement m postal
i trasferimento m postale
e transferencia f postal
n overmaking f per post; overschrijving f
  per post
d Postüberweisung f

1570 maker
f souscripteur m
i sottoscrittore m
e firmante m; suscriptor m
n trekker m; afgever m
d Aussteller m

1571 manage v; administer v
f administrer; gérer
i amministrare; dirigere
e administrar; regentear
n leiden; besturen; beheren
d verwalten; leiten

1572 managed economy
f économie f dirigée
i economia f pianificata
e economia f dirigida
n geleide economie f
d Planwirtschaft f

1573 management shares
f actions fpl d'administration
i azioni fpl d'amministrazione
e acciones fpl de administración
n aandelen npl in handen der directie;
  directieaandelen npl
d Vorstandsaktien fpl

1574 management trust
f société f d'investissement ayant le droit
  d'administration
i società di finanziamenti con diritto di
  amministrazione
e sociedad f de inversiones con derechos
  de administración
n beleggings- en beheermaatschappij f
d Kapitalanlagegesellschaft f mit Anlagen-
  verwaltung

1575 mandant; mandator
f mandant m
i mandante m
e mandante m
n opdrachtgever m
d Auftraggeber m; Vollmachtgeber m;
  Mandant m

1576 mandate
f mandat m
i mandato m
e mandato m
n opdracht f
d Auftrag m; Vollmacht f

* **mandator** → 1575

1577 mandatory
f mandataire m
i mandatario m
e mandatario m
n gevolmachtigde m; mandataris m
d Beauftragte(r) m; Bevollmächtiger m

1578 margin; spread
f marge f; différence f
i margine m; differenza f
e margen m; diferencia f
n marge f; differentie f
d Marge f; Differenz f; Spanne f

1579 marginal benefit
f avantage m marginal
i profitto m marginale; utilità f marginale
e beneficio m marginal
n marginaal voordeel n
d Grenznutzen m

1580 marginal cash reserves
f réserves fpl liquides marginales
i riserve fpl liquide marginali
e reservas fpl liquidas marginales
n marginale kasreserves fpl
d flüssige Grenzreserven fpl; liquide Grenzreserven fpl

1581 marginal efficiency of capital
f efficacité f marginale du capital
i produttività f marginale del capitale
e eficiencia f marginal del capital;
  productividad f marginal del capital
n marginale productiviteit f van het
  kapitaal
d Grenzleistungsfähigkeit f des Kapitals

1582 marginal letter of credit
f lettre f de crédit marginale
i lettera f di credito stampata al margine
  di una cambiale

e carta *f* de crédito impresa al margen de
una letra de cambio
n wisselkredietbrief *m*
d Wechselkreditbrief *m*

1583 marine insurance; sea insurance
f assurance *f* maritime
i assicurazione *f* marittima
e seguro *m* marítimo
n zeeverzekering *f*; zeeassurantie *f*
d Seeversicherung *f*

1584 marine insurance policy
f police *f* d'assurance maritime
i polizza *f* d'assicurazione marittima
e póliza *f* de seguro marítimo
n polis *f* van zeeverzekering
d Seeversicherungspolice *f*

1585 marine (insurance) underwriters
f compagnie *f* d'assurances maritimes
i compagnia *f* d'assicurazione marittima
e compañía *f* de seguros marítimos
n zeeassuradeurs *mpl*; zeeverzekeraars
mpl
d Seeversicherungsgesellschaft *f*

1586 market
f marché *m*
i mercato *m*
e mercado *m*; plaza *f*
n markt *f*
d Markt *m*

1587 marketable security
f titre *m* négociable
i titolo *m* negoziabile
e título *m* negociable
n verhandelbaar waardepapier *n*
d marktfähiges Wertpapier *n*

1588 market economy
f économie *f* de marché
i economia *f* di mercato
e economía *f* de mercado
n markteconomie *f*
d Marktwirtschaft *f*

1589 market overt
f marché *m* public
i mercato *m* aperto
e mercado *m* público
n open markt *f*
d offener Markt

1590 market price
f prix *m* de marché
i prezzo *m* di mercato
e precio *m* de plaza; precio *m* del mercado

n marktprijs *m*
d Marktpreis *m*

1591 market value
f valeur *f* marchande
i valore *m* nel mercato; valore *m* di
mercato
e valor *m* en plaza
n marktwaarde *f*
d Marktwert *m*

1592 marksman
f personne *f* qui signe d'une croix
i persona *f* che firma con un segno di
croce
e persona *f* que firma con una cruz
n iemand die met een kruisje tekent
d Person *f* die mit einem Kreuz unter-
zeichnet

1593 matching payment
f paiement *m* de contrepartie
i pagamento *m* di contropartita
e pago *m* de contrapartida
n vergelijkbare betaling *f*
d Ausgleichszahlung *f*

* **mature** *v* → 1140

* **maturity (of a bill of exchange)**
→ 1141

* **meeting of creditors** → 799

1594 memorandum of association
f acte *m* constitutif d'une société
i statuto *m* d'una società
e estatutos *mpl* de una sociedad; carta *f*
orgánica de una sociedad
n statuten *npl* van een vennootschap
d Gesellschaftsstatuten *npl*

1595 memorandum of deposit
f document *m* de dépôt
i nota *f* di deposito
e documento *m* de depósito
n depositonota *f*
d Hinterlegungsurkunde *f*

1596 mental incapacity
f incapacité *f* mentale
i incapacità *f* mentale
e incapacidad *f* mental
n ontoerekenbaarheid *f*
d Handlungsunfähigkeit *f*

1597 mercantile
f mercantile; commercial
i mercantile; commerciale

e mercantil; comercial
n handels-; koopmans-
d Handels-; kaufmännisch

1598 mercantile agent
f agent *m* de commerce
i agente *m* commerciale
e agente *m* de comercio
n handelsagent *m*
d Handelsvertreter *m*

1599 merchandise
f marchandise *f*
i merce *f*
e mercadería *f*; mercancía *f*
n koopwaar *f*; waar *f*
d Ware *f*

* **merchant bank** → 11

1600 metayer contract
f contrat *m* de métayage
i contratto *m* di mezzadria
e contrato *m* de aparcería
n pachtovereenkomst *f* waarbij de pachter
   de helft van de oogst afstaat
d Naturalpachtvertrag *m*

1601 minimum cash ratio
f coefficient *m* minimum d'encaisse
i coefficiente *m* minimo di riserva legale
e coeficiente *m* mínimo de encaje
n minimale kasreservecoëfficiënt *m*
d Mindestreservekoeffizient *m*

1602 minimum cash requirement
f encaisse *f* minimum obligatoire
i percentuale *f* di riserva minima
   obbligatoria
e porcentaje *m* de reserva obligatoria
n verplichte kasreserve *f*
d Mindestreservesatz *m*

1603 mint
f hôtel *m* de la Monnaie; hôtel *m* des
   Monnaies; Monnaie *f*
i zecca *f*
e casa *f* de moneda; ceca *f*
n munt *f*; munthuis *n*; muntgebouw *n*
d Münzamt *n*; Münzstätte *f*; Münze *f*

1604 mint par
f parité *f* entre le cours et la valeur
   métallique des monnaies
i parità *f* fra il corso ed il valore metallico
   delle monete
e paridad *f* entre el tipo de cambio y el
   valor metálico de las monedas

n muntpariteit *f*
d Münzparität *f*

1605 mint price
f nombre *m* de pièces qu'on peut frapper
   d'une certaine quantité d'or ou d'argent
i numero *m* di monete che entrano in una
   determinata quantità di oro o argento
e número *m* de monedas que entran en
   una cantidad determinada de oro o plata
n aantal *n* munten welke uit een bepaalde
   hoeveelheid goud of zilver geslagen
   kunnen worden
d Anzahl *f* der Münze die aus einer
   bestimmten Menge Gold oder Silber
   geprägt werden können

1606 minutes *(of proceedings)*
f procès-verbal *m*
i processo *m* verbale; verbale *m*; atti *mpl*
e actas *fpl*
n notulen *fpl*; proces-verbaal *n*
d Protokoll *n*

1607 monetary
f monétaire
i monetario
e monetario
n monetair; geld-; munt-
d Geld-; Münz-

1608 monetary authorities
f autorités *fpl* monétaires
i autorità *fpl* monetarie
e autoridades *fpl* monetarias
n geldoverheid *f*
d Devisenbehörden *fpl*

1609 monetary reserves
f réserves *fpl* monétaires
i riserve *fpl* monetarie
e reservas *fpl* monetarias
n geldreserves *fpl*
d Währungsreserven *fpl*

1610 monetary stock
f masse *f* monétaire; stock *m* monétaire
i massa *f* monetaria
e masa *f* monetaria
n geldvoorraad *m*; geldvolume *n*
d gesamter Geldbestand *m*

1611 monetary stringency
f austérité *f* monétaire
i austerità *f* monetaria
e austeridad *f* monetaria
n geldschaarste *f*
d Geldverknappung *f*

1612 monetary unit
 f unité *f* monétaire
 i unità *f* monetaria
 e unidad *f* monetaria
 n munteenheid *f*
 d Münzeinheit *f*; Geldeinheit *f*

1613 money; currency
 f monnaie *f*; argent *m*; espèces *fpl*
 i denaro *m*
 e dinero *m*; peculio *m*
 n geld *n*
 d Geld *n*

* **money at call** → 501

1614 money illusion
 f illusión *f* monétaire
 i illusione *f* monetaria; valore *m* illusorio della moneta
 e ilusión *f* monetaria; valor *m* ilusorio del dinero
 n geldillusie *f*; illusieve waarde *f* van het geld
 d illusorischer Wert *m* des Geldes

1615 money income
 f revenu *m* monétaire
 i rendita *f* monetaria
 e ingreso *m* monetario
 n geldinkomen *n*
 d Währungseinkünfte *fpl*; Einkassierung *f*

1616 money lender
 f prêteur *m*
 i prestatore *m*
 e prestamista *m/f*
 n geldschieter *m*
 d Geldverleiher *m*

1617 money market
 f marché *m* monétaire
 i mercato *m* monetario
 e mercado *m* monetario
 n geldmarkt *f*
 d Geldmarkt *m*

1618 money market papers
 f instruments *mpl* du marché monétaire
 i titoli *mpl* di mercato monetario; valori *mpl* di mercato monetario
 e títulos *mpl* del mercado monetario; valores *mpl* del mercado monetario
 n geldmarktpapieren *npl*
 d Geldmarktpapiere *npl*

1619 money market rate
 f taux *m* de l'argent hors bank
 i tasso *m* del mercato monetario
 e tasa *f* del mercado monetario
 n geldmarktkoers *m*
 d Geldmarktsatz *m*

1620 money order; postal order
 f mandat *m* de poste; mandat-poste *m*
 i vaglia *m* postale; mandato *m* postale
 e mandato *m* postal; giro *m* postal
 n postwissel *n*
 d Postanweisung *f*

1621 money supply
 f masse *f* monétaire; disponibilités *fpl* monétaires
 i massa *f* monetaria (in circolazione); offerta *f* monetaria
 e oferta *f* monetaria; circulante *m*
 n geldvolume *n*; geldhoeveelheid *f*
 d Geldmenge *f*; Geldvolumen *n*

1622 monometallism
 f monométallisme *m*
 i monometallismo *m*
 e monometalismo *m*
 n monometallisme *n*
 d Monometallismus *n*

1623 monopolize *v*
 f monopoliser
 i monopolizzare
 e monopolizar
 n monopoliseren
 d monopolisieren

1624 monopoly
 f monopole *m*
 i monopolio *m*
 e monopolio *m*
 n monopolie *n*; alleenhandel *m*; alleenverkoop *m*
 d Monopol *n*; Alleinhandel *m*; Alleinvertrieb *m*

1625 mora
 f délai *m*; retard *m*
 i mora *f*
 e mora *f*
 n uitstel *n*; achterstand *m*
 d Verzug *m*

1626 moratorium
 f moratorium *m*
 i moratoria *f*
 e moratoria *f*
 n moratorium *n*; uitstel *n* van betaling
 d Moratorium *n*; Zahlungsaufschub *m*

1627 mortgage
 f hypothèque *f*

i ipoteca f
e hipoteca f
n hypotheek f
d Hypothek f

1628 mortgage v; **hypothecate** v
f hypothéquer
i ipotecare
e hipotecar
n bezwaren met hypotheek; hypotheek
nemen op; verhypothekeren; belenen
d verpfänden; hypothekarisch belasten;
belasten mit einer Hypothek

* **mortgage** *(US)* → **969**

1629 mortgageable
f hypothécable
i ipotecabile
e hipotecable
n vatbaar voor hypotheek
d verpfändbar

1630 mortgage bank
f banque f hypothécaire
i banca f ipotecaria
e banco m hipotecario
n hypotheekbank f
d Hypothekenbank f

1631 mortgage bond
f titre m hypothécaire
i cartella f ipotecaria
e título m hipotecario
n pandbrief m; hypotheekbrief m
d Hypothekenbrief m; Hypothekenpfand-
brief m

1632 mortgage debenture
f obligation f hypothécaire
i obbligazione f ipotecaria
e obligación f hipotecaria
n hypothecaire obligatie f
d hypothekarisch gesicherte Schuldverschreibung f

1633 mortgage deed
f contrat m hypothécaire
i cartella f ipotecaria; contratto m
ipotecario
e escritura f hipotecaria
n hypotheekakte f; hypothecair contract n
d Hypothekenbrief m

1634 mortgagee
f créancier m hypothécaire
i creditore m ipotecario
e acreedor m hipotecario
n hypotheekhouder m; hypotheekgever m

d Hypothekengläubiger m; Pfandgläubiger m

1635 mortgage loan
f prêt m hypothécaire; prêt m sur
hypothèque
i prestito m ipotecario
e préstamo m hipotecario
n hypothecaire lening f; lening f onder
hypothecair verband; lening f op
hypotheek
d Hypothekendarlehen n

1636 mortgager; mortgagor
f débiteur m hypothécaire
i debitore m ipotecario
e deudor m hipotecario
n hypotheeknemer m
d Hypothekenschuldner m; Pfand-
schuldner m

1637 movable estate
f biens mpl meubles
i beni mpl mobili
e bienes mpl muebles
n roerend goed n
d bewegliches Vermögen n

1638 multilateral payments
f paiements m multilatéraux
i pagamenti mpl multilaterali
e pagos mpl multilaterales
n multilaterale betalingen fpl
d multilaterale Zahlungen fpl

1639 multiplier effect
f effet m multiplicateur
i effetto m moltiplicatore
e efecto m multiplicador
n vermenigvuldigingseffect n
d Vergrösserungseffekt m

1640 municipal bank
f banque f municipale
i banca f comunale
e banco m municipal
n gemeentelijke bank f
d Kommunalbank f

1641 mutilated cheque
f chèque m mutilé
i assegno m mutilato
e cheque m mutilado
n verminkte cheque m; beschadigde
cheque m
d beschädigter Scheck m

N

1642 naked bond
f obligation f sans garantie
i obbligazione f non assicurata
e obligación f desprovista de seguro
n niet gegarandeerde obligatie f
d unbesicherte Schuldverschreibung f

1643 name bond
f assurance f de garantie personnelle
i assicurazione f di garanzia personale
e seguro m de garantía personal
d Personengarantieversicherung f

1644 national accounts
f comptes mpl nationaux
i conti mpl nazionali
e cuentas fpl nacionales
n nationale rekeningen fpl
d volkswirtschaftliche Gesamtrechnung f;
gesamtwirtschaftliche Rechnung f

1645 national bank
f banque f nationale
i banca f nazionale
e banco m nacional
n centrale bank f; nationale bank f;
staatsbank f
d Nationalbank f; Staatsbank f

1646 national income
f revenu m national
i rendita f nazionale
e ingreso m nacional
n nationaal inkomen n
d Volkseinkommen n; Nationalein-
kommen n

1647 national product
f produit m national
i prodotto m nazionale
e producto m nacional
n nationaal product n
d Sozialprodukt n

1648 negative balance
f solde m négatif
i saldo m negativo; bilancia f deficitaria
e saldo m negativo
n negatief saldo n
d negativer Saldo m

1649 negative rate of interest
f taux m d'intérêt négatif
i tasso m d'interesse negativo
e tipo m de interés negativo

n negatieve rentevoet m
d negativer Zinssatz m

1650 negotiable
f négociable
i negoziabile
e negociable
n verhandelbaar; verkoopbaar
d begebbar; marktfähig; verkäuflich

1651 negotiable securities; negotiable papers
f titres mpl négociables; valeurs fpl
négociables
i titoli mpl negoziabili; valori mpl
negoziabili
e títulos mpl negociables; valores mpl
negociables
n verhandelbare waardepapieren npl
d begebbare Wertpapiere npl

1652 negotiate v
f négocier
i negoziare
e negociar
n verhandelen; onderhandelen
d verhandeln; handeln; begeben

1653 negotiations
f négociations fpl
i trattative fpl; negoziazioni fpl
e negociaciones fpl
n onderhandelingen fpl
d Verhandlungen fpl

1654 negotiator
f négociateur m
i negoziatore m
e negociador m
n onderhandelaar m
d Unterhändler m

1655 net
f net; sans déduction
i netto; senza sconto
e neto; sin descuento
n netto
d Netto-; Rein-

1656 net amount
f montant m net
i importo m netto
e monto m neto
n nettobedrag n
d Nettobetrag m; Reinbetrag m

1657 net income
f revenu m net
i introito m netto
e ingreso m neto

n netto-inkomen n
d Nettoeinkommen m; Reinertrag m

1658 net interest
f intérêt m net
i interesse m netto
e interés m neto
n netto-interest m
d Nettozinsen mpl

1659 net profit
f bénéfice m net
i profitto m netto; utile m netto; beneficio
m netto
e beneficio m neto; ganancia f neta
n nettowinst f
d Nettogewinn m; Reingewinn m

1660 net value
f valeur f nette
i valore m netto
e valor m neto
n nettowaarde f
d Nettowert m

1661 net worth
f actif m net
i attivo m netto
e patrimonio m
n netto actief n
d Eigenkapital n; Eigenmittel n

1662 new issue of shares
f émission f d'actions nouvelles
i emissione f di nuove azioni
e emisión f de acciones nuevas
n emissie f van nieuwe aandelen; uitgifte f
van nieuwe aandelen
d Ausgabe f junger Aktien

1663 night depository *(US)*; **night safe**
f coffre m de nuit
i deposito m notturno
e depósito m nocturno; depósito m fuera
de hora
n nachtkluis f
d Nachttresor m

1664 nominal
f nominal
i nominale
e nominal
n nominaal
d Nenn-; Nominal-; nominell

* **nominal account** → 1347

1665 nominal capital
f capital m nominal

i capitale m nominale
e capital m nominal
n nominaal kapitaal n
d Nennkapital n; Stammkapital n

* **nominal value** → 1160

1666 nominate v
f nommer; désigner
i nominare; designare
e nombrar; designar
n benoemen; kandidaat stellen
d ernennen; vorschlagen

1667 non-apportionable annuity
f annuité f non versée en cas de décès
i annualità f senza pagamento in caso di
morte
e anualidad f sin pago por muerte
n lijfrente f zonder uitkering bij overlijden
d Leibrente f ohne Zahlung im Todesfall

1668 non-assessable stock
f actions fpl non imposables
i azioni fpl non tassabili
e acciones fpl no gravables
n belastingvrije aandelen npl
d steuerfreie Aktien fpl

1669 non-cash input
f facteur m de production non financier
i fattore m di produzione non monetario
e insumo m no monetario
n geldloze productiefactor m
d bargeldloser Produktionsfaktor m

1670 non-collectable
f non percevable; non encaissable
i non percepibile
e no cobrable
n niet inbaar; niet incasseerbaar
d nicht eintreibbar

1671 non-cumulative dividend
f dividende m non cumulatif
i dividendo m non cumulativo
e dividendo m no cumulativo
n niet cumulatief dividend n
d nicht kumulative Dividende f

1672 non-member bank
f banque f hors de la chambre de
compensation
i banco m fuori della camera di
compensazione
e banco m fuera de la cámara de
compensación
n bank f die buiten de clearing staat

d Bank *f* die nicht der Clearingvereinigung
angehört

1673 non-member broker; outside broker
f courtier *m* libre
i sensale *m* libero
e corredor *m* libre
n niet aangesloten makelaar *m*
d freier Makler *m*

**1674 non-negotiable non-interest-bearing
note**
f bon *m* non négociable ne portant pas
intérêt
i nota *f* di debito non negoziabile e priva
di interessi
e pagaré *m* no negociable y sin intereses
n niet verhandelbaar renteloos
schuldbewijs *n*
d nicht verhandelbare Schuldverschreibung *f*

1675 non-operating income
f revenus *mpl* hors-exploitation
i rendita *f* non proveniente dalle
operazioni
e ingresos *mpl* no provenientes de las
operaciones
n inkomsten *fpl* niet voortvloeiende uit de
productie; toevallige baten *fpl*
d betriebsfremde Erträgnisse *fpl*

1676 non-par bank
f banque *f* hors du système de
compensation
i banco *m* fuori del sistema di
compensazioni
e banco *m* fuera del sistema de
compensaciones
n bank *f* buiten het clearingsysteem
d Bank *f* ausserhalb des Ausgleichsystems

1677 non-profit organization
f organisme *m* sans but lucratif
i organizzazione *f* senza fini di lucro
e organización *f* sin fines de lucro
n non-profit organisatie *f*
d gemeinnützige Organisation *f*

1678 non-recurring receipts
f recettes *fpl* exceptionnelles
i entrate *fpl* eccezionali
e ingresos *mpl* extraordinarios
n buitengewone inkomsten *fpl*
d ausserordentliche Einkommen *npl*

1679 non-taxable
f non imposable
i non tassabile

e libre de impuestos; no gravable
n onbelastbaar; niet belastbaar
d steuerfrei; nicht steuerpflichtig

1680 non-transferable
f non transférable
i non trasferibile
e intransferible; no transferible
n niet vatbaar voor overdracht; niet
transfereerbaar; niet overdraagbaar
d unübertragbar

1681 no-par stock
f action *f* sans valeur nominale
i azione *f* senza valore nominale
e acción *f* sin valor nominal
n aandeel *n* zonder nominale waarde
d Aktie *f* ohne Nominalwert; nennwertlose
Aktie *f*

1682 no-par value
f valeur *f* non-pair
i valore *m* non alla pari
e valor *m* no a la par
n waarde *f* buiten pari
d Nicht-Pariwert *m*

1683 nostro account
f notre compte *m*
i conto *m* nostro
e nuestra cuenta *f*
n nostrorekening *f*
d Nostrokonto *n*

1684 notary public
f notaire *m*
i notaro *m*; notaio *m*
e notario *m*; escribano *m*
n notaris *m*
d Notar *m*

* **note of hand** → 1890

1685 notice
f notification *f*; préavis *m*
i avviso *m*; notifica *f*
e advertencia *f*; notificación *f*
n bericht *n*; kennisgeving *f*; advies *n*
d Benachrichtigung *f*; Bekanntmachung *f*

1686 notification
f notification *f*
i notifica *f*
e notificación *f*
n kennisgeving *f*; bekendmaking *f*
d Mitteilung *f*; Bekanntmachung *f*

1687 notify *v*
f notifier

  i notificare
  e notificar
  n kennis geven van; aankondigen
  d mitteilen; bekanntgeben; bekanntmachen;
    zur Kenntnis bringen

1688 null and void
  f nul et non avenu
  i nullo e di nessun valore
  e nulo y sin valor
  n ongeldig; nietig; van nul en gener waarde
  d null und nichtig

1689 nullify *v*
  f annuler
  i annullare
  e anular
  n annuleren; nietig verklaren
  d annullieren; für nichtig erklären

O

1690 occupation accident; occupational injury
f accident m de travail
i accidente m sul lavoro; infortunio m sul lavoro
e accidente m de trabajo
n arbeidsongeval n; beroepsongeval n
d Arbeitsunfall m; Berufsunfall m

1691 offer v
f offrir
i offrire
e ofrecer; ofertar
n aanbieden; bieden
d anbieten

1692 offer
f offre f
i offerta f
e oferta f
n bod n; offerte f; aanbod n
d Offerte f; Angebot n

1693 office
f bureau m
i ufficio m
e oficina f
n kantoor n; bureau n
d Büro n

1694 official *(noun)*
f fonctionnaire m
i funzionario m
e funcionario m
n employé m
d Beamter m

1695 official *(adj.)*
f officiel
i ufficiale
e oficial
n officieel
d amtlich; offiziell

1696 official gold holdings
f stocks mpl d'or de l'Etat; avoirs mpl officiels d'or
i averi mpl ufficiali in oro
e tenencias fpl oficiales de oro
n officiële goudreserve f
d amtlicher Goldbestand m

1697 off-shore bank
f banque f off-shore
i banca f off-shore
e banco m extraterritorial; banco m off-shore

n off-shore bank f
d Off-shore-Bank f

1698 on-costs
f frais mpl généraux
i spese fpl generali; spese fpl indirette
e gastos mpl indirectos
n algemene onkosten mpl
d allgemeine Unkosten fpl

1699 on-lending
f réemprunt m
i riprestito m
e représtamo m
n wederuitlening f
d Wiederanleihe f; Wiederholungs-anleihe f; Wiederholungsdarlehen n

1700 open account
f compte m ouvert
i conto m aperto
e cuenta f abierta
n gewone rekening f
d offenes Konto n

1701 open cheque; uncrossed cheque
f chèque m ouvert; chèque m non barré
i assegno m aperto; assegno m no sbarrato
e cheque m abierto; cheque m sin cruzar
n open cheque m; ongekruiste cheque m
d offener Scheck m; ungekreuzter Scheck m

1702 open credit
f crédit m à découvert
i credito m allo scoperto
e crédito m al descubierto
n ongedekt krediet n
d offener Kredit m

1703 open economy
f économie f ouverte
i economia f aperta
e economía f abierta
n open economie f
d offene Wirtschaft f

1704 open-end investment company
f société f d'investissement à capital variable
i società f di investimenti con portafoglio di composizione variabile
e sociedad f de inversión con cartera de composición variable
n beleggingsmaatschappij f met variabel kapitaal
d Investitionsgesellschaft f mit wechseln-der Kapitalportefeuille

1705 opening capital
 f capital *m* initial
 i capitale *m* iniziale
 e capital *m* inicial
 n beginkapitaal *n*; aanvangskapitaal *n*
 d Anfangskapital *n*

1706 opening of account
 f ouverture *f* de compte
 i apertura *f* di conto
 e apertura *f* de cuenta
 n openen *n* van een rekening
 d Kontoeröffnung *f*

1707 opening price
 f premier cours *m*; cours *m* d'ouverture; cours *m* de début
 i prezzo *m* d'apertura; corso *m* d'apertura
 e precio *m* de apertura; tipo *m* de apertura
 n eerste koers *m*
 d Eröffnungspreis *m*; Anfangskurs *m*

1708 open policy
 f police *f* sans montant déclaré
 i polizza *f* senza valore dichiarato
 e póliza *f* sin valor declarado
 n open polis *f*
 d offene Police *f*

1709 operate v
 f opérer
 i operare
 e operar
 n zaken doen
 d operieren

1710 operating account
 f compte *m* d'exploitation
 i conto *m* di esercisio; conto *m* di operazioni
 e cuenta *f* de explotación; cuenta *f* de operación
 n exploitatierekening *f*
 d Betriebskonto *n*

1711 operating deficit
 f déficit *m* d'exercice
 i deficit *m* di esercizio
 e déficit *m* de ejercicio
 n bedrijfsverlies *n*; exploitatieverlies *n*
 d Betriebsverlust *m*

1712 operating expenses
 f dépenses *fpl* de fonctionnement; dépenses *fpl* d'exploitation
 i spese *fpl* di esercisio; spese *fpl* di operazioni
 e gastos *mpl* de explotación; gastos *mpl*

 de operación
 n bedrijfskosten *mpl*; exploitatiekosten *mpl*
 d Betriebskosten *fpl*

1713 operating losses
 f pertes *fpl* d'exploitation
 i perdite *fpl* di esercizio
 e pérdidas *fpl* de explotación
 n exploitatieverliezen *npl*
 d Betriebsverluste *mpl*

1714 operating ratio
 f coefficient *m* d'exploitation
 i coefficiente *m* di esercisio; coefficiente *m* di operazioni
 e coeficiente *m* de explotación
 n exploitatiecoëfficiënt *m*
 d Betriebskoeffizient *m*

1715 operating surplus
 f surplus *m* d'exploitation; bénéfices *mpl* d'exploitation
 i superavit *m* di funzionamento; superavit *m* di esercisio
 e superávit *m* de explotación; superávit *m* de operación
 n exploitatieoverschot *n*
 d Betriebsüberschuss *m*; Betriebsgewinn *m*

1716 operation
 f opération *f*
 i operazione *f*
 e operación *f*
 n zaak *f*; transactie *f*
 d Operation *f*; Geschäft *n*

1717 operational loan
 f prêt *m* de développement à court terme
 i prestito *m* per lo sviluppo a breve scandenza
 e préstamo *m* a corto plazo para desarrollo
 n kortlopende ontwikkelingslening *f*
 d kurzfristiger Entwicklungskredit *m*

1718 option dealing; option deal
 f opérations *fpl* à prime
 i operazioni *fpl* a premio
 e operaciones *fpl* de prima
 n premiehandel *m*
 d Prämiengeschäfte *npl*

1719 order
 f commande *f*; ordre *m*
 i ordine *m*; ordinazione *f*
 e orden *f*; pedido *m*
 n opdracht *f*; order *f*; bestelling *f*
 d Auftrag *m*; Order *f*; Bestellung *f*

1720 order cheque
f chèque *m* à ordre
i assegno *m* all'ordine
e cheque *m* a la orden
n ordercheque *m*
d Orderscheck *m*

1721 ordinary stock; common stock (US)
f action *f* ordinaire; action *f* de première
   émission
i azione *f* ordinaria; azione *f* di prima
   emissione
e acción *f* ordinaria; acción *f* de primera
   emisión
n gewoon aandeel *n*
d Stammaktie *f*

1722 organize v
f organiser
i organizzare
e organizar
n organiseren
d organisieren

1723 outflow of capital
f sortie *f* de capitaux
i fuga *f* di capitali; uscita *f* di capitali
e salida *f* de capital(es)
n afvloeiing *f* van kapitaal
d Kapitalabfluss *m*

1724 outlays; outgoings
f dépenses *fpl*; mises *fpl* de fonds;
   déboursements *mpl*
i spese *fpl*; sborsi *mpl*
e gastos *mpl*; desembolsos *mpl*;
   erogaciones *fpl*
n uitgaven *fpl*; uitbetaling *f*
d Ausgaben *fpl*; Auslagen *fpl*

1725 output
f production *f*; extrant *m*
i produzione *f*; prodotto *m*
e producción *f*; producto *m*
n productie *f*; product *n*
d Produktionsergebnis *n*; Ausstoss *m*

* **outside broker** → 1673

**1726 outstanding bonds; outstanding
   securities**
f obligations *fpl* en circulation
i obbligazioni *fpl* in circolazione
e bonos *mpl* en circulación
n uitstaande obligaties *fpl*
d im Umlauf befindliche Obligationen *fpl*

1727 outstanding coupon
f coupon *m* resté en souffrance

i cedola *f* non pagata
e cupón *m* no pagado
n achterstallige coupon *m*; nog niet
   betaalde coupon *m*
d ausstehender Kupon *m*; unbezahlter
   Kupon *m*

1728 outstanding debts
f dettes *fpl* en souffrance
i debiti *mpl* attivi
e deudas *fpl* activas
n uitstaande schulden *fpl*
d Aussenstände *mpl*

1729 outstanding expenses
f frais *mpl* à payer
i spese *fpl* non pagate
e gastos *mpl* pendientes de pago
n nog niet betaalde kosten *mpl*
d unbezahlte Ausgaben *fpl*

1730 outstanding external debt
f dette *f* extérieure non amortie
i debito *m* esterno pendente
e deuda *f* externa pendiente
n uitstaande buitenlandse schuld *f*
d ausstehende Auslandsschulden *fpl*

* **outstanding securities** → 1726

1731 overage loan
f prêt *m* destiné à couvrir un éventuel
   dépassement des coûts
i prestito *m* destinato a coprire eventuali
   eccessi di costi
e préstamo *m* para cubrir posibles excesos
   de costos
n lening *f* ter dekking van mogelijke
   kostenoverschrijdingen
d Kredit *m* um eventuelle Extraspesen zu
   decken

1732 overall deficit
f déficit *m* global
i deficit *m* globale
e déficit *m* global
n globaal tekort *n*
d Gesamtdefizit *n*

1733 overcapitalize v
f surcapitaliser
i supercapitalizzare
e sobrecapitalizar; supercapitalizar
n overkapitaliseren
d überkapitalisieren

1734 overcharge
f surcharge *f*
i sopraccarico *m*; maggiorazione *f*

e recargo *m*; sobrecarga *f*; aumento *m*
n toeslag *m*
d Zuschlag *m*; Aufschlag *m*

1735 overcredit *v*
f créditer en trop
i accreditare in eccesso
e acreditar en exceso
n te veel crediteren
d überkreditieren; zuviel gutschreiben

1736 overdebit *v*
f débiter en trop
i indebitare in eccesso
e debitar en exceso
n te veel debiteren
d überdebitieren; zuviel belasten

1737 overdepreciation
f surdépréciation *f*
i supersvalutazione *f*
e sobredepreciación *f*; superdepreciación *f*
n overmatige onderwaardering *f*; zeer hoge afschrijving *f*
d übermässige Entwertung *f*; übermässige Abschreibung *f*

1738 overdraft
f découvert *m*; solde *m* débiteur
i scoperto *m*
e sobregiro *m*; descubierto *m*
n overtrekking *f*
d Überziehung *f*; Überschreitung *f*

1739 overdraft facilities
f facilités *fpl* de découvert
i facilitazioni *fpl* per far fronte ad un eventuale scoperto
e servicio *m* de sobregiro
n kredietfaciliteiten *fpl*
d Überziehungskredit *m*; Dispositions-kredit *m*; Überziehungsmöglichkeit *f*

1740 overdraw *v* **an account**
f mettre un compte à découvert
i mandare un conto allo scoperto
e dejar una cuenta en descubierto; sobregirar
n een rekening overtrekken
d ein Konto überziehen

1741 overdrawn account
f compte *m* désapprovisionné
i conto *m* scoperto
e cuenta *f* sobregirada; cuenta *f* girada en descubierto
n overtrokken rekening *f*
d überzogenes Konto *n*

1742 overdue cheque
f chèque *m* échu
i assegno *m* scaduto; assegno *m* prescritto
e cheque *m* vencido; cheque *m* prescrito
n achterstallige cheque *m*
d verfallener Scheck *m*; überfälliger Scheck *m*

1743 overdue payment
f paiement *m* arriéré
i pagamento *m* arretrato
e pago *m* atrasado
n achterstallige betaling *f*
d rückständige Zahlung *f*

1744 overhead expenses
f frais *mpl* généraux
i spese *fpl* generali
e gastos *mpl* generales
n algemene onkosten *mpl*
d allgemeine Unkosten *fpl*

1745 overinsurance
f assurance *f* en excès
i assicurazione *f* in eccesso
e seguro *m* en exceso
n te hoge verzekering *f*
d Überversicherung *f*

1746 overinvestment
f placement *m* excessif
i investimento *m* eccesso
e inversión *f* en exceso
n te grote belegging *f*
d übermässige Geldanlage *f*; übermässige Investition *f*

1747 overpayment
f paiement *m* en excès
i pagamento *m* in eccesso
e pago *m* en exceso
n te hoge betaling *f*
d Überbezahlung *f*

1748 oversupply
f offre *f* excédentaire
i offerta *f* eccedentaria
e oferta *f* excesiva
n te groot aanbod *n*
d Überangebot *n*

1749 overvalue *v*
f surévaluer
i supervalutare
e tasar en exceso; sobrevaluar
n overwaarderen
d überbewerten; überwerten

1750 owe v
  f devoir
  i dovere
  e deber; adeudar
  n schuldig zijn
  d schulden; schuldig sein

1751 own v
  f posséder
  i possedere
  e poseer
  n bezitten
  d besitzen

1752 owner
  f possesseur *m*; propriétaire *m*
  i possessore *m*; proprietario *m*
  e poseedor *m*; posesor *m*; propietario *m*
  n bezitter *m*; eigenaar *m*
  d Besitzer *m*; Eigentümer *m*; Inhaber *m*

P

1753 paid
f payé; acquitté
i pagato
e pagado; pago
n betaald
d bezahlt

1754 paid-up capital
f capital *m* versé
i capitale *m* versato
e capital *m* integrado
n volgestort kapitaal *n*
d eingezahltes Kapital *n*

1755 paid-up policy
f police f intégralement payée
i polizza f interamente pagata
e póliza f enteramente pagada
n volgestorte polis f
d voll eingezahlte Police f

1756 paid-up shares; full-paid shares
f actions *fpl* intégralement payées; actions
fpl libérées; actions *fpl* entièrement
versées
i azioni *fpl* interamente pagate
e acciones *fpl* enteramente pagadas
n volgestorte aandelen *npl*
d voll eingezahlte Aktien *fpl*; Vollaktien
fpl

1757 paper
f document *m*
i documento *m*
e documento *m*
n document *n*
d Dokument *n*

1758 paper
f valeur f
i valore *m*
e valor *m*
n waardepapier *n*
d Wertpapier *n*

1759 paper currency; paper money
f papier-monnaie *m*
i carta f moneta
e papel *m* moneda
n papiergeld *n*
d Papiergeld *n*

1760 paper profits
f bénéfices *mpl* fictifs
i profitti *mpl* fittizi
e ganancias *fpl* ficticias

n schijnwinst f
d Scheingewinne *mpl*

1761 par *(adj.)*
f au pair
i alla pari
e a la par
n pari
d pari

1762 par *(noun)*
f valeur f nominale
i valore *m* nominale
e valor *m* nominal
n nominale waarde f
d Nennwert *m*

1763 parallel financing
f financement *m* parallèle
i finanziamento *m* parallelo
e financiación f paralela; financiamiento
m paralelo
n parallelfinanciering f
d Parallelfinanzierung f; Parallelanleihe f

1764 parallel market
f marché *m* parallèle; marché *m* libre
i mercato *m* parallelo di divise; mercato *m*
libero
e mercado *m* libre de cambios; mercado *m*
paralelo
n vrije deviezenmarkt f
d Parallelmarkt *m*; freier Devisenmarkt *m*

1765 parcel of shares
f paquet *m* d'actions
i pacco *m* d'azioni
e paquete *m* de acciones
n aandelenpakket *n*
d Aktienpaket *n*

* parcener → 753

1766 par collection
f encaissement *m* au pair
i incasso *m* alla pari
e cobro *m* a la par
n incasso *n* a pari
d Inkasso *n* zum Pariwert

1767 par of exchange
f parité f des changes
i parità f cambiaria
e paridad f cambiaria
n wisselpariteit f
d Wechselparität f

1768 participate *v*
f participer

i partecipare
e participar
n deelnemen
d teilnehmen; beteiligt sein

1769 participating annuity
f annuité *f* ayant part dans les bénéfices
i annualità *f* con partecipazione ai guadagni
e anualidad *f* con participación en las ganancias
n rente *f* met winstdeling
d Rente *f* mit Gewinnbeteiligung

1770 participating preference shares
f actions *fpl* de préférence ayant part dans les bénéfices
i azioni *fpl* di preferenza con partecipazione al beneficio
e acciones *fpl* de preferencia con participación en el beneficio
n winstdelende preferente aandelen *npl*
d Vorzugsaktien *fpl* mit Teilhaberschaft am Gewinn

1771 participating stock
f capital *m* d'actions ayant part dans les bénéfices
i capitale *m* azionario con partecipazione al beneficio
e capital *m* en acciones con participación en el beneficio
n winstdelend aandelenkapitaal *n*
d Aktienkapital *n* mit Teilhaberschaft am Gewinn

* **participation loan** → **2281**

1772 partition
f partage *m*
i spartizione *f*
e repartición *f*; reparto *m*
n verdeling *f*
d Aufteilung *f*

1773 partner
f associé *m*
i socio *m*
e socio *m*
n vennoot *m*; compagnon *m*
d Teilhaber *m*; Partner *m*; Gesellschafter *m*

1774 partnership
f société *f*
i società *f*
e sociedad *f*
n vennootschap *f*; compagnonschap *n*
d Gesellschaft *f*; Teilhaberschaft *f*

1775 partnership assets
f biens *mpl* de la société; actif *m* de la société
i beni *mpl* della società; attivo *m* sociale
e bienes *mpl* de la sociedad; activo *m* social
n activa *npl* der vennootschap
d Gesellschaftsvermögen *n*

1776 partnership debts
f dettes *fpl* de la société; passif *m* social
i debiti *mpl* della società; passivo *m* della società
e deudas *fpl* de la sociedad; pasivo *m* social
n schulden *fpl* der vennootschap
d Gesellschaftsschulden *fpl*

1777 partnership liabilities
f passif *m* social
i passivo *m* sociale
e pasivo *m* social
n verplichtingen *fpl* der vennootschap
d Verpflichtungen *fpl* einer Gesellschaft

1778 par value
f valeur *f* au pair
i valore *m* alla pari
e valor *m* a la par
n pariwaarde *f*
d Pariwert *m*

1779 passbook *(US)*; **bank book**
f livret *m* bancaire
i libretto *m* bancario
e libreta *f* de banco
n bankboekje *n*
d Bankbuch *n*

1780 passenger clause
f clause *f* indemnisatrice des passagers
i clausola *f* d'indennizzo dei passeggeri
e cláusula *f* de indemnización de pasajeros
n passagiersclausule *f*
d Reisebestimmungen *fpl*; Ersatzklausel *f* bei Reiseversicherungen der Passagiere

1781 passive debts
f dettes *fpl* non productives d'intérêt
i debiti *mpl* passivi
e deudas *fpl* que no producen intereses
n renteloze schulden *fpl*
d unverzinsliche Schulden *fpl*

1782 patent
f brevet *m*
i brevetto *m*
e patente *f*

n octrooi n; patent n
d Patent n

1783 patent v
f breveter
i brevettare
e patentar
n octrooi verlenen; patenteren
d patentieren

1784 patent rights
f droits m de brevet
i diritti mpl di brevetto
e derechos mpl de patente
n octrooirechten npl
d Patentrechte npl

1785 pattern of investment
f structure f de l'investissement
i composizione f degli investimenti
e composición f de la inversión
n investeringspatroon n
d Investitionsgefüge n

1786 pawn v; **hock** v
f mettre en gage
i impegnare
e empeñar; pignorar
n verpanden
d verpfänden; lombardieren

1787 pawn bank; pawn office
f mont-de-piété m
i monte m di pietà
e monte m de piedad
n bank f van lening; pandhuis n;
lommerd m
d Pfandbank f

1788 pawnbroker
f prêteur m (sur gages)
i prestatore m (su pegno)
e prestamista m/f (sobre prenda)
n lommerdhouder m; pandjesbaas m
d Pfandleiher m

1789 pawnbroking
f prêts mpl sur gage
i prestiti mpl su pegno
e préstamos mpl pignoraticios
n leningen fpl op onderpand
d Pfandleihgeschäfte npl

1790 pawnee
f créancier-gagiste m
i creditore m con pegno
e acreedor m prendario
n pandhouder m
d Pfandgläubiger m; Pfandinhaber m

* **pawn office** → 1787

1791 pay v
f payer; régler
i pagare
e pagar; abonar
n betalen
d zahlen; bezahlen

1792 payable
f payable
i pagabile
e pagadero
n betaalbaar
d zahlbar

1793 payable on demand
f exigible à vue; paiable à vue
i pagabile a vista; pagabile a presentazione
e pagadero a la vista; pagadero a presentación
n betaalbaar op vertoon; betaalbaar op zicht
d zahlbar bei Sicht; zahlbar auf Verlangen

1794 payable on presentation
f payable sur présentation
i pagabile a presentazione
e pagadero a presentación
n betaalbaar bij aanbieding
d zahlbar bei Vorlage

1795 payable to order
f payable à ordre
i pagabile all'ordine
e pagadero a la orden
n betaalbaar aan order
d zahlbar an Order

1796 payback period
f période f de récuperation; période f de recouvrement
i periodo m di ricupero; periodo m di rimborso
e período m de recuperación; período m de reembolso
n remboursperiode f
d Kapitalrückflussdauer f

1797 payee
f bénéficiaire m
i beneficiario m
e beneficiario m
n begunstigde m; ontvanger m
d Zahlungsempfänger m

1798 payer
f payeur m
i pagatore m

e pagador *m*
n betaler *m*
d Zahler *m*; Zahlmeister *m*

1799 payer of a bill
f preneur *m* d'une traite
i prenditore *m* di una cambiale
e tomador *m* de una letra
n koper *m* van een wissel
d Wechseleinnehmer *m*

* paying-in slip → 801

1800 paying teller
f caissier *m* payeur
i cassiere-pagatore *m*
e cajero-pagador *m*
n kassier *m* voor uitbetalingen
d Kassierer *m* für Auszahlungen

1801 payment
f paiement *m*
i pagamento *m*
e pago *m*
n betaling *f*
d Zahlung *f*; Bezahlung *f*

1802 payment arrears
f arriérés *mpl* de paiement
i ritardo *m* nel pagamento; pagamenti *mpl* arretrati
e atraso *m* en los pagos
n achterstallige betalingen *fpl*; betalingsachterstand *m*
d rückständige Zahlungen *fpl*; Zahlungs-rückstände *mpl*

1803 payment bond
f garantie *f* de paiement
i garanzia *f* di pagamento
e fianza *f* de pago
n garantie *f* van betaling
d Zahlungsbürgschaft *f*

1804 payment in advance; advance payment; anticipated payment
f paiement *m* anticipé
i pagamento *m* anticipato
e pago *m* anticipado
n vooruitbetaling *f*
d Vorauszahlung *f*

1805 payment in full
f paiement *m* intégral
i pagamento *m* totale
e pago *m* total
n volledige betaling *f*
d Vollzahlung *f*

1806 payment in full
f versement *m* de libération (d'actions)
i versamento *m* a liberazione (di azioni)
e pago *m* de liberación (de acciones)
n volstorting *f* (van aandelen)
d Vollzahlung *f* (von Aktien)

1807 payment received
f pour acquit
i pagato
e pagado
n voldaan; betaling ontvangen
d Zahlung erhalten

1808 payments deficit
f déficit *m* de paiement
i deficit *m* di pagamento
e déficit *m* de pagos
n betalingstekort *n*
d Zahlungsbilanzdefizit *n*

1809 payments position
f situation *f* des paiements
i situazione *f* dei pagamenti
e estado *m* de los pagos; situación *f* de los pagos
n betalingspositie *f*
d Zahlungslage *f*

1810 payments restrictions
f restrictions *fpl* de paiements
i restrizione *f* dei pagamenti
e restricciones *fpl* en los pagos
n betalingsbeperkingen *fpl*
d Zahlungsbeschränkungen *fpl*

1811 pay v off
f payer; liquider
i pagare; liquidare
e pagar; liquidar
n betalen; afbetalen
d abzahlen; abbezahlen; auszahlen

1812 pay v up
f payer entièrement
i pagare interamente
e pagar por completo; saldar
n volstorten
d voll bezahlen; voll einzahlen

* peculation → 1065

1813 pecuniary
f pécuniaire
i pecuniario
e pecuniario
n geldelijk
d pekuniär; Geld-

1814 penalty clause
f clause f de pénalité
i clausola f penale
e cláusula f penal
n strafclausule f
d Strafklausel f; Strafbestimmungen fpl

1815 pension
f retraite f; pension f
i pensione f
e pensión f; jubilación f
n pensioen n
d Pension f

1816 pent-up demand
f demande f comprimée; demande f refoulée
i domanda f compressa; domanda f repressa
e demanda f reprimida
n gecomprimeerde vraag f
d beschränkte Nachfrage f; gepresste Nachfrage f

1817 per capita
f par tête
i per testa
e per capita; por cabeza
n per hoofd; per persoon
d pro Kopf

1818 per capita income
f revenu m par habitant; revenu m par tête
i rendita f individuale; entrate fpl per persona
e ingreso m per capita
n inkomen n per hoofd
d Pro-Kopf-Einkommen n

1819 per cent
f pour cent
i per cento
e por ciento
n percent; procent
d prozent

1820 percentage
f pourcentage m
i percentuale f
e porcentaje m
n percentage n
d Prozentsatz m

1821 percentage distribution
f ventilation f en pourcentage
i distribuzione f percentuale
e distribución f porcentual

n procentuele verdeling f
d prozentuale Verteilung f

1822 percentage point
f point m de pourcentage
i punto m percentuale
e punto m porcentual
n percentagepunt n
d Prozentpunkt m

1823 performance bond
f caution f de bonne fin; garantie f de bonne fin
i cauzione f per il buon fine; garanzia f per il buon fine
e fianza f de cumplimiento
n werkuitvoeringsgarantie f
d Gewährleistungsgarantie f

1824 permit
f permis m; licence f
i permesso m; licenza f
e permiso m; licencia f
n vergunning f; verlof n
d Erlaubnis f; Genehmigung f

* perpetual annuity → 1532

1825 perpetual bond
f titre m de rente viagère
i titolo m di rendita vitalizia
e título m de renta vitalicia
n obligatie f met lijfrente
d Leibrentenschein m

1826 perpetual debenture
f obligation f perpétuelle
i obbligazione f perpetua
e obligación f perpetua
n obligatie f zonder aflossingstermijn; eeuwigdurende obligatie f
d Dauerschuldverschreibung f

1827 personal bond
f garantie f personnelle
i cauzione f personale
e fianza f personal
n persoonlijke garantie f
d persönliche Garantie f

1828 personal chattels
f biens mpl meubles; biens mpl personnels
i beni mpl mobili; beni mpl personali
e bienes mpl muebles; bienes mpl personales
n roerende goederen npl; persoonlijke bezittingen fpl
d Mobilien fpl; bewegliches Vermögen n

1829 personal loan *(US)*
f prêt m personnel (sans garantie)
i prestito m personale (senza garanzia)
e préstamo m personal (sin garantía)
n persoonlijke lening f (zonder borgstelling)
d persönliches Darlehen n (ohne Garantie)

1830 personal security
f garantie f personnelle; garantie f sans documents
i garanzia f personale; garanzia f senza documenti
e garantía f personal; garantía f sin documentos
n persoonlijke borgstelling f; garantie f zonder documenten
d persönliche Bürgschaft f; nicht durch Dokumente gedeckte Sicherheit f

* **petition** → 319

1831 physical assets
f valeurs fpl matérielles
i valori mpl materiali
e valores mpl materiales
n tastbare activa npl
d materielle Vermögenswerte mpl

1832 physical investment
f investissement m matériel
i investimento m materiale; investimento m in attivo fisso
e inversión f en activos fijos
n investering f in vaste activa
d Investition f in festen Aktiven

1833 pipeline credit
f fonds mpl engagés mais non encore versés
i credito m in corso di risoluzione
e crédito m en tramitación
n krediet n in behandeling
d in Verhandlung befindlicher Kredit m

1834 pledge
f gage m
i pegno m
e prenda f
n pand n
d Pfand n

1835 pledge loan
f prêt m sur gage
i prestito m su pegno
e préstamo m pignoraticio
n pandlening f
d Pfandanleihe f

1836 ploughed-back profits
f bénéfices mpl réinvestis
i utilità fpl reinvestite
e utilidades fpl reinvertidas
n herbelegde winsten fpl
d reinvestierte Gewinne mpl

1837 policy
f police f
i polizza f
e póliza f
n polis f
d Police f

* **policy of insurance** → 1414

* **poll tax** → 543

* **pool** → 2280

1838 possessory title
f titre m de possession
i titolo m di proprietà
e título m de propiedad
n titel m van eigendom; eigendomstitel m; eigendomsbewijs n; certificaat n van eigendom
d Besitztitel m; Besitzurkunde f

* **postal order** → 1620

1839 postal savings bank
f casse f d'épargne postale
i cassa f di risparmio postale
e caja f de ahorro postal
n postspaarbank f
d Postsparkasse f

1840 posted values
f mercuriale f
i valori mpl di mercato
e valores mpl de mercado
n marktwaarden fpl; genoteerde waarden fpl
d Marktwerte mpl

* **potential stock** → 2379

1841 pound
f livre f
i lira f
e libra f
n pond n
d Pfund n

1842 power of attorney
f pouvoir m; procuration f
i procura f
e poder m

n procuratie f; volmacht f
d Vollmacht f

1843 precarious loan
f commodat m précaire
i prestito m senza termine fisso
e comodato m sin plazo fijo
n lening f zonder vaste termijn
d unsicheres Darlehen n

1844 pre-emption
f droit m de préemption; option f d'achat
i diritto m di precedenza nell'acquisto
e derecho m de prioridad en la compra
n voorkoopsrecht n
d Vorkaufsrecht n

1845 preference bond
f titre m privilégié
i titolo m privilegiato
e título m privilegiado
n preferente obligatie f
d Vorzugsobligation f

**1846 preference share; preference stock;
priority share**
f action f de préférence; action f
privilégiée; action f de priorité
i azione f di priorità; azione f privilegiata
e acción f de preferencia
n preferent aandeel n; prioriteitsaandeel n
d Vorzugsaktie f; Prioritätsaktie f

1847 preferential creditor
f créancier m privilégié
i creditore m privilegiato
e acreedor m privilegiado
n preferente schuldeiser m; bevoorrechte
schuldeiser m
d bevorrechtigter Gläubiger m; Vorzugs-
gläubiger m

**1848 preferential debt; preferred debt;
privileged debt**
f dette f privilégiée
i debito m privilegiato
e deuda f privilegiada
n preferente schuld f
d bevorrechtete Schuld f

1849 preferential payment
f paiement m privilégié
i pagamento m preferenziale
e pago m preferencial
n preferente betaling f
d Vorzugszahlung f

* **preferred debt** → 1848

1850 preferred dividend
f dividende m de priorité
i dividendo m privilegiato
e dividendo m privilegiado
n preferent dividend n
d Vorzugsdividende f

1851 prefinancing
f préfinancement m
i finanziamento m previo
e prefinanciamiento m; financiamiento m
previo
n voorfinanciering f
d Vorfinanzierung f

1852 prematured loan
f prêt m dont on exige le remboursement
anticipé
i prestito m la cui scadenza è stata
anticipata
e préstamo m cuyo vencimiento se ha
adelantado
n lening f met vervroegde vervaldatum
d Darlehen n mit Vorauszahlungstermin

1853 premium
f prime f
i premio m
e prima f
n premie f
d Prämie f

1854 premium bond
f bond m à prime
i buono m di premio
e bono m de prima
n premie-obligatie f; lot n
d Prämienschein m

1855 premium on foreign exchange
f prime f de change
i premio m cambiario
e prima f cambiaria; prima f de cambio
n deviezenpremie f
d Devisenaufgeld n

* **prepaid interest** → 2373

1856 prepayment
f paiement m d'avance
i pagamento m anticipato
e pago m anticipado; pago m por
adelantado
n vooruitbetaling f
d Vorauszahlung f

1857 prescribe v
f prescrire
i prescrivere

e prescribir
n verjaren
d vorschreiben; verjähren

1858 prescription
f prescription f
i prescrizione f
e prescripción f
n verjaring f
d Verjährung f

1859 prescriptive right
f droit m de prescription
i diritto m di prescrizione
e derecho m de prescripción
n recht n van verjaring
d Verjährungsrecht n

1860 "present again" *(words sometimes written by a banker upon a cheque unpaid because of insufficient funds)*
f "présenter de nouveau"
i "presentare di nuovo"
e "presentar de nuevo"
n "weer aanbieden"
d "wieder vorlegen"

1861 presentment for acceptance
f présentation f pour acceptation
i presentazione f all'accettazione
e presentación f para aceptación
n aanbieding f ter acceptatie
d Vorlage f zur Annahme; Vorlage f zum Akzept

1862 presentment for payment
f présentation f pour paiement
i presentazione f al pagamento
e presentación f para el pago
n aanbieding f ter betaling
d Vorlage f zur Zahlung

1863 present value
f valeur f actualisée
i valore m aggiornato
e valor m actualizado
n actuele waarde f
d Gegenwartswert m

1864 prevailing market rate
f cours m du marché
i tasso m vigente di mercato
e tipo m vigente en el mercado; tasa f vigente en el mercado
n geldende marktkoers m
d marktgängiger Satz m

1865 price elasticity
f élasticité f par rapport au prix; élasticité-

prix f
i elasticità f del prezzo
e elasticidad-precio f; elasticidad f con respecto al precio
n prijselasticiteit f
d Preiselastizität f

1866 price escalation clause
f clause f de révision des prix
i clausola f relativa all'aumento dei prezzi
e cláusula f sobre aumento de precio
n prijsindexclausule f
d Preisgleitklausel f

1867 price swing
f fluctuation f entre deux prix
i fluttuazione f dei prezzi
e fluctuación f de precios; oscilación f de precios
n prijsfluctuatie f; prijsschommeling f
d Preisschwankung f

1868 primary reserves
f réserves fpl primaires
i riserve fpl primarie
e reservas fpl primarias
n primaire reserves fpl
d gesetzliche Rücklagen fpl

1869 prime bill of exchange
f première f de change
i prima f di cambio
e primera f de cambio
n prima-wissel m
d Primawechsel m

1870 prime rate
f taux m préférentiel
i tasso m d'interesse preferenziale
e tipo m de interés preferencial
n bankdisconto n; preferentiële rente f
d Kreditzins m für erstklassige Kunden

* **principal** → 507

* **priority share** → 1846

1871 prior lien
f droit m prioritaire de rétention
i diritto m privilegiato di ritenzione
e derecho m prioritario de retención
n bevoorrecht verband n
d bevorrechtigtes Zurück-behaltungsrecht n; bevorrechtigtes Pfandrecht n

1872 private bank
f banque f privée
i banca f privata

e banco *m* privado
n particuliere bank *f*
d Privatbank *f*

1873 privilege
f privilège *m*
i privilegio *m*
e privilegio *m*
n privilege *n*; voorrecht *n*
d Privileg *n*; Vorrecht *n*

* **privileged debt** → **1848**

1874 prize
f prix *m*; récompense *f*
i premio *m*; ricompensa *f*
e premio *m*; recompensa *f*
n prijs *m*; beloning *f*
d Preis *m*; Belohnung *f*

1875 probate
f acte *m* probatif d'un testament
i prova *f* ufficiale di un testamento
e acta *f* probativa de un testamento
n rechtsgeldig afschrift *n* van een
  testament
d gerichtliche Testamentbestätigung *f*

1876 probate *v*
f valider un testament
i omologare un testamento
e validar un testamento
n een testament rechtsgeldig verklaren
d ein Testament gerichtlich bestätigen
  lassen

1877 probate register
f registre *m* de testaments légalement
  valides
i registro *m* di testamenti legalmente
  validi
e registro *m* de testamentos válidos
  legalmente
n register *n* van rechtsgeldige testamenten
d Testamentshinterlegungsstelle *f*

1878 proceeds of a credit; proceeds of a loan
f fonds *mpl* provenant d'un crédit
i fondi *mpl* provenienti da un credito
e fondos *mpl* de un crédito
n kredietfonds *n*
d Kreditfonds *m*; Fonds *m* eines Kredits

1879 processing of a loan
f traitement *m* de crédit
i studio *m* di un prestito; esame *m* di un
  prestito
e tramitación *f* de un préstamo

n kredietbehandeling *f*
d Kreditverhandlung *f*

1880 procuration
f procuration *f*; mandat *m*
i procura *f*; mandato *m*
e procuración *f*; poder *m*
n procuratie *f*; volmacht *f*
d Prokura *f*; Vollmacht *f*

1881 productive investment
f placement *m* profitable
i investimento *m* produttivo
e inversión *f* productiva
n winstgevende belegging *f*
d lohnende Investition *f*; einträgliche
  Investition *f*

1882 profit
f profit *m*; bénéfice *m*; gain *m*
i profitto *m*; beneficio *m*; guadagno *m*
e beneficio *m*; ganancia *f*
n winst *f*
d Gewinn *m*; Profit *m*

1883 profitability; earning power
f rentabilité *f*
i rendimento *m*; profitto *m*; rendita *f*
e rentabilidad *f*
n rentabiliteit *f*
d Rentabilität *f*; Rendite *f*

1884 profit-and-loss account; profit-and-loss statement
f compte *m* de profits et pertes
i conto *m* profitti e perdite
e cuenta *f* de pérdidas y ganancias
n winst-en-verliesrekening *f*; verlies-en-
  winstrekening *f*
d Gewinn-und-Verlustkonto *n*; Erfolgs-
  rechnung *f*

1885 profiteer *v*
f faire des bénéfices excessifs; prêter à
  usure
i ottenere benefici esorbitanti; prestare a
  usura
e obtener beneficios exorbitantes; prestar a
  usura
n buitensporige winsten maken; uitlenen
  tegen woekerrente
d aussergewöhnliche Gewinne einstecken;
  leihen auf Wucherzins

1886 profit seeking
f à but lucratif
i con fini di lucro
e con fines lucrativos

n met winstbejag
d zu einträglichen Zwecken *mpl*

1887 program loan
f prêt-programme *m*
i prestiti *mpl* per programmi
e préstamo *m* para programas
d Anleihe *f* für Bauprogramme

1888 progress payment
f acompte *m*
i acconto *m* parziale; pagamento *m*
   parziale
e pago *m* parcial
n gedeeltelijke betaling *f*
d Teilzahlung *f*

1889 project loan
f prêt-projet *m*
i prestito *m* per un progetto
e préstamo *m* para un proyecto
n projectlening *f*
d Projektkredit *m*; Anleihe *f* für Projekte

1890 promissory note; note of hand; iou
f billet *m*; promesse *f*
i pagherò *m*
e vale *m*; pagaré *m*
n promesse *f*
d Schuldschein *m*; Solawechsel *m*

1891 proof of debt
f titre *m* de créance
i titolo *m* di debito; prova *f* di debito
e comprobante *m* de deuda
n schuldbewijs *n*
d Schuldtitel *m*

1892 property
f propriété *f*
i proprietà *f*
e propiedad *f*
n eigendom *n*; bezit *n*
d Eigentum *n*; Besitz *m*

1893 property dividend
f dividende *m* en nature
i dividendo *m* in natura
e dividendo *m* en especie
n dividend *n* in natura
d Dividende *f* in Form von Güter

1894 property income
f recettes *fpl* domaniales; revenus *mpl*
   domaniaux
i entrate *fpl* domaniali; rendite *fpl* su
   proprietà pubbliche
e renta *f* sobre propiedades públicas

n onroerend-goed-inkomsten *fpl*
d Einkommen *n* aus Volkseigentum

1895 proportion
f proportion *f*
i proporzione *f*
e proporción *f*
n evenredigheid *f*; verhouding *f*
d Verhältnis *n*

1896 proportional
f proportionnel
i proporzionale
e proporcional
n evenredig
d proportional; verhältnismässig

* **proprietary** → **1900**

1897 proprietary equity
f valeur *f* liquide d'une propriété
i valore *m* liquido di una proprietà
e valor *m* liquido de una propiedad
n contante waarde *f* van een eigendom
d Barbetrag *m* aus einem Grundbesitz

1898 proprietary interest
f participation *f* au capital
i interesse *m* patrimoniale;
   partecipazione *f*
e interés *m* patrimonial; participación *f*
n eigendomsinterest *m*; deelneming *f*
d Anteilzinsen *mpl*

1899 proprietary right; proprietorship
f droit *m* de propriété
i diritto *m* di proprietà
e derecho *m* de propiedad
n eigendomsrecht *n*
d Eigentumsrecht *n*

1900 proprietor; proprietary
f propriétaire *m*
i proprietario *m*
e propietario *m*
n eigenaar *m*
d Eigentümer *m*

* **proprietorship** → **1899**

1901 pro-rate
f au prorata
i al prorata
e a prorrata
n naar rato; naar verhouding
d nach Verhältnis

1902 prorate *v*
f partager proportionnellement

i ripartire al prorata
e prorratear
n toewijzen naar rato; evenredig verdelen
d berechnen nach Verhältnis

1903 protectionism
f protectionnisme *m*
i protezionismo *m*
e proteccionismo *m*
n protectionisme *n*
d Schutzsystem *n*

1904 protest charges
f frais *mpl* de protêt
i spese *fpl* di protesto
e gastos *mpl* de protesto
n protestkosten *mpl*
d Protestkosten *fpl*

1905 protested bill
f traite *f* protestée
i cambiale *f* protestata
e letra *f* protestada
n geprotesteerde wissel *m*
d protestierter Wechsel *m*

1906 provable debts
f dettes *fpl* démontrables
i debiti *mpl* che si possono provare
e deudas *fpl* que pueden probarse
n bewijsbare schulden *fpl*
d nachweisbare Schulden *fpl*

1907 prove *v*
f prouver; démontrer
i provare; dimostrare
e probar; demostrar
n bewijzen; staven
d beweisen; nachweisen; beglaubigen

1908 provident fund
f fonds *m* de prévoyance
i fondo *m* di previdenza
e fondo *m* de previsión
n voorzorgsfonds *n*
d Fürsorgefonds *m*

1909 provision
f prévision *f*
i disposizione *f*
e disposición *f*
n bestemming *f*; dispositie *f*
d Bestimmung *f*; Vorsorge *f*

1910 proxy
f mandataire *m*; procureur *m*
i mandatario *m*; procuratore *m*
e apoderado *m*

n gemachtigde *m*
d Bevollmächtigter *m*

1911 proxy holder
f fondé *m* de pouvoir
i detentore *m* d'una procura
e poderhabiente *m*
n procuratiehouder *m*; houder *m* van een volmacht
d Vollmachtsbesitzer *m*

1912 public account
f compte *m* public
i conto *m* pubblico
e cuenta *f* pública
n overheidsrekening *f*
d Staatskonto *n*

1913 public credit
f crédit *m* de l'Etat
i credito *m* pubblico
e crédito *m* público
n staatskrediet *n*
d Staatskredit *m*; öffentlicher Kredit *m*

1914 public funds
f deniers *mpl* publics; fonds *mpl* publics
i fondi *mpl* pubblici
e fondos *mpl* públicos
n overheidsgelden *npl*
d Staatsgelder *npl*

1915 purchase price; purchase money
f prix *m* d'achat
i prezzo *m* d'acquisto
e precio *m* de compra
n koopprijs *m*
d Kaufpreis *m*

1916 put and call
f option *f* double
i opzione *f* doppia
e opción *f* doble
n dubbele optie *f*; "put" en "call"
d Stell(age)geschäft *n*

1917 qualified acceptance
f acceptation f conditionnelle
i accettazione f condizionata
e aceptación f condicional
n voorwaardelijke acceptatie f
d bedingtes Akzept n; bedingte Annahme f

1918 qualified endorsement
f endos m sous réserves; endossement m
  conditionnel
i girata f condizionata
e endoso m condicional
n voorwaardelijk endossement n
d bedingtes Indossament n

1919 qualifying shares
f actions fpl de garantie
i azioni fpl abilitanti; azioni fpl di
  garanzia
e acciones fpl habilitantes; acciones fpl
  de garantía
n garantieaandelen npl
d Qualifikationsaktien fpl

1920 quantity theory of money
f théorie f quantitative de la monnaie
i teoria f quantitativa del denaro
e teoría f cuantitativa del dinero
n kwalitatieve theorie f van het geld
d Quantitätstheorie f des Geldes

1921 quarterage
f montant m du trimestre
i importo m trimestrale
e monto m trimestral
n kwartaalbedrag n
d Quartalsbetrag m

1922 quasi-money
f quasi-monnaie f
i quasidenaro m
e cuasidinero m
n bijnageld n
d Quasi-Geld n

1923 quasi-negotiable instrument
f document m quasi-négotiable
i documento m quasi-negoziabile
e documento m casi negociable
n quasi-verhandelbaar document n
d quasi-begebbares Wertpapier n; quasi-
  übertragbares Wertpapier n

1924 quick assets
f actif m négociable
i attivo m di rapida liquidazione

e activo m realizable
n beschikbaar actief n
d leicht realisierbare Aktiva npl

* **quick ratio → 40**

1925 quitclaim
f cession f d'un droit; renonciation f
i cessione f di un diritto; rinuncia f
e cesión f de un derecho; renuncia f
n afstand m van rechten
d Rechtübertragung f; Verzichtleistung f

* **quittance → 1951**

1926 quota
f quote-part f; contingent m
i quota f
e cuota f; cupo m
n contingent n; quota f
d Kontingent n; Rate f

1927 quotation
f cote f
i quotazione f
e cotización f
n notering f
d Notierung f

1928 quote v
f coter
i quotare
e cotizar
n noteren
d notieren

R

1929 rack rent
f loyer *m* maximum
i affitto *m* massimo
e alquiler *m* máximo
n maximaal huurbedrag *n*
d erreichbare Höchstmiete *f*

1930 raise *v*
f augmenter; accroître
i aumentare
e aumentar
n verhogen
d erhöhen

1931 raise
f augmentation *f*; accroissement *m*;
  hausse *f*
i aumento *m*
e aumento *m*
n verhoging *f*; stijging *f*
d Erhöhung *f*

1932 raise *v* **a protest**
f émettre un protêt
i emettere un protesto
e emitir un protesto
n protest aantekenen
d Protest erheben

1933 raised cheque
f chêque *m* majoré frauduleusement
i assegno *m* aumentato fraudolentamente
e cheque *m* aumentado fraudulentamente
n cheque *m* waarvan het bedrag door
  vervalsing verhoogd is
d Scheck *m* gefälscht durch Erhöhung des
  Betrages

1934 raise *v* **funds**
f se procurer des fonds
i ottenere fondi
e obtener fondos
n gelden bijeenbrengen
d Geldmittel beschaffen

1935 raise *v* **money**
f se procurer de l'argent
i procurare denaro
e obtener dinero
n geld bijeenbrengen
d Geld beschaffen; Geldmittel auftreiben

1936 rate
f cours *m*; taux *m*
i corso *m*; tasso *m*
e tipo *m*; tasa *f*

n koers *m*; voet *m*
d Kurs *m*; Satz *m*

**1937 rate of exchange; course of exchange;
     exchange rate**
f cours *m* de change; taux *m* de change
i tasso *m* di cambio; corso *m* delle valute
e tipo *m* de cambio
n wisselkoers *m*
d Wechselkurs *m*

1938 rate of return; yield rate
f taux *m* de rendement
i tassa *f* di rendimento
e tipo *m* de rendimiento
n rendementspercentage *n*
d Ertragsrate *f*

1939 ready money
f argent *m* liquide; argent *m* comptant
i fondi *mpl* liquidi; contanti *mpl*
e dinero *m* en efectivo; dinero *m* contante
n liquide middelen *npl*; liquiditeiten *fpl*;
  contant geld *n*; contanten *npl*
d flüssige Mittel *npl*; Bargeld *n*

1940 real estate; real assets
f biens *mpl* immeubles; propriété *f*
  immobilière
i beni *mpl* immobili
e bienes *mpl* inmuebles; propiedad *f*
  inmobiliaria
n onroerende goederen *npl*
d unbewegliches Vermögen *n*; Grundeigentum *n*

1941 real interest rate
f taux *m* d'intérêt réel
i tasso *m* reale di interessi
e tipo *m* real de interés
n werkelijk rentepercentage *n*; effectief
  rentepercentage *n*
d Realzins *m*

1942 realizable
f réalisable
i realizzabile
e realizable
n verkoopbaar; realiseerbaar
d realisierbar; begebbar; börsengängig; verkäuflich

1943 realization value
f valeur *f* de réalisation
i valore *m* di liquidazione
e valor *m* de liquidación
n liquidatiewaarde *f*; waarde *f* in geval van
  verkoop
d Liquidationswert *m*; Realisationswert *m*

1944 realize v
 f réaliser; liquider
 i realizzare; liquidare
 e realizar; liquidar
 n verkopen; te gelde maken
 d realisieren; liquidieren

1945 realty
 f immeubles mpl; biensfonds mpl
 i beni mpl immobili
 e inmuebles mpl; bienes mpl raíces
 n onroerend goed n
 d Immobilien fpl; Grundbesitz m

1946 reappraisal
 f réévaluation f
 i rivalutazione f
 e reavaluación f; reavalúo m;
   revalorización f
 n herwaardering f
 d Neubewertung f; Neuschätzung f

1947 reappraise v
 f réévaluer
 i rivalutare
 e reavaluar; revalorizar
 n herwaarderen
 d neubewerten

1948 reasonable price
 f prix m modique
 i prezzo m ragionevole
 e precio m razonable
 n redelijke prijs m
 d annehmbarer Preis m

* **rebate** → 892

1949 recapitalization
 f recapitalisation f; augmentation f de
   capital
 i ricapitalizzazione f
 e recapitalización f; refuerzo m de capital
 n herkapitalisatie f
 d Neukapitalisierung f

1950 recapitalize v
 f fournir du nouveau capital
 i ricapitalizzare
 e recapitalizar
 n herkapitaliseren
 d nochmals kapitalisieren; neu finanzieren

1951 receipt; quittance
 f reçu m; quittance f
 i quietanza f; ricevuta f
 e recibo m; finiquito m
 n kwijting f; kwitantie f
 d Quittung f

1952 receipt in full
 f quittance f pour solde
 i quietanza f per saldo; ricevuta f a saldo
 e recibo m por saldo; recibo m total
 n volledige kwijting f
 d Quittung f per Saldo

1953 receivables
 f effets mpl à recevoir
 i conti mpl da incassare
 e cuentas fpl por cobrar; cuentas fpl a
   cobrar
 n vorderingen fpl
 d Forderungen fpl

1954 receiver
 f receveur m
 i ricevitore m
 e recibidor m
 n ontvanger m
 d Empfänger m

1955 receiver in lunacy
 f gardien m des biens d'un dément
 i amministratore m dei beni d'un demente
 e administrador m de los bienes de un
   demente
 n beheerder m van het vermogen van een
   geesteszieke
 d Vermögenspfleger m für einen
   Geisteskranken

1956 receiving teller *(US)*
 f employé m de banque qui contrôle les
   chèques reçus
 i impiegato m di banca che fa il controllo
   degli assegni ricevuti
 e empleado m de banco que verifica los
   cheques recibidos
 n bankemployé m die inkomende cheques
   controleert
 d Scheckkontrolleur m

1957 recipient
 f destinataire m
 i destinatario m
 e destinatario m
 n geadresseerde m
 d Adressat m

1958 reciprocal contract
 f contrat m bilatéral; contrat m
   synallagmatique
 i contratto m bilaterale
 e contrato m bilateral
 n wederzijds contract n
 d gegenseitiger Kontrakt m

1959 reckon *v*
f calculer
i calcolare
e calcular
n rekenen; berekenen
d rechnen; berechnen; kalkulieren

* **recompense** → 2093

1960 reconstruction
f reconstruction f; réorganisation f
i ricostruzione f
e reconstrucción f; reorganización f
n reconstructie f; wederopbouw m; reorganisatie f
d Wiederaufbau m

1961 reconveyance
f rétrocession f (d'une propriété après le paiement de l'hypothèque)
i retrocessione f (di una proprietà dopo il pagamento della ipoteca)
e retraspaso m (de una propiedad luego de pagada la hipoteca)
n herregistratie f (van eigendom na aflossing van de hypotheek)
d Rückübereignung f (nach Zahlung der Hypothek)

1962 record *v*
f enregistrer
i registrare
e registrar
n registreren
d registrieren; eintragen

1963 record
f enregistrement m
i registro m; registrazione f
e registro m
n register n; registratie f
d Register n; Eintrag m

1964 recover *v*
f recouvrer; récupérer
i ricuperare
e recuperar
n terugkrijgen
d wiedererlangen

1965 recoverable
f recouvrable; récupérable
i ricuperabile
e recuperable
n inbaar
d eintreibbar

1966 redeem *v*
f amortir; purger; racheter; rembourser

i ammortizzare; riscatare; rimborsare
e amortizar; rescatar; reembolsar
n amortiseren; afkopen; aflossen; delgen
d tilgen; amortisieren; rückzahlen; auslösen; ablösen; kündigen

1967 redeemable
f amortissable; rachetable; remboursable
i ammortizzabile; riscatabile; rimborsabile
e amortizable; rescatable; reembolsable
n amortiseerbaar; afkoopbaar; aflosbaar
d tilgbar; amortisierbar; rückzahlbar; auslösbar; ablösbar; kündbar

1968 redeemable loan
f prêt m amortissable
i prestito m ammortizzabile
e préstamo m amortizable
n aflosbare lening f
d Tilgungsdarlehen n

1969 redemption
f amortissement m; rachat m; remboursement m
i ammortizzazione f; rimborso m
e amortización f; reembolso m
n aflossing f; amortisatie f
d Tilgung f; Amortisation f; Rückzahlung f

1970 rediscount
f réescompte m
i risconto m
e redescuento m
n herdisconto n
d Rediskont m

1971 rediscount ceiling
f plafond m de réescompte
i limite m massimo di risconto
e limite m de redescuento
n herdisconteringsplafond n
d Rediskontplafond m; Rediskontgrenze f

1972 redraft
f retraite f; rechange m
i rivalsa f
e letra f de resaca
n herwissel m
d Rückwechsel m; Ricambiowechsel m

1973 re-exchange
f montant m d'une retraite
i importo m d'una rivalsa
e importe m de una letra de resaca
n bedrag n van een herwissel
d Rückwechselbetrag m

1974 refinancing of maturing bonds
f refinancement m d'obligations venant à

échéance
i rifinanziamento *m* di buoni scaduti
e refinanciación *f* de bonos a su vencimiento
n herfinanciering *f* van vervallen obligaties
d Refinanzierung *f* von fälligen Obligationen

1975 reflation
f relance *f*
i rilancio *m*; ripresa *f*; reflazione *f*
e reflación *f*
n reflatie *f*
d Reflation *f*

1976 refund *v*
f rembourser
i rimborsare
e reembolsar
n terugbetalen
d zurückerstatten; rückzahlen; rückvergüten

* **refund** → **1980**

1977 refundable
f remboursable
i rimborsabile
e reembolsable
n aflosbaar
d rückzahlbar

* **refunding** → **1980**

1978 refunding bond
f bon *m* de remboursement
i buono *m* di rimborso
e bono *m* de reintegro
n aflosbare obligatie *f*
d Ablösungsschuldverschreibung *f*

1979 refunding mortgage
f hypothèque *f* de remboursement
i ipoteca *f* di rimborso
e hipoteca *f* de reintegración
n rembourshypotheek *f*
d Ablösungshypothek *f*

1980 refundment; refund; refunding
f remboursement *m*
i rimborso *m*; restituzione *f*
e reembolso *m*; restitución *f*; reintegro *m*
n terugbetaling *f*
d Rückerstattung *f*; Rückzahlung *f*; Vergütung *f*; Ablösung *f*

1981 refusal
f refus *m*; non-acceptation *f*
i rifiuto *m*

e rechazo *m*
n weigering *f*
d Ablehnung *f*; Weigerung *f*; Absage *f*

1982 refuse *v*
f refuser; rejeter
i rifiutare
e rechazar
n weigeren
d ablehnen; verweigern

1983 register
f registre *m*; inscription *f*
i registro *m*; registrazione *f*; iscrizione *f*
e registro *m*; inscripción *f*
n register *n*; registratie *f*
d Register *n*; Verzeichnis *n*; Eintragung *f*

1984 register *v*
f enregistrer
i registrare
e registrar
n registreren
d registrieren

1985 registered bond
f titre *m* nominatif
i titolo *m* al nominativo
e título *m* nominativo
n op naam gesteld effect *n*
d Namenspapier *n*

1986 registered coupon bonds
f titres *mpl* nominatifs à coupon d'intérêt
i titoli *mpl* nominativi con cedola d'interessi
e títulos *mpl* nominativos con talón de interés
n effecten *npl* op naam, voorzien van couponbladen
d Namenspapiere *npl* mit Zinsschein

1987 registered debenture
f obligation *f* nominative
i obbligazione *f* al nominativo
e obligación *f* nominativa
n obligatie *f* op naam
d Namensobligation *f*

1988 registered share
f action *f* nominative
i azione *f* nominativa
e acción *f* nominativa
n aandeel *n* op naam
d Namensaktie *f*

1989 register of charges
f registre *m* de charges
i registro *m* dei gravami

e registro *m* de gravámenes
n lastenregister *n*
d Register *n* für Grundstücksbelastungen

1990 register of mortgages
  f registre *m* des hypothèques
  i registro *m* delle ipoteche
  e registro *m* de hipotecas
  n hypotheekregister *n*
  d Hypothekenregister *n*

1991 register of title deeds
  f registre *m* de titres de propriété
  i registro *m* di titoli di proprietà
  e registro *m* de títulos de propiedad
  n kadaster *n*
  d Grundbuchamt *n*

1992 registrar of mortgages
  f conservateur *m* des hypothèques
  i conservatore *m* del registro delle ipoteche
  e custodio *m* del registro de hipotecas
  n hypotheekbewaarder *m*
  d Grundbuchrichter *m*

1993 registration of charges
  f enregistrement *m* de charges
  i registrazione *f* dei gravami
  e registro *m* de gravámenes
  n registratie *f* van lasten
  d Eintragung *f* von Belastungen

1994 registration of deeds
  f enregistrement *m* de documents
  i registrazione *f* di documenti
  e registro *m* de documentos
  n registratie *f* van documenten
  d Eintragung *f* von Urkunden

1995 registration of transfers
  f enregistrement *m* de transferts
  i registrazione *f* dei trasferimenti
  e registro *m* de transferencias
  n registratie *f* van overdrachten
  d Registrierung *f* von Übertragungen

1996 regulations
  f règlements *mpl*
  i disposizioni *fpl*; regolamenti *mpl*
  e disposiciones *fpl*; reglamentos *mpl*
  n regelingen *fpl*; verordeningen *fpl*
  d Verordnungen *fpl*

1997 rehabilitate *v*
  f réhabiliter
  i riabilitare
  e rehabilitar

n rehabiliteren
d rehabilitieren

1998 rehabilitation
  f réhabilitation *f*
  i riabilitazione *f*
  e rehabilitación *f*
  n rehabilitatie *f*
  d Rehabilitierung *f*; Normalisierung *f*

1999 rehypothecate *v*
  f réhypothéquer
  i reipotecare
  e rehipotecar
  n herhypothekeren
  d wiederverpfänden; weiterverpfänden

2000 reimburse *v*; **repay** *v*
  f rembourser
  i rimborsare
  e reembolsar
  n terugbetalen; vergoeden
  d rückzahlen; rückvergüten; vergüten

2001 reimbursement; repayment
  f remboursement *m*
  i rimborso *m*
  e reembolso *m*
  n terugbetaling *f*; rembours *n*
  d Rückzahlung *f*; Rembours *m*

2002 reinstate *v*
  f réintégrer; rétablir; réparer
  i rimettere; riporre; riparare
  e reponer; reparar
  n herstellen; vergoeden
  d wiedereinsetzen; Ersatz leisten; ersetzen

2003 reinstatement
  f rétablissement *m*
  i reintegrazione *f*
  e reposición *f*
  n herstel *n*
  d Wiedereinsetzung *f*

2004 reinstatement
  f réparation *f*
  i risarcimento *m*
  e reparación *f*
  n vergoeding *f*
  d Ersatzleistung *f*

2005 reinsurance
  f réassurance *f*
  i riassicurazione *f*
  e reaseguro *m*
  n herverzekering *f*
  d Rückversicherung *f*

2006 reinsure *v*
  f réassurer
  i riassicurare
  e reasegurar
  n herverzekeren
  d rückversichern

2007 reinvest *v*
  f réinvestir; replacer; remployer
  i reinvestire
  e reinvertir
  n herbeleggen
  d wiederanlegen

2008 reinvestment
  f réinvestissement *m*; nouvel investissement *m*; remploi *m*
  i reinvestimento *m*; investimento *m* nuovo
  e reinversión *f*
  n herbelegging *f*; opnieuw investeren *n*
  d Wiederanlage *f*; Neuinvestition *f*

2009 reissuable notes
  f billets *mpl* de banque pouvant être remis en circulation
  i banconote *fpl* che si possono mettere di nuovo in circolazione
  e billetes *mpl* de banco que pueden ponerse de nuevo en circulación
  n bankbiljetten *npl* die wederom in omloop gebracht kunnen worden
  d wieder ausgebbare Banknoten *fpl*

2010 reissue
  f nouvelle émission *f*
  i nuova emissione *f*
  e nueva emisión *f*
  n nieuwe emissie *f*; nieuwe uitgifte *f*; heruitgifte *f*
  d Wiederausgabe *f*

2011 reissue of a bill of exchange
  f renouvellement *m* d'une lettre de change
  i riemissione *f* di una lettera di cambio
  e reemisión *f* de una letra de cambio
  n heruitgifte *f* van een wissel
  d Wiederausgabe *f* von einem Wechsel

2012 reject *v*
  f rejeter; repousser; réprouver
  i rigettare; respingere
  e rechazar; rehusar
  n verwerpen; afslaan; weigeren
  d ablehnen; zurückweisen

2013 re-lease *v*
  f relouer
  i riaffittare
  e realquilar; rearrendar
  n opnieuw verpachten; opnieuw verhuren
  d wiedervermieten

2014 release *v*
  f libérer; décharger
  i liberare; scaricare; rinunciare
  e liberar; exonerar; renunciar; ceder
  n ontheffen
  d befreien; freistellen; entlasten; verzichten

2015 release
  f libération *f*; décharge *f*
  i liberazione *f*
  e liberación *f*; descargo *m*
  n vrijgeven *n*
  d Freigabe *f*; Erlassung *f*

* remission → 974

2016 remit *v*
  f remettre
  i rimettere
  e remitir; remesar
  n overmaken; remitteren
  d überweisen; senden; remittieren

2017 remittance
  f remise *f*; envoi *m* de fonds; versement *m*
  i rimessa *f*; versamento *m*
  e remesa *f*; remisión *f*
  n remise *f*; zending *f*; overmaking *f*
  d Überweisung *f*; Rimesse *f*

2018 remittee
  f destinataire *m* (d'une remise)
  i destinatario *m* (di una rimessa)
  e destinatario *m* (de una remesa)
  n ontvanger *m* (van een remise)
  d Empfänger *m* (einer Rimesse)

2019 remitter
  f envoyeur *m* (d'une remise)
  i remittente *m* (di una rimessa)
  e remitente *m* (de una remesa)
  n zender *m* (van een remise)
  d Remittent *m* (einer Rimesse)

2020 remunerate *v*
  f rémunérer
  i rimunerare
  e remunerar
  n belonen; betalen
  d belohnen; bezahlen

2021 remuneration
  f rémunération *f*
  i rimunerazione *f*
  e remuneración *f*

n beloning *f*; remuneratie *f*; betaling *f*
voor bewezen diensten
d Belohnung *f*; Lohn *m*; Zahlung *f*

2022 renegotiable
f rénégociable
i rinegoziabile
e renegociable
n wederom verhandelbaar
d wiederbegebbar; wiederverwertbar;
wiederverkäuflich

2023 renegotiate *v*
f rénégocier
i rinegoziare
e volver a negociar; renegociar
n wederom verhandelen; wederom
verkopen
d wiederbegeben; wiederverwerten; wiederverkaufen; wiederverhandeln

2024 renew *v*
f renouveler
i rinnovare
e renovar
n vernieuwen; hernieuwen
d erneuern

2025 renewal
f renouvellement *m*; prolongation *f*;
prorogation *f*
i rinnovo *m*; proroga *f*
e renovación *f*; prórroga *f*
n vernieuwing *f*; hernieuwing *n*;
verlenging *f*; prolongatie *f*
d Erneuerung *f*; Verlängerung *f*; Prolongation *f*

2026 renounce *v*
f renoncer
i rinunciare
e renunciar
n afzien; afstand doen
d verzichten; Abstand nehmen

2027 renouncement
f renonciation *f*
i rinuncia *f*
e renuncia *f*
n afstand *m*
d Verzicht *m*; Verzichtleistung *f*

2028 rent
f loyer *m*; prix *m* de location; fermage *m*
i affitto *m*; locazione *f*
e alquiler *m*; arriendo *m*
n huur *f*; pacht *f*
d Miete *f*; Pacht *f*

2029 rent *v*
f louer; prendre en location
i affittare
e alquilar; arrendar
n huren; pachten
d mieten

2030 rental
f loyer *m* d'une propriété
i affitto *m* di una proprietà
e alquiler *m* de una propiedad
n huuropbrengst *f*
d Mietertrag *m*

2031 rent collector
f encaisseur *m* de loyers
i esattore *m* di affitti
e cobrador *m* de alquileres
n huurincasseerder *m*
d Mieteneinzieher *m*

2032 rentier
f rentier *m*
i titolare *m* di una rendita; rentista *m/f*
e rentista *m/f*
n rentenier *m*; rentetrekker *m*
d Rentner *m*

* **repay** *v* → 2000

* **repayment** → 2001

2033 repeater loan
f prêt-relais *m*
i prestito *m* complementare
e préstamo *m* complementario
n aanvullende lening *f*
d Ergänzungsanleihe *f*; zusätzliche Anleihe *f*

2034 rescheduling of debt
cf. **debt rearrangement**
f rééchelonnement *m* de la dette;
aménagement *m* de la dette
i riscaglionamento *m* del servizio di un
debito
e reestructuración *f* de la deuda
n herstructurering *f* van de schuld
d Neuordnung *f* der Schulden; Umschich-
tung *f* der Schulden

2035 rescind *v*
f rescinder; annuler
i rescindere; annullare
e rescindir; anular
n opheffen; annuleren
d aufheben; rückgängig machen; annullieren

2036 rescindible
f rescindable; annulable
i rescindibile; annullabile
e rescindible; anulable
n ophefbaar; annuleerbaar
d aufhebbar; annullierbar

2037 rescission
f rescision f
i rescissione f
e rescisión f
n opheffing f
d Aufhebung f

2038 rescission bond
f titre m émis pour garantie annulée
i titolo m emesso per garanzie annullate
e título m emitido por garantías anuladas
n schuldbekentenis f afgegeven met ongeldige garanties
d Schuldverschreibung f zur Ablösung ungültig ausgegebener Garantien

2039 resell v
f revendre
i rivendere
e revender
n wederverkopen; opnieuw verkopen; doorverkopen
d wiederverkaufen

2040 reserve v
f réserver
i riservare
e reservar
n reserveren; voorbehouden
d reservieren; vorbehalten; zurückhalten

2041 reserve currency
f monnaie f de réserve
i divisa f di riserva
e divisas fpl de reserva
n reservevaluta f
d Reservewährung f

2042 reserved interest
f intérêt m douteux; intérêt m incertain
i interesse m non sicuro
e interés m dudoso; interés m inseguro
n twijfelachtige interest m
d zweifelhafte Zinszahlung f

2043 reserved liability
f capital m en actions réservé en cas de liquidation des affaires
i capitale m in azioni riservato per il caso di conclusione di affari
e capital m en acciones reservado para el caso de conclusión de negocios

n niet gestort kapitaal n dat slechts voor liquidatiedoeleinden opgevorderd kan worden
d Aktienkapital n bereitgestellt für Geschäftsabschlüsse

2044 reserve funds
f fonds mpl de réserve
i fondi mpl di riserva
e fondos mpl de reserva
n reservefondsen npl; reservemiddelen npl
d Reservefonds mpl

2045 reserve gap
f déficit m de resources
i insufficienza f di mezzi; insufficienza f di fondi
e insuficiencia f de recursos; brecha f de recursos
n tekort n aan reserves; reservekloof f
d Mangel m an Reserven

2046 reserve ratio
f ratio m de liquidité; coefficient m de liquidité
i coefficiente m di liquidità; coefficiente m di riserva
e coeficiente m de liquidez; coeficiente m de reservas
n liquiditeitscoëfficiënt m
d Flüssigkeitskoeffizient m

2047 reserve requirement
f réserves fpl obligatoires
i riserva f obbligatoria
e reserva f obligatoria; encaje m legal
n verplichte reserve f; wettelijke reserve f
d Reservesoll m; gesetzliche Reserve f; Mindestreserve f

2048 reserve(s)
f réserve(s) f(pl)
i riserva f; riserve fpl
e reserva(s) f(pl)
n reserve(s) f(pl)
d Reserve(n) f(pl); Rücklage(n) f(pl)

* **residuary devisee** → 2050

2049 residuary estate; residual
f héritage m résiduel
i eredità f residuale
e herencia f residual
n residu n van de nalatenschap
d Restnachlass m

2050 residuary legatee; residuary devisee
f légataire m résiduel; dernier héritier m

i erede *m* del rimanente
e legatario *m* residual
n erfgenaam *m* na aftrek der legaten
d Nachvermächtnisnehmer *m*

2051 residue
  f résidu *m*; reste *m*
  i residuo *m*; resto *m*
  e residuo *m*; resto *m*
  n overschot *n*; rest *f*
  d Rest *m*

2052 resource(s)
  f ressource(s) *f(pl)*
  i risorsa *f*; risorse *fpl*; ricorsi *mpl*
  e recurso(s) *m(pl)*
  n hulpbron(nen) *f(pl)*; bron(nen) *f(pl)*;
     hulpmiddel(len) *n(pl)*; geldmiddelen *npl*
  d Hilfsmittel *n(pl)*; Geldmittel *n(pl)*

2053 respite
  f répit *m*; prolongation *f*
  i proroga *f*; respiro *m*; dilazione *f*
  e prórroga *f*; plazo *m*
  n uitstel *n*; wachttijd *m*; respijt *n*
  d Bedenkzeit *f*; Respekttage *mpl*;
     Zahlungsaufschub *m*

2054 respondentia
  cf. **bottomry bond**
  f prêt *m* hypothécaire sur la cargaison
     d'un navire
  i prestito *m* ipotecario sul carico di una
     nave
  e préstamo *m* hipotecario sobre la carga
     de un navío
  n hypothecaire lening *f* op de
     scheepslading
  d Hypothekengeld *n* auf die Schiffsladung

2055 responsibility
  f solvabilité *f*
  i solvenza *f*
  e solvencia *f*
  n soliditeit *f*
  d Solidität *f*

2056 responsibility
  f responsabilité *f*
  i responsabilità *f*
  e responsabilidad *f*
  n verantwoordelijkheid *f*
  d Verantwortlichkeit *f*

2057 responsible
  f solvable
  i solvente
  e solvente

n solide; betrouwbaar
d solid

2058 responsible
  f responsable
  i responsabile
  e responsable
  n verantwoordelijk
  d verantwortlich

2059 rest
  f arrêté *m* de compte
  i saldo *m* di conto
  e saldo *m* de cuenta
  n saldo *n* van de rekening
  d Rechnungssaldo *m*

2060 restitution
  f restitution *f*
  i restituzione *f*
  e restitución *f*
  n terugbetaling *f*; teruggave *f*
  d Rückzahlung *f*; Rückgabe *f*; Rücker-
     stattung *f*

2061 restrict *v*
  f restreindre; limiter
  i restringere; limitare
  e restringir; limitar
  n beperken
  d einschränken; beschränken

2062 restricted credit
  f crédit *m* restreint
  i credito *m* limitato
  e crédito *m* restringido
  n beperkt krediet *n*
  d beschränkter Kredit *m*

2063 restriction
  f restriction *f*
  i restrizione *f*
  e restricción *f*
  n beperking *f*
  d Einschränkung *f*; Beschränkung *f*

2064 restrictions on transfers
  f restrictions *fpl* sur les transferts
  i restrizione *f* dei trasferimenti di fondi
  e restricciones *fpl* a las transferencias
  n beperkingen *fpl* op overmakingen
  d Beschränkung *f* der Geldüberweisungen

2065 restrictive endorsement
  f endossement *m* restrictif
  i girata *f* ristretta
  e endoso *m* restrictivo
  n beperkend endossement *n*

d Rektaindossament *n*; beschränktes
Giro *n*

2066 retain *v*
f retenir; garder
i ritenere; trattenere
e retener; guardar
n terughouden; weerhouden; inhouden
d zurückbehalten; wahren; vorbehalten

2067 retained earnings; retained profits
f bénéfices *mpl* retenus; bénéfices *mpl*
non distribués
i guadagni *mpl* trattenuti; guadagni *mpl*
distribuiti; profitti *mpl* non distribuiti
e utilidades *fpl* retenidas; utilidades *fpl*
incorporadas; utilidades *fpl* no
distribuidas; ganancias *fpl* no
distribuidas
n niet uitgekeerde winsten *fpl*; ingehouden
winsten *fpl*
d zurückbehaltene Gewinne *mpl*; nicht aus-
geschüttete Gewinne *mpl*; einbehaltene
Erträge *mpl*

2068 retained income
f revenus *mpl* retenus
i redditi *mpl* trattenuti
e ingresos *mpl* retenidos
n ingehouden inkomsten *fpl*
d zurückbehaltenes Einkommen *n*

* **retained profits** → 2067

2069 retaining fee
f avance *f* (faite à un avocat)
i onorario *m* anticipato (a un avvocato)
e adelanto *m*; anticipo *m* (hecho a un
abogado)
n voorschot *n* (aan een advocaat)
d (Anwalts)Vorschuss *m*

2070 retention money
f retenue *f* de garantie
i ritenzione *f* di garanzia
e retención *f* de garantía
n ingehouden waarborgsom *f*
d einbehaltene Garantiesumme *f*; einbehaltene Sicherheitssumme *f*

* **retire** *v* → 1332

2071 retire *v* **a debt**
f rembourser une dette
i pagare un debito
e cancelar una deuda; pagar una deuda
n een schuld betalen
d eine Schuld bezahlen; eine Schuld
einlösen

2072 retribute *v*
f rétribuer
i retribuire
e retribuir
n belonen; vergelden
d belohnen; vergelten

2073 retroactive
f rétroactif
i retroattivo
e retroactivo
n terugwerkend
d rückwirkend

2074 retroactive financing; back financing
f financement *m* rétroactif
i finanziamento *m* retroattivo
e financiamiento *m* retroactivo
n retroactieve financiering *f*
d rückwirkende Finanzierung *f*

2075 retroactivity
f rétroactivité *f*
i retroattività *f*
e retroactividad *f*
n terugwerkende kracht *f*
d Rückwirkung *f*

2076 return
f rendement *m*
i reddito *m*
e rendimiento *m*
n rendement *n*; opbrengst *f*
d Ertrag *m*; Rendite *f*

2077 returned cheque
f chèque *m* refusé
i assegno *m* respinto
e cheque *m* rechazado
n geweigerde cheque *m*
d zurückgewiesener Scheck *m*

2078 return of investment
f remboursement *m* de l'investissement
i ricupero *m* del investimento
e recuperación *f* de la inversión
n herkrijging *f* van de belegging
d Erstattung *f* der Investition

2079 return on investment
f rentabilité *f* de l'investissement
i rendimento *m* dell'investimento
e rendimiento *m* de la inversión
n beleggingsrendement *n*
d Anlageverzinsung *f*; Investitionszinsen
mpl

2080 returns
f chèques *mpl* et lettres *fpl* de change

retournés
i assegni *mpl* e cambiali *fpl* restituiti
e cheques *mpl* y letras *fpl* devueltos
n geretourneerde cheques *mpl* en wissels
  mpl
d retournierte Schecks *mpl* und Wechsel
  mpl

2081 returns to scale
f rendements *mpl* d'échelle
i rendimento *m* scalare
e rendimiento *m* a escala
n schaalrendement *n*
d Skalenerträge *mpl*

2082 revaluation
f réévaluation *f*
i rivalutazione *f*
e revalúo *m*; revaluación *f*
n waardering *f*; revaluatie *f*
d Neubewertung *f*; Umwertung *f*

* **revenue** → **1361**

2083 revenue account
f compte *m* de résultat
i conto *m* di introiti
e cuenta *f* de ingresos
n inkomstenrekening *f*
d Ertragsrechnung *f*

2084 revenue stamp
f timbre *m* fiscal
i bollo *m* fiscale
e timbre *m* fiscal
n belastingzegel *n*
d Steuermarke *f*

2085 reverse stock cheque
f document *m* employé pour le paiement
  d'actions acquises sur marché étranger
i strumento *m* usato per pagare azioni
  acquistate in un centro straniero
e instrumento *m* usado para el pago de
  acciones adquiridas en un mercado
  extranjero
n document *n* strekkende tot betaling van
  in het buitenland verworven aandelen
d Anweisung *f* zur Zahlung auf aus-
  ländischem Markt gekaufter Aktien

2086 reversion; reversionary interest
f réversion *f*; droit *m* de retour
  successoral
i riversione *f*; diritto *m* di riversione;
  diritto *m* di successione
e reversión *f*; derecho *m* de reversión;
  derecho *m* de sucesión
n terugkering *f*; recht *n* van terugkering;

recht *n* van opvolging
d Rückfall *m*; Rückfallrecht *n*; Anwart-
  schaft *f*; Anwartschaftsrecht *n*

2087 reversionary
f réversible
i reversibile
e reversible
n bij versterf op iemand overgaand
d anwartschaftlich

* **reversionary interest** → **2086**

2088 reversioner
f détenteur *m* du droit de retour
  successoral
i detentore *m* del diritto di successione
e detentor *m* del derecho de sucesión
n persoon wie bij overleving van een ander
  een bepaald recht toevalt
d Anwartschaftsberechtigter *m*

2089 revocable credit
f crédit *m* révocable
i credito *m* revocabile
e crédito *m* revocable
n herroepbaar krediet *n*
d widerruflicher Kredit *m*

2090 revoke *v*
f révoquer; annuler
i revocare; annullare
e revocar; anular
n herroepen; intrekken
d widerrufen; rückgängig machen

2091 revolving credit
f accréditif *m* automatiquement
  renouvelable
i credito *m* rinovabile automaticamente
e crédito *m* renovable automáticamente
n automatisch hernieuwd krediet *n*
d automatisch sich erneuerndes
  Akkreditiv *n*

2092 revolving fund
f fonds *m* renouvelable
i fondo *m* rinovabile
e fondo *m* renovable
n hernieuwbare fondsen *npl*
d sich erneuernde Fonds *mpl*

2093 reward; recompense
f récompense *f*; rémunération *f*
i ricompensa *f*
e recompensa *f*; gratificación *f*
n beloning *f*; vergoeding *f*; loon *n*
d Belohnung *f*; Lohn *m*

2094 rigid trust
f société f à investissements restreints
i società f d'investimenti limitati
e sociedad f de inversiones restringidas
n maatschappij f met beperkt investeringskapitaal
d Trust m mit beschränkter Kapitalanlage

2095 rig v the market
f provoquer une hausse factice à la Bourse
i provocare un rialzo artificiale dei prezzi della Borsa
e provocar un alza artificial de los precios en la Bolsa
n een kunstmatige koersstijging veroorzaken
d eine künstliche Kurssteigerung an der Börse hervorrufen

2096 risk capital
f capital m de spéculation
i capitale m di speculazione
e capital m de especulación
n speculatie-kapitaal n
d Spekulationskapital n

2097 robbery insurance; theft insurance
f assurance f contre le vol
i assicurazione f contro il furto
e seguro m contra robos
n berovingsverzekering f
d Raubüberfallversicherung f

2098 rollover
f renouvellement m; refinancement m
i rifinanziamento m
e refinanciamiento m
n herfinanciering f
d Neufinanzierung f; Refinanzierung f

2099 root of title
f document m de propriété
i scrittura f di proprietà
e escritura f de propiedad
n eigendomsbewijs n
d Eigentumsurkunde f

2100 royalty
f redevance f
i diritto m da pagare; "royalty" m
e regalía f; participación f en los ingresos
n royalty f; aandeel n in de opbrengst
d Ertragsanteil m; Royalty f

* **rubber check** *(US)* → 1489

2101 runaway inflation
f inflation f galopante
i inflazione f galoppante

e inflación f galopante; inflación f desenfrenada
n galopperende inflatie f
d galoppierende Inflation f; rasende Inflation f

2102 running costs
f frais mpl d'exploitation
i spese fpl d'esercizio
e gastos mpl de explotación
n bedrijfskosten mpl; exploitatiekosten mpl
d Betriebskosten fpl

S

2103 safe; safe box; strong box
f coffre-fort *m*
i cassaforte *f*
e caja *f* fuerte; caja *f* de caudales
n kluis *f*; safe *f*
d Safe *n*; Schrankfach *n*

2104 safe-deposit box
f boîte *f* de coffre-fort
i cassa *f* di sicurezza
e caja *f* de seguridad
n kluisloket *n*; safeloket *n*
d Schliessfach *n*; Safe *n*

2105 safe investment
f placement *m* sûr
i investimento *m* sicuro
e inversión *f* segura
n veilige belegging *f*
d sichere Anlage *f*; mündelsichere
   Kapitalanlage *f*

2106 safe-keeping
f bonne garde *f*
i custodia *f*
e custodia *f*
n bewaring *f*
d sicherer Gewahrsam *m*

2107 salary
f traitement *m*; appointements *mpl*;
   salaire *m*
i salario *m*
e salario *m*
n salaris *n*; loon *n*
d Gehalt *n*; Lohn *m*

2108 sale
f vente *f*
i vendita *f*
e venta *f*
n verkoop *m*
d Verkauf *m*

2109 sales price
f prix *m* de vente
i prezzo *m* di vendita
e precio *m* de venta
n verkoopprijs *m*
d Verkaufspreis *m*

2110 sales tax
f taxe *f* sur les ventes
i tassa *f* sopra le vendite
e impuesto *m* a las ventas

n omzetbelasting *f*
d Umsatzsteuer *f*

2111 save *v*; spare *v*
f épargner; économiser
i risparmiare; economizzare
e ahorrar; economizar
n sparen; besparen; bezuinigen
d sparen; einsparen; ersparen

2112 saver
f épargnant *m*
i risparmiatore *m*
e ahorrista *m/f*; ahorrador *m*
n spaarder *m*
d Sparer *m*

2113 savings
f épargne *f*; économie *f*
i risparmio *m*; economia *f*
e ahorro *m*; economía *f*
n besparing *f*; spaarzaamheid *f*
d Ersparnis *f/n*; Sparsamkeit *f*

**2114 savings account; special interest account
   (US); thrift account *(US)***
f compte *m* d'épargne
i conto *m* di risparmio
e cuenta *f* de ahorros
n spaarrekening *f*
d Sparkonto *n*

2115 savings and loan association
f société *f* d'épargne et de crédit
i società *f* di risparmio e di credito
e sociedad *f* de ahorro y crédito
   inmobiliario
n bouwspaarkas *m*
d Bausparkasse *f*

2116 savings bank
f caisse *f* d'épargne
i cassa *f* di risparmio
e caja *f* de ahorro
n spaarbank *f*; spaarkas *f*
d Sparkasse *f*; Sparbank *f*

2117 savings bonds
f bons *mpl* d'épargne
i titoli *mpl* di risparmio
e bonos *mpl* de ahorro
n spaarobligaties *fpl*; "savings bonds" *mpl*
d "Savings bonds" *mpl*; kleingestückelte
   Obligationen *fpl*

2118 savings deposit
f dépôt *m* d'épargne
i deposito *m* a risparmio
e depósito *m* de ahorros

n spaardeposito n; spaartegoed n
d Spareinlage f

2119 scale of charges
f barème m de redevances
i scala f di spese
e escala f de derechos a pagar
n kostentabel f; kostenschaal f
d Gebührentabelle f

2120 scare on the stock exchange
f panique m à la Bourse
i panico m nella Borsa
e pánico m en la Bolsa
n paniek f op de Beurs
d Panik f auf der Börse

2121 scrip certificate; scrip
f certificat m provisoire (de titres)
i certificato m provvisorio (di titoli)
e certificado m provisional (de títulos)
n voorlopig certificaat n (van aandelen of obligaties)
d Interimsschein m (einer Obligation oder Aktie)

* **SDR** → **2201**

* **sea insurance** → **1583**

2122 seal
f cachet m; scellé m; sceau m
i sugello m; sigillo m
e sello m
n zegel n
d Siegel n

2123 seasonal credit
f crédit m saisonnier
i credito m stagionale
e crédito m estacional
n seizoenkrediet n
d Saisonkredit m

2124 seasonal movements
f mouvements mpl saisonniers
i movimenti mpl stagionali
e variaciones fpl estacionales
n seizoenschommelingen fpl
d saisonale Schwankungen fpl

2125 seasoned securities
f valeurs fpl confirmées
i valori mpl accreditati
e valores mpl acreditados
n gerenommeerde waardepapieren npl
d gut renommierte Wertpapiere npl; Standardpapiere npl

2126 secondary (line of) reserves
f réserves fpl de deuxième rang
i linea f secondaria di riserve
e linea f secundaria de reservas
n secundaire reserves fpl
d sekundäre Reserven fpl

2127 secondary securities
f valeurs fpl de deuxième rang
i valori mpl di secondo ordine
e valores mpl de segundo orden
n secundaire waardepapieren npl
d sekundäre Wertpapiere npl

2128 second-class papers
f valeurs fpl de second ordre; valeurs fpl de deuxième classe
i valori mpl di seconda classe
e valores mpl de segunda clase
n minder solide waardepapieren npl; waardepapieren npl van de tweede orde
d zweitklassige Wertpapiere npl

2129 second mortgage; junior mortgage
f seconde hypothèque f; deuxième hypothèque f
i seconda ipoteca f
e segunda hipoteca f
n tweede hypotheek f
d nachstellige Hypothek f

2130 sector loan
f prêt-secteur m
i prestito m settoriale
e préstamo m sectorial; préstamo m para un sector
n sectorlening f; sectorkrediet n
d Sektoranleihe f

2131 secure v
f mettre en sûreté; protéger
i mettere al sicuro; proteggere
e poner en seguridad; proteger
n zekerstellen; veiligstellen
d sicherstellen; schützen

2132 secure v **a loan**
f garantir un prêt; obtenir un prêt
i garantire un prestito; ottenere un prestito
e garantizar un préstamo; obtener un préstamo
n een lening garanderen; een lening verkrijgen
d eine Anleihe besichern; eine Anleihe bekommen

2133 secured creditor
f créancier m garanti
i creditore m garantito

e acreedor *m* asegurado
n gedekte schuldeiser *m*
d sichergestellter Gläubiger *m*

2134 securities
f titres *mpl*; valeurs *fpl*
i titoli *mpl*; valori *mpl*
e títulos *mpl*; valores *mpl*
n waardepapieren *npl*; effecten *npl*
d Wertpapiere *npl*; Effekten *pl*

* **securities market** → **2244**

2135 security
f garantie *f*; gage *m*; nantissement *m*
i garanzia *f*; pegno *m*
e garantía *f*; prenda *f*
n garantie *f*; waarborg *m*
d Garantie *f*; Sicherheit *f*; Pfand *n*

2136 security deposit
f dépôt *m* de garantie
i deposito *m* di garanzia
e depósito *m* de garantía
n garantiedeposito *n*
d Sicherstellungsdepot *n*

2137 segregated account *(US)*
f compte *m* séparé (pour le paiement de chèques, lettres de change, etc.)
i conto *m* separato (per il pagamento di assegni, cambiali, ecc.)
e cuenta *f* separada (para el pago de cheques, letras, etc.)
n aparte rekening *f*; speciale rekening *f* (voor de betaling van cheques, wissels, enz.)
d Sonderkonto *n* (zur Zahlung von Schecks, Wechseln, usw.)

2138 seisin; seizin
f saisine *f*; possession *f*; prise *f* de possession
i possesso *m*; presa *f* in possesso
e posesión *f*; toma *f* de posesión
n saisine *f*; bezit *n*; inbezitneming *f*
d Besitz *m*; Besitzergreifung *f*

2139 seize *v*; **sequestrate** *v*; **sequester** *v*
f saisir; confisquer
i confiscare; sequestrare
e confiscar; incautarse de; embargar
n beslag leggen op; in beslag nemen
d beschlagnahmen; belegen mit Beschlag

* **seizin** → **2138**

2140 seizure; sequestration
f saisie *f*; confiscation *f*; séquestration *f*

i confisca *f*; sequestro *m*
e confiscación *f*; incautación *f*; secuestro *m*
n beslagneming *f*; beslaglegging *f*
d Beschlagnahme *f*

2141 self-financing
f autofinancement *m*
i autofinanziamento *m*
e autofinanciamiento *m*
n zelffinanciering *f*
d Selbstfinanzierung *f*; Eigenfinanzierung *f*

2142 sell *v*
f vendre
i vendere
e vender
n verkopen
d verkaufen

2143 selling rate
f cours *m* vendeur
i cambio *m* di vendita
e tipo *m* vendedor
n verkoopkoers *m*
d Verkaufskurs *m*

2144 senior debt
f dette *f* privilégiée
i debito *m* principale; debito *m* privilegiato
e deuda *f* prioritaria
n voorkeursschuld *f*
d vorrangige Schuld *f*

2145 senior mortgage
f hypotèque *f* de priorité
i ipoteca *f* di priorità
e hipoteca *f* de prioridad
n voorkeurshypotheek *f*
d Vorrangshypothek *f*

2146 senior shares
f actions *fpl* de priorité
i azioni *fpl* di priorità
e acciones *fpl* de prioridad
n prioriteitsaandelen *npl*; voorkeursaandelen *npl*
d Vorzugsaktien *fpl*

* **sequester** *v* → **2139**

2147 sequestered account
f compte *m* sous procès judiciaire
i conto *m* soggetto a processo giudiziario
e cuenta *f* sujeta a proceso judicial
n rekening *f* onder wettelijk beslag gesteld

d Konto *n* unter gerichtlicher Zwangsver-
waltung

* **sequestrate** *v* → 2139

* **sequestration** → 2140

2148 service charge
f frais *mpl* bancaires d'administration
i spese *fpl* di amministrazione;
commissione *f* bancaria per operazioni
su conti
e gastos *mpl* bancarios de administración
n administratiekosten *mpl*
d Kontobearbeitungsgebühr *f*

2149 set of exchange
f lettre *f* de change émise en plusieurs
exemplaires
i cambiale *f* in vari esemplari
e letra *f* de cambio en varios ejemplares
n wissel *m* uitgegeven in meerdere
exemplaren
d Satz-Wechsel *m*

2150 settle *v*
f liquider; régler
i liquidare; saldare; regolare
e liquidar; saldar; arreglar
n liquideren; afrekenen; verrekenen;
vereffenen; betalen
d liquidieren; regeln; begleichen; abmachen

2151 settlement
f liquidation *f*; règlement *m*
i liquidazione *f*; regolamento *m*
e liquidación *f*; arreglo *m*
n afrekening *f*; liquidatie *f*; betaling *f*;
vereffening *f*; verrekening *f*
d Liquidation *f*; Begleichung *f*; Abrechnung *f*

2152 settlement account
f compte *m* de liquidation
i conto *m* di liquidazione
e cuenta *f* de liquidación
n liquidatierekening *f*
d Liquidationskonto *n*

2153 shadow exchange rate
f taux *m* de change de référence
i tasso *m* di cambio di riferimento
e tipo *m* de cambio de cuenta
n referentiekoers *m*
d Referenzkurs *m*

2154 shadow price
f prix *m* de référence; prix *m* comptable
i prezzo *m* di riferimento; prezzo *m*

contabile
e precio *m* de cuenta; precio *m* sombra
n rekeningprijs *m*
d Referenzpreis *m*

2155 sham dividend
f dividende *m* fictif
i dividendo *m* fittizio
e dividendo *m* ficticio
n schijndividend *n*
d fiktive Dividende *f*; Scheindividende *f*

2156 sham title
f titre *m* faux
i titolo *m* falso
e título *m* falso
n verkeerd stuk *n*; onecht stuk *n*; vals
stuk *n*
d falscher Titel *m*

2157 share
f action *f*
i azione *f*
e acción *f*
n aandeel *n*
d Aktie *f*

2158 share *v*
f compartir; partager; répartir; diviser;
participer
i ripartire; dividere; partecipare
e compartir; repartir; dividir; participar
n verdelen; aandeel hebben; deelnemen
d verteilen; teilnehmen

2159 share
f part *f*
i parte *f*
e parte *f*
n deel *n*
d Teil *m*

**2160 share capital; capital stock *(US)*; stock
capital; equity capital**
f capital-actions *m*; capital *m* social
i capitale *m* azionario; capitale *m* sociale
e capital *m* en acciones; capital *m* social
n aandelenkapitaal *n*
d Aktienkapital *n*; Eigenkapital *n*

**2161 share certificate; stock certificate; share
warrant; stock warrant; stock trust
certificate; certificate of stock**
f certificat *m* d'actions; titre *m* d'actions
i certificato *m* d'azioni
e certificado *m* de acciones
n aandelencertificaat *n*; certificaat *n* van
aandelen
d Aktienzertifikat *n*; Aktienschein *m*

* **shareholder** → **2245**

2162 share list
f cote f de la Bourse
i listino m di Borsa
e lista f de cotizaciones bursátiles
n beurslijst f; aandelenlijst f
d Kursblatt n der Börse;
  Aktienkurszettel m

2163 share pusher
f placier m de valeurs douteuses
i venditore m di valori non sicuri
e colocador m de valores dudosos
n verkoper m van dubieuze aandelen
d betrügerischer Aktienverkäufer m

* **share warrant** → **2161**

2164 share warrant to bearer
f certificat m d'actions au porteur
i certificato m d'azioni al portatore
e certificado m de acciones al portador
n certificaat n van aandelen aan toonder
d Inhaberaktienzertifikat n

2165 shift of short-term funds
f déplacement m de fonds à court terme
i spostamento m di fondi a breve
  scandenza
e movimiento m de fondos a corto plazo
n verschuiving f in kortlopende fondsen
d kurzfristige Verschiebung f der Gelder

2166 shilling
f schilling m
i scellino m
e chelín m
n shilling m
d Schilling m

2167 shipper's draft
f traite f de l'expéditeur
i tratta f dello speditore
e letra f del embarcador
n verscheperswissel m
d Tratte f des Verladers

2168 shipping shares
f actions fpl de compagnies de navigation;
  valeurs fpl de navigation
i azioni fpl di compagnie di navigazioni;
  valori mpl marittimi
e acciones fpl de compañías de
  navegación; valores mpl marítimos
n scheepvaartaandelen npl
d Schiffahrtsaktien fpl

2169 shortage
f pénurie f; déficit m
i penuria f; scarsità f; deficit m
e escasez f; déficit m
n krapte f; tekort n
d Knappheit f; Verknappung f; Defizit n

2170 shortfalls
f insuffisance f
i insufficienza f
e insuficiencia f; falta f
n tekort n
d Lücke f

2171 short-term bill
f lettre f à court terme
i cambiale f a breve scadenza
e letra f a corto plazo
n kortlopende wissel m; wissel m op korte
  termijn
d kurzfristiger Wechsel m; Wechsel m auf
  kurze Sicht

2172 short(-term) loan
f emprunt m à courte échéance
i prestito m a breve scadenza
e préstamo m a corto plazo
n kortlopende lening f; lening f op korte
  termijn
d kurzfristige Anleihe f; kurzfristiges Darlehen n

2173 at sight
f à vue
i a vista
e a la vista
n op zicht
d bei Sicht

2174 sight v a bill
f présenter une lettre de change à
  l'acceptation
i presentare una cambiale all'accettazione
e presentar una letra a la aceptación
n een wissel doen accepteren
d einen Wechsel zum Akzept vorlegen

2175 sight assets
f avoirs mpl à vue
i averi mpl a vista; attivi mpl a vista
e activos mpl a la vista
n direct opvorderbare activa npl
d Sichtaktiva npl; Sichtguthaben n

2176 sight bill; sight draft
f traite f à vue; effet m à vue
i tratta f a vista; cambiale f a vista
e letra f a la vista

n zichtwissel *m*
d Sichttratte *f*; Sichtwechsel *m*

2177 sight deposit
  f dépôt *m* à vue
  i deposito *m* a vista
  e depósito *m* a la vista
  n direct opvraagbaar tegoed *n*
  d Sichteinlage *f*

  * **sight draft** → **2176**

2178 sight letter of credit
  f lettre *f* de crédit à vue
  i lettera *f* di credito a vista
  e carta *f* de crédito a la vista
  n zichtkredietbrief *m*
  d Sichtakkreditiv *n*

2179 sight liabilities
  f engagements *mpl* à vue
  i impegni *mpl* a vista; obbligazioni *fpl* a vista
  e obligaciones *fpl* a la vista
  n direct opvorderbare passiva *npl*
  d Sichtverbindlichkeiten *fpl*

2180 sight rate
  f cours *m* à vue
  i cambio *m* a vista
  e cambio *m* a la vista
  n zichtkoers *m*
  d Sichtkurs *m*

2181 sign *v*
  f signer
  i firmare
  e firmar
  n ondertekenen; tekenen
  d unterschreiben; unterzeichnen; zeichnen

2182 signature
  f signature *f*
  i firma *f*
  e firma *f*
  n ondertekening *f*; handtekening *f*
  d Unterschrift *f*

2183 signature book
  f registre *m* de signatures
  i registro *m* delle firme
  e registro *m* de firmas
  n register *n* van handtekeningen
  d Unterschriftenverzeichnis *n*

  * **silent partner** *(US)* → **2187**

2184 simple interest
  f intérêts *mpl* simples

  i interessi *mpl* semplici
  e interés *m* simple
  n eenvoudige interest *m*
  d einfache Verzinsung *f*

2185 single creditor
  f créditeur *m* unique
  i creditore *m* unico
  e acreedor *m* único
  n alleencrediteur *m*; enige crediteur *m*
  d einziger Gläubiger *m*

2186 sinking fund
  f fonds *m* d'amortissement
  i fondo *m* d'ammortamento
  e fondo *m* de amortización
  n amortisatiefonds *n*
  d Amortisationsfonds *m*; Schuldentilgungsfonds *m*

2187 sleeping partner *(GB)*; **silent partner** *(US)*
  f associé *m* commanditaire; commanditaire *m*; bailleur *m* de fonds
  i socio *m* accomandante; socio *m* occulto
  e socio *m* comanditario
  n stille vennoot *m*
  d stiller Teilhaber *m*; Kommanditär *m*

2188 sliding-scale clause
  f clause *f* d'échelle mobile
  i clausola *f* di scala mobile
  e cláusula *f* de escala móvil
  n staffelclausule *f*
  d Staffelklausel *f*

2189 social accounts
  f comptes *mpl* nationaux
  i conti *mpl* sociali
  e cuentas *fpl* sociales
  n sociale rekeningen *fpl*
  d Sozialkonten *npl*

2190 social insurance
  f assurance *f* sociale
  i assicurazione *f* sociale
  e seguro *m* social
  n sociale verzekering *f*
  d Sozialversicherung *f*

2191 soft currency
  f monnaie *f* faible
  i valuta *f* debole; moneta *f* debole
  e moneda *f* blanca
  n zwakke valuta *f*
  d weiche Währung *f*

2192 soft loan
  f prêt *m* assorti de conditions de faveur

i prestito *m* a condizioni di favore
e préstamo *m* en condiciones favorables
n voordelig krediet *n*
d vorteilhafter Kredit *m*

2193 sola bill; sola of exchange
f seule *f* de change
i sola *f* di cambio
e única *f* de cambio
n sola-wissel *m*
d Solawechsel *m*

2194 solicitor
f avoué *m*
i procuratore *m*
e procurador *m*
n procureur *m*; zaakwaarnemer *m*
d Rechtsanwalt *m*

* **solvency** → 804

2195 solvent
f solvable
i solvente; solvibile
e solvente
n solvent
d solvent; zahlungsfähig

2196 solvent debt
f dette *f* recouvrable
i debito *m* solvibile
e deuda *f* exigible y cobrable
n inbare schuld *f*
d zahlungsfähige Schuld *f*

2197 sound
f solide
i solvente
e sólido
n solide
d solid

* **spare** *v* → 2111

2198 spare capital
f fonds *mpl* disponibles
i fondi *mpl* disponibili
e fondos *mpl* disponibles
n beschikbare gelden *npl*; beschikbaar kapitaal *n*
d flüssiges Kapital *n*

2199 special crossing
f barrement *m* spécial (d'un chèque)
i sbarramento *m* speciale (di un assegno)
e cruce *m* especial (de un cheque)
n op bijzondere wijze kruisen *n* (van een cheque)
d spezielle Kreuzung *f* (von Schecks)

2200 special deposit
f dépôt *m* spécial
i deposito *m* speciale
e depósito *m* especial
n deposito *n* met speciale bestemming
d Sonderdepot *n*

2201 special drawing rights; SDR
f droits *mpl* de tirage spéciaux; DTS
i diritti *mpl* speciali di operazione; DSO
e derechos *mpl* especiales de giro; DEG
n speciale trekkingsrechten *npl*; STR
d Sonderziehungsrechte *npl*; SZR

2202 special endorsement
f endossement *m* complet
i girata *f* intera
e endoso *m* completo
n compleet endossement *n*; volwaardig endossement *n*
d ausgefülltes Giro *n*; Vollgiro *n*

* **special interest account** *(US)* → 2114

2203 specie
f espèces *fpl* monnayées; numéraire *m*
i moneta *f* metallica
e efectivo *m*; numerario *m*; especie *f* monetaria
n klinkende munt *f*
d Hartgeld *n*; klingende Münze *f*

* **specie points** → 1297

2204 speculate *v*
f spéculer
i speculare
e especular
n speculeren
d spekulieren

2205 speculate *v* **for a fall**
f spéculer à la baisse
i speculare sul ribasso
e especular a la baja
n speculeren à la baisse
d spekulieren auf Baisse

2206 speculate *v* **for a rise**
f spéculer à la hausse
i speculare sul rialzo
e especular al alza
n speculeren à la hausse
d spekulieren auf Hausse

2207 speculation
f spéculation *f*
i speculazione *f*
e especulación *f*

n speculatie *f*
d Spekulation *f*

2208 speculative transactions
  f opérations *fpl* de spéculation
  i affari *mpl* di speculazione
  e negocios *mpl* especulativos
  n speculatieve transacties *fpl*
  d Spekulationsgeschäfte *npl*

2209 speculator
  f spéculateur *m*
  i speculatore *m*
  e especulador *m*
  n speculant *m*
  d Spekulant *m*

2210 spend *v*; **expend** *v*
  f dépenser
  i spendere
  e gastar
  n uitgeven
  d ausgeben

2211 spin-off; split-off
  f échange *m* d'actions
  i scambio *m* di azioni
  e cambio *m* de acciones
  n aandelenruil *m*
  d Umtausch *m* von Aktien

2212 split funding
  f programme *m* de formation de capital
  i programma *m* di formazione di capitale
  e programa *m* de formación de capital
  d Vermögensbildungsprogramm *n*

* **split-off** → 2211

2213 split *v* **shares**
  f partager des actions
  i distribuire azioni
  e repartir acciones
  n aandelen splitsen
  d Aktien splitten

2214 spot exchange rate
  f taux *m* de change au comptant
  i tasso *m* di cambio in contanti
  e tipo *m* de cambio al contado
  n contante wisselkoers *m*
  d Devisenkassakurs *m*

2215 spread
  f différence *f* entre deux types d'intérêts
  i differenza *f* fra due tipi di interessi
  e diferencia *f* entre dos tipos de interés
  n renteverschil *n*
  d Zinsspanne *f*

* **spread** → 1578

2216 stability
  f stabilité *f*
  i stabilità *f*
  e estabilidad *f*
  n bestendigheid *f*; stabiliteit *f*
  d Beständigkeit *f*; Stabilität *f*

2217 stabilization fund
  f fonds *m* de stabilisation
  i fondo *m* di stabilizzazione
  e fondo *m* de estabilización
  n stabilisatiefonds *n*
  d Stabilisierungsgelder *npl*

2218 staff guarantee fund
  f fonds *m* de garantie bancaire
  i fondo *m* di garanzia bancaria
  e fondo *m* de garantía bancaria
  n bankgarantiefonds *n*
  d Bankgarantiefonds *m*

2219 stagflation
  f stagflation *f*
  i stagflazione *f*
  e estagflación *f*
  n stagflatie *f*
  d Stagflation *f*

2220 stale cheque
  f chèque *m* prescrit
  i assegno *m* prescritto
  e cheque *m* prescrito
  n vervallen cheque *m*
  d verjährter Scheck *m*

2221 stamp
  f timbre *m*
  i bollo *m*
  e sello *m*; timbre *m*
  n zegel *n*; stempel *m*
  d Stempel *m*

2222 stamp duty
  f droit *m* de timbre
  i diritto *m* di bollo
  e derecho *m* de sellos
  n zegelrecht *n*
  d Stempelgebühr *f*

2223 stamped paper
  f papier *m* timbré
  i carta *f* bollata
  e papel *m* sellado
  n gezegeld papier *n*
  d Stempelpapier *n*

2224 standard gold
f or *m* au titre
i oro *m* fino
e oro *m* fino
n fijngoud *n*
d Feingold *n*

2225 standard of value
f étalon *m* de valeur
i tipo *m* di valore
e tipo *m* de valor
n waardestandaard *m*; waardemeter *m*
d Wertmesser *m*; Wertmassstab *m*

2226 standard rate of interest
f taux *m* d'intérêt courant
i tasso *m* corrente di interesse
e tipo *m* de interés vigente
n geldig interestpercentage *n*
d gültiger Zinssatz *m*

2227 stand-by agreement
f accord *m* d'aide éventuelle
i accordo *m* d'aiuto contingente
e acuerdo *m* contingente; acuerdo *m* stand-by
n stand-by-overeenkomst f
d Bereitschaftsabkommen *n*; Stützungsabkommen *n*

2228 stand-by loan
f prêt *m* conditionnel
i prestito *m* contingente
e préstamo *m* contingente
n stand-by-krediet *n*
d Stützungsanleihe f; Beistandkredit *m*; Stand-by-Darlehen *n*

2229 stated capital
f capital *m* déclaré
i capitale *m* dichiarato
e capital *m* declarado
n opgegeven kapitaal *n*
d angegebenes Kapital *n*

2230 statement of account
f relevé *m* de compte
i estratto-conto *m*
e estado *m* de cuenta
n rekening-courantafschrift *n*; uittreksel *n* uit de rekening-courant
d Kontoauszug *m*; Rechnungsauszug *m*

2231 statement of condition (US)
f solde *m* journalier
i bilancio *m* giornaliero
e informe *m* diario; balance *m* diario
n dagbalans f
d Tagesbericht *m*; Tagesbilanz f

2232 state-owned bank
f banque f d'Etat
i banca f dello Stato
e banco *m* del Estado
n staatsbank f
d staatliche Bank f; Staatsbank f

2233 statute
f statut *m*
i statuto *m*
e estatuto *m*
n statuut *n*
d Statut *n*

* statutory mortgage → 1508

2234 statutory receipt
f reçu *m* légal
i ricevuta f legale
e recibo *m* legal
n wettelijk ontvangstbewijs *n*
d gesetzlich vorgeschriebene Quittung f

2235 statutory reserves
f réserves *fpl* statutaires
i riserve *fpl* statutarie
e reservas *fpl* estatutarias
n verplichte reserves *fpl*
d Reserven *fpl* vorgeschrieben nach den Satzungen

2236 sterling area
f zone f sterling
i area f della sterlina
e área f de la esterlina
n sterlinggebied *n*; sterlingblok *n*
d Sterlingblock *m*

2237 sterling bonds
f obligations *fpl* payables en sterling
i obbligazioni *fpl* pagabili in sterline
e obligaciones *fpl* pagaderas en esterlina
n sterlingobligaties *fpl*
d Sterlingobligationen *fpl*

2238 stipulation
f stipulation f
i stipulazione f
e estipulación f
n voorwaarde f; bepaling f
d Festsetzung f; Bedingung f

2239 stock
cf. **stocks**
f capital *m*; capital *m* social
i capitale *m*; capitale *m* sociale
e capital *m*; capital *m* social
n kapitaal *n*; maatschappelijk kapitaal *n*
d Kapital *n*; Stammkapital *n*

2240 stock accounting
f comptabilité f matières
i contabilità f delle esistenze
e contabilidad f de existencias
n voorraadboekhouding f
d Lagerbuchführung f

2241 stockbroker
f courtier m en valeurs; agent m de change
i sensale m di borsa; sensale m di cambio
e corredor m de bolsa; corredor m de cambios
n beursmakelaar m
d Börsenmakler m

* **stock capital** → 2160

* **stock certificate** → 2161

* **stock cheque** → 935

2242 stock dilution; stock watering
f dilution f du capital
i diluzione f di capitale
e dilución f del capital
n kapitaalontwaarding f
d Verwässerung f des Kapitals; Kapitalentwertung f

2243 stock dividend
f dividende m en actions
i dividendo m in azioni
e dividendo m en acciones
n stockdividend n
d Dividende f in Form von Aktien

* **stock draft** → 935

2244 stock exchange; securities market
f bourse f des valeurs
i borsa f (dei) valori
e bolsa f de valores
n effectenbeurs f
d Effektenbörse f

2245 stockholder; shareholder
f actionnaire m/f; porteur m d'actions; détenteur m d'actions
i azionista m/f; possessore m di azioni
e accionista m/f; tenedor m de acciones
n aandeelhouder m
d Aktionär m; Aktieninhaber m

2246 stockholders' meeting
f assemblée f d'actionnaires
i assemblea f di azionisti
e asamblea f de accionistas
n aandeelhoudersvergadering f;

vergadering f van aandeelhouders
d Aktionärsversammlung f

2247 stockjobber; jobber
f courtier m intermédiaire de bourse
i intermediario m fra agenti di borsa
e intermediario m de corredores de bolsa
n tussenmakelaar m
d Zwischenmakler m

2248 stock option
f option f de souscription d'actions
i opzione f di compera di azioni
e opción f de compra de acciones
n stock-optie f
d Bezugsrecht n auf neue Aktien; Aktienverkaufsrecht n

2249 stock power *(US)*
f pouvoir m pour la vente de valeurs
i procura f per la vendita di valori
e carta-poder f para la venta de valores
n volmacht f tot verkoop van waardepapieren
d Vollmacht f zum Verkauf von Wertpapieren; Effektenverkaufsvollmacht f

2250 stocks
f actions fpl; valeurs fpl; titres mpl
i azioni fpl; valori mpl; titoli mpl
e acciones fpl; valores mpl; títulos mpl
n aandelen npl; waarden fpl; waardepapieren npl
d Aktien fpl; Werte mpl; Wertpapiere npl

* **stock trust certificate** → 2161

* **stock warrant** → 2161

* **stock watering** → 2242

2251 stop v payment of a cheque
f bloquer un chèque
i sospendere il pagamento di un assegno
e detener el pago de un cheque; suspender el pago de un cheque
n de betaling van een cheque opschorten
d einen Scheck sperren

2252 straddle
f opération f à cheval
i opzione f di comperare o vendere nella borsa
e operación f de bolsa con opción de compra o venta; opción f doble
n stellage f
d Stell(age)geschäft n

2253 straight bill of lading *(US)*
  f connaissement *m* à personne dénommée
  i polizza *f* di carico nominativa
  e conocimiento *m* de embarque
     nominativo; conocimiento *m* de embarque no traspasable
  n connossement *n* op naam
  d Namenskonnossement *n*

2254 straight letter of credit
  f lettre *f* de crédit acceptée et irrévocable
  i credito *m* confermato ed irrevocabile
  e carta *f* de crédito confirmada e irrevocable
  n onherroepelijk geconfirmeerd accreditief *n*
  d bestätigtes und unwiderrufliches Akkreditiv *n*

* **stringency** → **1192**

2255 strip of maturities
  f tranche *f* verticale d'un prêt
  i porzione *f* di ciascuna delle somme in scandenza di un prestito
  e porción *f* de cada uno de los vencimientos de un préstamo
  n deel *n* van elk van de vervaldagen van een lening
  d Teil *m* von jeder verfallenen Anleihesumme

2256 strip participation
  f participation *f* à toutes les échéances d'un prêt
  i partecipazione *f* a ciascuna delle scadenze di un prestito
  e participación *f* en cada uno de los vencimientos de un préstamo
  n deelname *f* in alle vervaldagen van een lening
  d Anleihebeteiligung *f*

* **strong box** → **2103**

* **strong currency** → **1319**

2257 strong room
  f cave *f* des coffres-forts
  i deposito *m* di sicurezza
  e depósito *m* de seguridad
  n kluis *f*
  d Stahlkammer *f*; Tresor *m*

2258 structural inflation
  f inflation *f* structurelle
  i inflazione *f* strutturale
  e inflación *f* estructural

  n structurele inflatie *f*
  d strukturbedingte Inflation *f*

2259 subborrower
  f emprunteur *m* secondaire
  i mutuatario *m* secondario
  e subprestatario *m*
  n secundaire leningnemer *m*
  d nachstelliger Entleiher *m*

2260 sublease
  f sous-location *f*
  i subaffitto *m*
  e subarriendo *m*
  n onderverhuring *f*
  d Unterpacht *f*; Untervermietung *f*

2261 sublease *v*; **sublet** *v*
  f sous-louer
  i subaffittare
  e subarrendar
  n onderverhuren
  d weiterverpachten; untervermieten

2262 subordinate lender
  f prêteur *m* non privilégié
  i prestatore *m* subordinato
  e prestamista *m/f* subordinado
  n ondergeschikte leninggever *m*
  d nachstelliger Verleiher *m*

2263 subscribe *v*
  f souscrire
  i sottoscrivere
  e suscribir
  n inschrijven
  d unterzeichnen; zeichnen

2264 subscribed capital
  f capital *m* souscrit
  i capitale *m* sottoscritto
  e capital *m* suscrito
  n volteekend kapitaal *n*
  d gezeichnetes Kapital *n*

2265 subsidiary loan
  f prêt *m* subsidiaire
  i prestito *m* sussidiario
  e préstamo *m* subsidiario
  n plaatsvervangende lening *f*
  d Nebenanleihe *f*

2266 subsidize *v*
  f fournir des subsides; subventionner
  i sussidiare; sovvenzionare
  e subsidiar; subvencionar
  n subsidiëren
  d unterstützen; unterstützen durch Staatsgelder

2267 subsidy
f subside *m*; subvention *f*
i sussidio *m*; sovvenzione *f*
e subsidio *m*; subvención *f*
n subsidie *f/n*
d Unterstützung *f*; Subvention *f*

2268 substitution of debt
f novation *f* de créance
i trapasso *m* di debito
e traspaso *m* de deuda
n schuldvervanging *f*
d Schuldübernahme *f*

2269 sunk cost
f coûts *mpl* irréversibles
i costo *m* non ricorrente del capitale
e costo *m* no recurrente de capital
n eenmalige kosten *mpl*
d einmalige Kosten *fpl*

2270 supplementary finance
f financement *m* supplémentaire
i finanziamento *m* supplementario
e financiamiento *m* supplementario
n aanvullende financiering *f*
d Extrafinanzierung *f*

2271 suppliers credit
f crédit-fournisseur *m*
i credito *m* di fornitori
e crédito *m* de proveedores
n leverancierskrediet *n*
d Lieferantenkredit *m*

2272 supply and demand
f l'offre *f* et la demande *f*
i offerta *f* e domanda *f*
e la oferta *f* y la demanda *f*
n vraag *f* en aanbod *n*
d Angebot *n* und Nachfrage *f*

* surety → 1314

2273 surety bond
f garantie *f*
i garanzia *f*
e garantía *f*
n borgstelling *f*
d Garantie *f*

2274 surplus
f surplus *m*
i eccedenza *f*
e superávit *m*
n surplus *n*
d Überschuss *m*

2275 surplus dividend
f dividende *m* supplémentaire; superdividende *m*
i superdividendo *m*; extradividendo *m*
e dividendo *m* suplementario; dividendo *m* extraordinario
n surplusdividend *n*; aanvullend dividend *n*
d Superdividende *f*; ausserordentliche Dividende *f*

2276 surplus reserves *(US)*
f réserves *fpl* à fins spéciales
i riserve *fpl* per fini speciali
e fondos *mpl* reservados para fines especiales
n bijzondere reserves *fpl*; reserves *fpl* voor speciale doeleinden
d zweckgebundene Rücklagen *fpl*

2277 suspense account
f compte *m* provisoire
i conto *m* provvisorio
e cuenta *f* provisional
n voorlopige rekening *f*
d vorläufiges Konto *n*; transitorisches Konto *n*

2278 swaps
f crédit *m* réciproque
i credito *m* reciproco
e crédito *m* recíproco
n wederzijds krediet *n*
d gegenseitiger Kredit *m*

2279 sworn declaration
f déclaration *f* sous serment
i dichiarazione *f* sotto giuramento
e declaración *f* jurada
n beëdigde verklaring *f*
d vereidigte Erklärung *f*

2280 syndicate; pool
f syndicat *m*; consortium *m*
i sindacato *m*; consorzio *m*
e sindicato *m*; consorcio *m*
n syndicaat *n*; consortium *n*
d Syndikat *n*; Konsortium *n*

2281 syndicate loan *(US)*; participation loan
f crédit *m* syndical
i credito *m* del consorzio
e crédito *m* de sindicato
n lening *f* verstrekt door een syndicaat
d Konsortialkredit *m*

2282 syndication fee
f droit *m* d'entrée dans un consortium bancaire

i diritto *m* d'entrata in un consorzio
   bancario
e derecho *m* de ingreso en un consorcio
   bancario
n entreeloon *n* in een bankconsortium
d Recht *n* von einem Bankkonsortium Mit-
   glied zu sein

T

2283 tacit mortgage
 f hypothèque f légale
 i ipoteca f legale
 e hipoteca f legal
 n stilzwijgende hypotheek f
 d stillschweigende Hypothek f; stilliegende Hypothek f

2284 tacking
 f rattachement m de deux hypothèques
 i unione f di due ipoteche
 e unión f de dos hipotecas
 n onder één verband brengen n van twee hypotheken; samenvoegen n van twee hypotheken
 d Hypothekenvereinigung f

2285 taker
 f preneur m; acheteur m
 i prenditore m; compratore m
 e tomador m; comprador m
 n nemer m; koper m
 d Einnehmer m; Abnehmer m; Käufer m

* **take** v **up** → 1332

2286 take v **up shares**
 f souscrire à des actions
 i sottoscrivere azioni
 e subscribir acciones
 n aandelen opnemen
 d Aktien zeichnen; Aktien beziehen

2287 talon
 f talon m
 i talloncino m
 e talón m
 n talon m
 d Talon m; Allonge f

2288 tariff
 f tarif m
 i tariffa f
 e tarifa f
 n tarief n
 d Tarif m

2289 tax
 f impôt m
 i imposta f; tassa f
 e impuesto m
 n belasting f
 d Steuer f; Abgabe f; Last f

2290 tax v; **burden** v
 f imposer; grever

 i gravare
 e gravar
 n belasten; belasting heffen van
 d besteuern; belasten

2291 taxable
 f imposable
 i tassabile
 e gravable; imponible
 n belastbaar
 d steuerbar; besteuerbar

2292 taxable income; assessed income
 f revenu m imposable
 i reddito m soggetto a tasse; entrate fpl soggette a imposte
 e ingreso m imponible; ingreso m sujeto a impuestos
 n belastbaar inkomen n
 d steuerpflichtiges Einkommen n

2293 taxable profits
 f gains mpl imposables
 i guadagni mpl soggette a imposte
 e ganancias fpl sujetas a impuestos
 n belastbare winst f
 d steuerpflichtige Verdienste mpl

2294 taxable value
 f valeur f imposable
 i valore m tassabile
 e valor m gravable
 n belastbare waarde f
 d steuerpflichtiger Wert m; steuerbarer Wert m

2295 taxation
 f imposition f
 i tassazione f
 e fijación f de impuestos
 n aanslag m; belasting f
 d Steuerveranlagung f; Besteuerung f

2296 tax credit
 f crédit m d'impôt
 i credito m tributario; bonifica f fiscale
 e crédito m tributario; bonificación f fiscal
 n belastingvermindering f
 d Steuergutschrift f; Steuervergünstigung f

2297 tax evasion
 f fraude f fiscale
 i evasione f fiscale
 e evasión f tributaria; evasión f fiscal
 n belastingontduiking f
 d Steuerflucht f; Steuerhinterziehung f

2298 technical overdraft
 f découvert m technique

i scoperto *m* formale
e sobregiro *m* aparente; descubierto *m* formal
n formele overtrekking *f*
d technische Kontoüberziehung *f*

* **telegraphic transfer** → **491**

2299 teller *(US)*
f caissier *m*
i cassiere *m*
e cajero *m*
n kassier *m*
d Kassierer *m*

2300 teller proof
f contrôle *m* de caisse
i riscontro *m* di cassa; verifica *f* di cassa
e control *m* de caja
n kascontrole *f*; kas opmaken *n*
d Kassenabschluss *m*; Kassenrevision *f*

2301 teller stamp *(US)*
f timbre *m* de caisse
i timbro *m* di cassa; timbro *m* del cassiere
e sello *m* de caja
n kassiersstempel *n*
d Kassenstempel *m*

2302 tel quel rate
f cours *m* tel quel; cours *m* net
i corso *m* tel quel; prezzo *m* netto
e cotización *f* tal cual; precio *m* neto
n nettokoers *m*
d Telquelkurs *m*; Nettokurs *m*

2303 temporary annuity
f annuité *f* temporaire
i annualità *f* temporale
e anualidad *f* temporaria
n tijdelijke rente *f*
d Zeitrente *f*

2304 tenant
f locataire *m*
i affittuario *m*; inquilino *m*
e inquilino *m*
n huurder *m*; pachter *m*
d Mieter *m*; Pächter *m*

2305 tender
f offre *f*
i offerta *f*
e oferta *f*
n aanbod *n*
d Kostenanschlag *m*

2306 tenor of a bill
f échéance *f* d'une lettre

i scadenza *f* di una cambiale
e vencimiento *m* de una letra
n looptijd *m* van een wissel
d Verfallzeit *f* eines Wechsels

2307 term
f échéance *f*; terme *m*
i scadenza *f*
e vencimiento *m*; plazo *m*
n termijn *m*; looptijd *m*
d Verfall *m*; Laufzeit *f*; Termin *m*; Frist *f*

2308 termination
f annulation *f*; résiliation *f*
i storno *m*
e anulación *f*; rescisión *f*
n annulering *f*
d Storno *m*

* **term loan** → **2315**

2309 terms of payment
f conditions *fpl* de paiement
i condizioni *fpl* di pagamento
e condiciones *fpl* de pago
n betalingsvoorwaarden *fpl*; voorwaarden *fpl* van betaling
d Zahlungsbedingungen *fpl*

2310 testament
f testament *m*
i testamento *m*
e testamento *m*
n testament *n*
d Testament *n*

* **theft insurance** → **2097**

* **thrift account** *(US)* → **2114**

2311 tight credit policy
f politique *f* de resserrement du crédit
i politica *f* creditizia restrittiva
e política *f* de restricción crediticia
n kredietbeperkingspolitiek *f*
d restriktive Kreditpolitik *f*

2312 tightening of credit
f resserrement *m* du credit
i restrizione *f* del credito
e restricciones *fpl* crediticias; contracción *f* del crédito
n kredietbeperking *f*
d Verschärfung *f* der restriktiven Kreditpolitik

2313 time bill; time draft
f lettre *f* de change à échéance fixe
i cambiale *f* a scadenza fissa

e letra f a plazo fijo
n wissel m met vaste looptijd
d Zeitwechsel m

2314 time deposit
f dépôt m à terme
i deposito m a termine fisso
e depósito m a plazo fijo
n deposito n op vaste termijn
d befristete Einlage f

* time draft → 2313

2315 time loan; term loan
f prêt m à terme fixe
i prestito m a scadenza fissa
e préstamo m a plazo fijo
n lening f op vaste termijn
d befristetes Darlehen n

2316 time policy
f police f à terme
i polizza f a termine fisso
e póliza f con vencimiento fijo
n polis f voor een vaste termijn
d zeitlich befristete Police f

2317 title
f titre m; droit m
i titolo m; diritto m
e título m; derecho m
n titel m; recht n; aanspraak f
d Titel m; (Rechts)anspruch m

2318 title deeds
f titres mpl de propriété
i titoli mpl di proprietà
e títulos mpl de propiedad
n titels mpl van eigendom; eigendomstitels mpl; bewijzen npl van eigendom; eigendomsbewijzen npl
d Eigentumsurkunden fpl; Besitzurkunden fpl

2319 token coin; token money
f monnaie f d'appoint
i moneta f divisionale
e moneda f divisionaria
n pasmunt f
d Scheidemünze f

2320 token payment
f paiement m partiel en reconnaissance de dette
i pagamento m parziale in riconoscimento di un debito
e pago m parcial en reconocimiento de una deuda
n gedeeltelijke betaling f ten bewijze van

een bestaande schuld
d Teilzahlung f in Anerkenntnis einer Schuld

2321 trade
f commerce m; négoce m
i commercio m; negozio m
e comercio m; negocio m
n handel m; bedrijf n
d Handel m; Geschäft n

2322 trade v
f commercer; négocier
i commerciare; negoziare
e comerciar; negociar
n handelen; handel drijven; verhandelen
d handeln; Handel treiben

2323 trade acceptance
f acceptation f de commerce
i accettazione f commerciale
e aceptación f comercial
n handelsaccept n
d Handelsakzept n

* trade balance → 272

2324 trade bill
f lettre f de change commerciale; effet m de commerce
i cambiale f di commercio; effetto m commerciale
e letra f de cambio comercial; efecto m de comercio
n handelswissel m; commerciële wissel m
d Handelswechsel m; Warenwechsel m

2325 trade deficit
f déficit m commercial
i deficit m commerciale
e déficit m comercial
n tekort n op de handelsbalans
d Handelsdefizit n

2326 trade note; trade paper
f document m commercial
i documento m commerciale
e documento m comercial
n handelsdocument n
d Handelsdokument n

2327 trading account
f compte m en bénéfice brut
i conto m entrate lorde
e cuenta f de beneficios en bruto
n exploitatierekening f
d Bruttogewinnkonto n

* trading capital → 2443

2328 trading year
f exercice *m*
i esercizio *m*
e ejercicio *m*
n boekjaar *n*
d Geschäftsjahr *n*

2329 transaction
f transaction *f*; affaire *f*
i transazione *f*; affare *m*
e transacción *f*; negocio *m*
n transactie *f*; zaak *f*
d Transaktion *f*; Abschluss *m*

2330 transfer *v*
f transférer
i trasferire
e transferir
n overdragen; overmaken
d übertragen

2331 transfer
f transfert *m*; versement *m*; cession *f*
i trasferimento *m*; trapasso *m*; cessione *f*
e transferencia *f*; traspaso *m*; cesión *f*
n overdracht *f*; overmaking *f*;
    overboeking *f*
d Transfer *m*; Überweisung *f*; Übertrag *m*

2332 transferable
f transférable
i trasferibile
e transferible
n overdraagbaar
d übertragbar

2333 transferable securities
f valeurs *fpl* négociables; valeurs *fpl*
    mobilières
i valori *mpl* trasferibili; valori *mpl*
    mobiliari
e valores *mpl* negociables; valores *mpl*
    mobiliarios
n overdraagbare waardepapieren *npl*
d übertragbare Wertpapiere *npl*

2334 transfer fee
f frais *mpl* de transfert
i spese *fpl* di trasferimento
e gastos *mpl* de transferencia
n overdrachtskosten *mpl*
d Übertragungsgebühr *f*; Transfergebühr *f*

**2335 transfer of shares; transmission of
    shares**
f transfert *m* d'actions
i trasferimento *m* di azioni
e transferencia *f* de acciones

n overdracht *f* van aandelen
d Aktienübertragung *f*

2336 transfer order
f ordre *m* de transfert
i ordine *m* di trasferimento
e orden *f* de transferencia
n order *f* tot overdracht
d Übertragungsanweisung *f*

2337 transit bill
f passavant *m*
i bolletta *f* di transito
e pase *m*
n geleidebiljet *n*
d Transitschein *m*

2338 transit duty
f droit *m* de transit
i diritto *m* di transito
e derecho *m* de tránsito
n transitobelasting *f*
d Transitzoll *m*

* **transmission of shares** → 2335

**2339 traveller's cheques; circular cheques;
    circular notes**
f chèques *mpl* de voyage
i assegni *mpl* per viaggiatori
e cheques *mpl* de viajero
n reischeques *mpl*
d Reiseschecks *mpl*; Traveller-Schecks
    mpl

2340 traveller's letter of credit
f lettre *f* de crédit de voyageur
i lettera *f* di credito per viaggiatori
e carta *f* de crédito de viajero
n reiskredietbrief *m*
d Reisekreditbrief *m*

2341 treasure
f trésor *m*
i tesoro *m*
e tesoro *m*
n schat *m*
d Schatz *m*

2342 treasurer
f trésorier *m*
i tesoriere *m*
e tesorero *m*
n penningmeester *m*; thesaurier *m*
d Schatzmeister *m*

2343 treasury
f Trésor *m*; Trésor *m* public
i Tesoro *m*; Tesoro *m* Pubblico

e Tesoro *m*; Tesorería *f*
n Schatkist *f*
d Schatzamt *n*

2344 treasury bill; treasury note
f bon *m* du Trésor
i buono *m* del Tesoro
e bono *m* del Tesoro
n schatkistbon *m*; schatkistbiljet *n*
d Schatzwechsel *m*

2345 treasury bond
f obligation *f* du Trésor
i obbligazione *f* del Tesoro
e letra *f* de Tesorería
n schatkistobligatie *f*
d Schatzanweisung *f*

* **treasury note** → **2344**

2346 trust
f trust *m*
i trust *m*; consorzio *m* monopolistico
e trust *m*; consorcio *m* monopolístico
n trust *m*
d Trust *m*

2347 trust company
f société *f* fiduciaire
i società *f* fiduciaria
e compañía *f* fiduciaria
n trustmaatschappij *f*
d Treuhandgesellschaft *f*

2348 trust deed
f acte *m* fiduciaire
i scrittura *f* fiduciaria
e escritura *f* fiduciaria
n trustakte *f*
d Treuhandvertrag *m*

2349 trustee
f syndic *m*; administrateur *m*
i fiduciario *m*; amministratore *m*
e síndico *m*; administrador *m*
n trustee *m*; beheerder *m*;
bewindvoerder *m*; gevolmachtigde *m*
d Treuhänder *m*; Verwalter *m*

2350 trust funds
f fonds *mpl* fiduciaires
i fondi *mpl* fiduciari
e fondos *mpl* bajo administración
fiduciaria
n beheerfondsen *npl*
d Treuhandfonds *mpl*

2351 trust letter
f lettre *f* fiduciaire

i lettera *f* fiduciaria
e carta *f* fiduciaria
n trustbrief *m*
d Treuhandschein *m*

2352 trust mortgage
f hypothèque *f* fiduciaire
i ipoteca *f* fiduciaria
e hipoteca *f* fiduciaria
n trusthypotheek *f*
d Sicherungshypothek *f*; treuhänderisch
verwaltete Hypothek *f*

2353 two-tier loan
f prêt *m* à deux étages
i prestito *m* a due livelli
e préstamo *m* en dos niveles
n lening *f* in twee niveaus
d zweistufige Anleihe *f*

U

2354 ultimate balance
f dernier solde *m*
i bilancio *m* finale
e último balance *m*
n eindbalans *f*
d letzte Bilanz *f*

2355 unadjusted liabilities
f passif *m* non réglé
i passivo *m* transitorio
e pasivo *m* transitorio
n onafgewikkelde verplichtingen *fpl*; nog lopende verplichtingen *fpl*
d schwebende Verbindlichkeiten *fpl*

2356 unallotted shares
f actions *fpl* non réparties
i azioni *fpl* non distribuite
e acciones *fpl* no distribuidas
n niet toegewezen aandelen *npl*
d unverteilte Aktien *fpl*

2357 unappropriated funds
f fonds *mpl* sans emploi défini
i fondi *mpl* senza destinazione
e fondos *mpl* sin destino asignado
n fondsen *npl* zonder vaste bestemming
d nicht verwendete Fonds *mpl*

2358 unappropriated profits; undivided profits
f bénéfices *mpl* non distribués
i profitti *mpl* non assegnati
e beneficios *mpl* sin destino asignado
n onverdeelde winst *f*; niet toegewezen winst *f*
d unverteilter Reingewinn *m*

2359 unappropriated surplus
f surplus *m* non distribué; excédent *m* disponible
i eccedenza *f* non assegnata
e superávit *m* sin asignar
n surplus *n* zonder vaste bestemming
d unverteilter Überschuss *m*

2360 unbalanced budget
f budget *m* non équilibré
i bilancio *m* non equilibrato
e presupuesto *m* desnivelado
n niet sluitende begroting *f*
d unausgeglichenes Budget *n*

2361 uncalled capital
f capital *m* non versé
i capitale *m* non versato
e capital *m* no integrado

n niet gestort kapitaal *n*
d nicht eingezahltes Kapital *n*

* **unclaimed balance** → **1017**

2362 unclean bill of lading
f connaissement *m* défectueux; connaissement *m* avec réserves
i polizza *f* di carico difettosa
e conocimiento *m* de embarque observado
n vuil connossement *n*; niet schoon connossement *n*
d fehlerhaftes Konnossement *n*

2363 uncollectable
f non encaissable
i non riscotibile
e incobrable
n niet inbaar; niet incasseerbaar
d nicht einziehbar; nicht einkassierbar

2364 unconfirmed credit
f crédit *m* non confirmé
i credito *m* non confermato
e crédito *m* no confirmado
n onbevestigd krediet *n*
d nicht bestätigtes Akkreditiv *n*

2365 uncredited
f non crédité
i non accreditato
e no acreditado
n niet gecrediteerd
d nicht gutgeschrieben; nicht kreditiert

* **uncrossed cheque** → **1701**

2366 undercapitalize *v*
f sous-capitaliser
i subcapitalizzare
e subcapitalizar
n onderkapitaliseren
d unterkapitalisieren

2367 underinvestment
f sous-investissement *m*
i investimento *m* insufficiente
e inversión *f* insuficiente
n onderinvestering *f*; onvoldoende investering *f*
d nicht ausreichende Investition *f*

2368 underlying mortgage
f hypothèque *f* de priorité
i ipoteca *f* precedente
e hipoteca *f* de prioridad
n voorrangshypotheek *f*
d Vorrangshypothek *f*

2369 undervalue v
f sous-estimer; sous-évaluer
i sottovalutare
e subestimar; tasar en menos
n onderwaarderen; schatten beneden de
   waarde
d unterbewerten; schätzen unter dem Wert

2370 underwriter
f assureur m
i assicuratore m
e asegurador m
n verzekeraar m; assuradeur m
d Versicherungsgeber m

2371 underwriter
f souscripteur m d'une émission d'actions
i sottoscrittore m di una emissione di
   azioni
e. suscriptor m de una emisión de acciones
n inschrijver m op een aandelenemissie
d Zeichner m einer Aktienausgabe

* undivided profits → 2358

2372 undrawn balance
f solde m disponible; solde m non utilisé
i saldo m non utilizzato
e saldo m no utilizado
n onopgenomen saldo n
d nicht in Anspruch genommener Saldo m

2373 unearned discount; prepaid interest
f escompte m fait en avance; intérêt m
   reçu par avance
i sconto m fatto anticipatamente; interesse
   m ricevuto in anticipo
e descuento m hecho por adelantado;
   interés m cobrado por adelantado
n rente f bij vooruitbetaling
d im voraus gemachter Abzug m; im
   voraus vorgenommener Zinsabzug m

2374 uneconomic
f non économique
i antieconomico
e antieconómico; no económico
n oneconomisch
d unwirtschaftlich

2375 unexpired insurance
f assurance f en vigueur
i assicurazione f esigibile
e seguro m vigente
n niet vervallen verzekering f; lopende
   verzekering f
d nicht abgelaufene Versicherung f; gültige
   Versicherung f

* unfunded debt → 1227

2376 unified mortgage
f hypothèque f consolidée
i ipoteca f consolidata
e hipoteca f consolidada
n geconsolideerde hypotheek f
d Einheitshypothek f

2377 unimpaired capital
f capital m net d'obligations
i capitale m non soggetto a gravami
e capital m libre de gravámenes
n onbelast kapitaal n
d steuerfreies Kapital n

2378 uninsured
f non assuré
i non assicurato
e sin asegurar
n niet verzekerd
d unversichert

**2379 unissued shares; unissued stock; poten-
tial stock**
f actions fpl non encore émises
i azioni fpl non emesse
e acciones fpl no emitidas
n niet uitgegeven aandelen npl
d nicht ausgegebene Aktien fpl

2380 unitary rate
f taux m unitaire
i tipo m di cambio unico
e tipo m de cambio único
n eenheidskoers m
d Einzelkurs m

2381 unit of account
f unité f de compte
i unità f di conto; unità f contabile
e unidad f de cuenta
n rekeneenheid f
d Rechnungseinheit f

2382 unit of value
f unité f de valeur
i unità f di valore
e unidad f de valor
n waarde-eenheid f
d Währungseinheit f

2383 unit teller
f caissier m payeur et receveur
i cassiere m pagatore e ricevitore
e cajero m pagador y recibidor
n betaal- en ontvangkassier m
d Kassierer m für Ein- und Auszahlungen

2384 unit value
f valeur f unitaire
i valore m unitario
e valor m unitario
n eenheidswaarde f
d Einheitswert m

2385 unlisted shares
f actions fpl non admises à la cote
officielle
i azioni fpl non registrate
e acciones fpl no inscritas
n niet ter beurze genoteerde aandelen npl
d an der Börse nicht notierte Aktien fpl;
nicht börsenfähige Aktien fpl

2386 unmarketable title
f titre m invendable
i titolo m invendibile
e título m incolocable
n onverkoopbaar waardepapier n
d unverkäufliches Wertpapier n

2387 unpaid
f impayé
i non pagato
e no pagado; sin pagar
n onbetaald
d unbezahlt

2388 unseasoned investment
f investissement m qui n'a pas encore
atteint son rendement normal
i investimento m non ancora pienamente
redditizio
e inversión f en vías de rendimiento pleno
n nog niet geheel rendabele belegging f
d noch nicht ganz rentable Investition f

2389 unsecured creditor
f créditeur m sans garantie
i creditore m non garantito
e acreedor m sin garantía
n ongedekte schuldeiser m
d ungesicherter Gläubiger m

2390 unsecured loan
f prêt m à découvert; emprunt m à
découvert; prêt m sans garantie; emprunt
m sans garantie
i prestito m non garantito
e empréstito m sin garantía; préstamo m
sin garantía
n ongedekte lening f
d unbesicherte Anleihe f; Anleihe f ohne
Deckung; Darlehen n ohne Deckung

2391 unspent credit balance
f reliquat m de crédit

i saldo m di credito utilizzato
e saldo-crédito m no utilizado
n ongebruikt kredietsaldo n
d nicht in Anspruch genommener Kredit-
Saldo m

2392 unsubscribed stock
f actions fpl non souscrites
i azioni fpl non sottoscritte
e acciones fpl no subscritas
n niet geplaatste aandelen npl
d nicht gezeichnete Aktien fpl

2393 untransferable
f non transférable
i intrasferibile
e intransferible
n niet overdraagbaar
d nicht übertragbar

2394 upward trend
f tendance f à la hausse
i tendenza f al rialzo
e tendencia f alcista
n opgaande tendens f
d steigende Tendenz f; Aufwärtstendenz f

2395 usance
f usage m
i usanza f
e usanza f
n usance f; usantie f
d Usance f

2396 usance
f délai m
i termine m; dilazione f
e plazo m
n uso n
d Frist f; Usofrist f

2397 usance bill
f lettre f de change à usance
i cambiale f a usanza
e letra f de cambio con vencimiento común
n usowissel m
d Usowechsel m

2398 usufruct
f usufruit m
i usufrutto m
e usufructo m
n vruchtgebruik n
d Niessbrauch m; Nutzniessung f

2399 usury
f usure f
i usura f
e usura f

n woeker *m*
d Wucher *m*

V

2400 valid
f valide; valable
i valido
e válido
n geldig
d gültig

2401 validity
f validité f
i validità f
e validez f
n geldigheid f
d Gültigkeit f

2402 valuables
f objets mpl de prix; objets mpl de valeur
i oggetti mpl di valore
e objetos mpl de valor; valores mpl
n kostbaarheden fpl
d Wertsachen fpl; Wertgegenstände mpl

2403 valuation
f évaluation f; estimation f
i stima f; valutazione f; tassazione f
e tasación f; estimación f
n schatting f; waardering f; waardeschatting f
d Schätzung f; Wertbestimmung f

2404 value
f valeur f
i valore m
e valor m
n waarde f
d Wert m

2405 value v
f évaluer; estimer
i stimare; valutare; tassare
e tasar; estimar
n schatten
d schätzen

2406 value added
f valeur f ajoutée
i valore m aggiunto
e valor m agregado; valor m añadido
n toegevoegde waarde f
d Mehrwert m

2407 value for collection
f valeur f à l'encaissement
i valore m per l'incasso
e valor m al cobro
n te incasseren waarde f
d Wert m zum Inkasso

2408 vault
f chambre f forte; salle f des coffres
i camera f del tesoro
e cámara f del tesoro
n kluis f
d Tresor m; Stahlkammer f

2409 vault cash *(US)*
f réserves fpl en espèces
i capitale m effettivo di riserva
e efectivo m en reserva
n liquide reserve f
d Barreserve f

2410 velocity of circulation
f vitesse f de circulation
i velocità f di circolazione
e velocidad f de circulación
n omloopsnelheid f
d Umlaufsgeschwindigkeit f

2411 venture capital
cf. **risk capital**
f capital m en actions ordinaires
i capitale m in azioni ordinarie
e capital m en acciones ordinarias
n gewone-aandelenkapitaal n
d Stammaktienkapital n

2412 void
f nul; sans valeur
i nullo; senza valore
e nulo; sin valor
n nietig; ongeldig
d nichtig; ungültig

2413 voluntary bankruptcy
f faillite f volontaire
i bancarotta f volontaria
e bancarrota f voluntaria
n vrijwillige faillissementsaanvrage f
d selbst beantragte Konkurserklärung f

2414 voting stock
f actions fpl donnant droit à voter
i azioni fpl con diritto di voto
e acciones fpl con derecho de voto
n aandelen npl met stemrecht
d Stimmrechtaktien fpl

2415 vouch v
f certifier; garantir
i attestare; garantire
e certificar; garantir
n getuigen; instaan voor
d bezeugen; bürgen

2416 voucher
f certificat m

   i certificato *m*
   e comprobante *m*
   n bewijsstuk *n*
   d Beleg *m*

W

2417 wage-price spiral
f spirale f prix-salaires
i spirale f salari-prezzi
e espiral f salarios-precios
n lonen- en prijzenspiraal f
d Lohn-Preis-Spirale f

2418 wager policy
f police f spéculative
i polizza f di gioco
e póliza f de juego
n risicopolis f
d Wettpolice f

2419 wage(s)
f paie f; salaire m
i paga f; salario m
e sueldo m; salario m
n loon n
d Lohn m

2420 wages cheque
f chèque m pour le paiement de salaires
i assegno m per il pagamento di salari
e cheque m para pago de salarios
n looncheque m
d Lohnscheck m

2421 warehouse warrant; dock warrant
f bulletin m de dépôt; warrant m
i certificato m di deposito
e conocimiento m de depósito
n opslagbewijs n
d Lagerschein m

2422 warrant
f mandat m; autorisation f
i mandato m; autorizzazione f
e mandato m; autorización f
n mandaat n; volmacht f; machtiging f
d Vollmacht f; Befugnis f

2423 warrant v
f autoriser
i autorizzare
e autorizar
n machtigen
d bevollmächtigen

2424 warrant
f garantie f
i garanzia f
e garantía f
n garantie f
d Sicherheit f

2425 warrant v
f garantir
i garantire
e garantir
n waarborgen; garanderen
d bürgen; garantieren

2426 warrant
f warrant m; bulletin m de gage
i nota f di pegno
e nota f de empeño
n warrant m; waarborgbewijs n
d Warrant m

2427 warrant
f traite f
i tratta f
e letra f
n traite f; wissel m
d Tratte f

2428 warranty
f garantie f
i garanzia f
e garantía f
n waarborg m
d Garantie f; Bürgschaft f

2429 wasting assets
f avoirs mpl défectifs
i beni mpl che perdono valore
e haberes mpl que pierden valor
n niet duurzame activa npl
d kurzlebige Aktiva npl

2430 watered capital
f capital m dilué
i capitale m svalorizzato
e capital m desvalorizado
n verwaterd kapitaal n; gedevaloriseerd kapitaal n
d verwässertes Kapital n

2431 watered stocks
f actions fpl dévalorisées
i azioni fpl svalorizzate
e acciones fpl desvalorizadas
n gedevaloriseerde aandelen npl; verwaterde aandelen npl
d verwässerte Aktien fpl

2432 waybill
f lettre f de voiture
i lettera f di vettura
e carta f de porte
n vrachtbrief m
d Frachtbrief m

2433 weight
f poids *m*
i peso *m*
e peso *m*
n gewicht *n*
d Gewicht *n*

2434 weighted average
f moyenne f pondérée
i media f ponderata
e media f ponderada; promedio *m*
ponderado
n gewogen gemiddelde *n*
d gewogener Durchschnitt *m*

2435 will
f testament *m*
i testamento *m*
e testamento *m*
n testament *n*
d Testament *n*

* **windbill → 20**

2436 window-dressing
f amélioration f fallacieuse d'un bilan
i camuffamento *m* di bilancio
e alteración f falaz de un balance
d Bilanzverschleierung f; Bilanzfrisur f

2437 wind v up
f clore; clôturer
i liquidare; concludere
e terminar; cancelar
n liquideren; afsluiten
d abschliessen; auflösen

2438 wipe v off a debt
cf. **pay v off**
f s'acquitter d'une dette
i estinguere un debito
e enjugar una deuda; cancelar una deuda
n een schuld aflossen
d eine Schuld abstatten

2439 withdraw v
f retirer; prélever
i ritirare
e retirar
n intrekken; terugtrekken
d einziehen; zurückziehen; entziehen

2440 withdrawal
f retrait *m*; prélèvement *m*
i ritiro *m*; prelevamento *m*
e retiro *m*
n intrekking f
d Entnahme f

2441 withdraw v from circulation
f retirer de la circulation
i ritirare della circolazione
e retirar de circulación
n uit de circulatie nemen
d ausser Umlauf setzen

2442 witness v
f témoigner; attester
i testimoniare; attestare
e atestiguar; testimoniar
n getuigen
d zeugen; bezeugen; beglaubigen

2443 working capital; trading capital
f capital *m* d'exploitation; fonds *m* de
roulement
i capitale *m* d'esercizio
e capital *m* de explotación; capital *m* en
giro; capital *m* de trabajo
n bedrijfskapitaal *n*
d Betriebskapital *n*

2444 working capital loan
f financement *m* du fonds de roulement
i credito *m* d'avviamento
e préstamo *m* para capital de trabajo
n werkkapitaalkrediet *n*; bedrijfskapitaal-
krediet *n*
d Betriebsmittelkredit *m*

2445 working credit
f crédit *m* d'exploitation
i credito *m* di sfruttamento
e crédito *m* de explotación
n bedrijfskrediet *n*
d Betriebskredit *m*

2446 worth
f valeur f
i valore *m*
e valor *m*
n waarde f
d Wert *m*

2447 write v down
f amortir de façon dégressive
i ridurre il valore nei libri; ammortizzare
parzialmente
e rebajar el valor en los libros; amortizar
parcialmente; castigar
n gedeeltelijk afschrijven
d abbuchen; teilweise abschreiben

2448 write v off
f amortir
i ammortizzare
e amortizar

  n afschrijven
  d abschreiben

2449 write-offs *(US)*
  f valeurs *fpl* non encaissables
  i valori *mpl* non riscotibili
  e valores *mpl* incobrables
  n afschrijvingen *fpl*
  d nicht einziehbare Werte *mpl*

Y

2450 yield *(on securities)*
 f rendement *m*
 i reddito *m*
 e rédito *m*; interés *m*
 n rendement *n*
 d Ertrag *m*; Rendite *f*

 * **yield rate** — **1938**

Z

2451 zero base budgeting
   f budget *m* à la base
   i bilancio *m* preventivo a partire da zero
   e presupuestación *f* a partir de cero
   n nulbasis-begroting *f*
   d ab Null festgestellter Voranschlag *m*

Français

abandon 594
acceptant 14
acceptant en faillite 314
acceptation 9
acceptation conditionnelle 1917
acceptation de banque 279
acceptation de commerce 2323
acceptation en blanc 393
acceptation postérieure 91
acceptation pure et simple 629
accepter 8
accepter (une lettre) 1332
accepteur 14
accepteur en faillite 320
accident de travail 1690
accident industriel 1385
accomplissement 1278
accord 102, 183, 331, 861
accord d'aide éventuelle 2227
accord de compensation 639
accord de crédit 785
accord de crédit de
    développement 961
accord de délégation de créance
    212
accorder 123
accord sur un produit de base
    681
accréditer 34
accréditif 1516
accréditif automatiquement
    renouvelable 2091
accroissement 1931
accroître 1930
accumulation 39
accumuler 35
accumuler, s'~ 35
accusé de réception 41
accuser réception de 42
achalandage 1301
achat à la hausse 467
acheter 483
acheter au comptant 487
acheteur 484, 2285
acompte 1402, 1888
acquéreur 44
acquérir 43
acquisition 45
acquit 974
acquitté 1753
acquitter 47, 973
acquitter des dettes 635
acquitter d'une dette, s'~ 2438
acte 893
acte constitutif d'une société
    1594
acte de cession 896
acte de donation 897
acte de garantie 781

acte de société 898
acte d'intervention 63
acte fiduciaire 2348
acte probatif d'un testament
    1875
acte unilatéral 899
actif 56, 198, 199
actif courant 822
actif de la société 1775
actif disponible 1538
actif flottant 1223
actif négociable 1924
actif net 1661
actif roulant 1223
action 52, 55, 2157
action de banque 328
action de préférence 1846
action de première émission
    1721
action de priorité 1846
actionnaire 2245
action nominative 1988
action ordinaire 1721
action privilégiée 1846
actions 1090, 2250
action sans valeur nominale
    1681
actions d'administration 1573
actions de compagnies de
    navigation 2168
actions de fondateur 1259
actions de garantie 1919
actions de préférence ayant
    part dans les bénéfices 1770
actions de priorité 2146
actions dévalorisées 2431
actions différées 911
actions donnant droit à voter
    2414
actions données en prime 428
actions entièrement versées
    1756
actions garanties 1313
actions gratuites 428
actions industrielles 1387
actions intégralement payées
    1756
actions libérées 1756
actions non admises à la cote
    officielle 2385
actions non encore émises 2379
actions non imposables 1668
actions non réparties 2356
actions non souscrites 2392
actuaire 64
addition 67
additionner 65
adjudicateur 228
administrateur 73, 2349

administratif 75
administration 74
administrer 1571
admission 77
adresse 68
adresser 69
adresser à, s'~ 159
adresser, s'~ 69
ad valorem 78
affaire 476, 861, 2329
affaires 476
affaire simulée 1036
affectation 111, 175
affectation des bénéfices 113
affectation des fonds (du prêt)
    112
affecter 110, 173
affidavit 88
affirmer 254
affrètement 90, 603
affréter 604
agent 96, 1161
agent de banqueroutier 315
agent de change 374, 452, 1111,
    2241
agent de commerce 1598
agio 100, 1470
agiotage 1470
agir 51
agrégat 97
agro-industries 103
ajourner 906
ajouter, s'~ 35
ajustement de change 1109
aliénable 104
aliénataire 107
aliénation 106
aliéner 105
allègement de la dette 878
alléguer 108
allocation de change 1110
allonge (d'une lettre de change)
    116
altération 129
amélioration fallacieuse d'un
    bilan 2436
aménagement de la dette 2034
amende 1196, 1250
amortir 134, 1966, 2448
amortir de façon dégressive
    2447
amortissable 1967
amortissement 132, 1969
amortissement dégressif 888
amortissement linéaire 1524
analyse des comptes 25
anatocisme 137
année budgétaire 1194, 1207
année civile 495

banque par actions 1481
banque pour le commerce 675
banque privée 1872
banque privilégiée 605
banqueroute 316
banqueroute frauduleuse 1263
banqueroutier 324
banques 299
banquier 294
baraterie 335
barème de redevances 2119
barrement spécial (d'un chèque) 2199
barres d'or ou d'argent 468
base de crédit 788
bénéfice 1882
bénéfice brut 1309
bénéfice net 644, 1659
bénéfices d'exploitation 1715
bénéfices fictifs 1760
bénéfices non distribués 1047, 2067, 2358
bénéfices réinvestis 1836
bénéfices retenus 2067
bénéficiaire 356, 1797
bénéficiaire alternatif 131
bénéficiaire d'une annuité 143
biens de capital 509, 514
biens de consommation 720
biens de la société 1775
biens d'équipement 514, 521
biens de succession assignés par un tribunal judiciaire 1088
biensfonds 1945
biens immeubles 1342, 1940
biens meubles 608, 1637, 1828
biens meubles d'une entreprise 1218
biens personnels 1057, 1828
bilan 265
bilan consolidé 710
bilan des titres 271
bilan d'inventaire 273
bilan périodique de chèques aux fins de contrôle 840
billet 1890
billet à longue échéance 1562
billet à ordre 378
billet de banque 306, 373
billet de complaisance 23
billets de banque 1305
billets de banque coupés en deux et envoyés séparément par la poste 1318
billets de banque pouvant être remis en circulation 2009
blanc, en ~ 392
bloquer 405

bloquer un chèque 2251
boîte de coffre-fort 2104
bômerie 440
bon 415, 865
bond à prime 1854
bond de revenus 1363
bon de remboursement 1978
bon du Trésor 817, 1125, 2344
bonification d'intérêts 1429
bonne affaire 333
bonne garde 2106
bon non négociable ne portant pas intérêt 1674
bons d'épargne 2117
bons d'équipement 1087
bordereau d'achat 735
bordereau de vente 735
bourse 442
bourse des valeurs 2244
bourse noire 390
brevet 1782
breveter 1783
brouillard 410
budget 456
budget administratif 76
budgétaire 458
budget à la base 2451
budget de devises 1112
budget de gestion 558
budget d'équipement 510
budget de trésorerie 558
budget d'investissement 510
budget non équilibré 2360
bulletin 1253
bulletin de chargement 381
bulletin de dépôt 2421
bulletin de gage 2426
bulletin de livraison 931
bureau 1693
bureau de comptabilité 774
bureau de douane 836
but lucratif, à ~ 1886

cachet 2122
caisse 547
caisse d'épargne 2116
caisse enregistreuse 574
caissier 566, 2299
caissier de banque 286
caissier en chef 1322
caissier payeur 1800
caissier payeur et receveur 2383
calcul 493, 693
calcul des frais 759
calculer 492, 694, 1959
calendrier 494
calendrier d'amortissement 133
cambiste 503
candidat 153

capacité d'absorption 5
capacité d'emprunt 438, 804
capacité d'endettement 438
capital 507, 2239
capital-actions 2160
capital autorisé 239
capital circulant 621, 1224
capital d'actions ayant part dans les bénéfices 1771
capital déclaré 2229
capital de spéculation 2096
capital d'exploitation 2443
capital dilué 2430
capital d'un trust 755
capital émis 1466
capital en actions différées 912
capital en actions ordinaires 2411
capital en actions réservé en cas de liquidation des affaires 2043
capital entièrement versé 1284
capital flottant 621
capital immobilisé 1209
capital improductif 859
capital inactif 859
capital initial 1705
capitalisation 525
capitaliser 526
capitaliste 524
capitalistique 523
capital national 536
capital net d'obligations 2377
capital nominal 1159, 1665
capital non versé 2361
capital oisif 1336
capital placé en biens immeubles 2424
capital productif 59
capital social 1480, 2160, 2239
capital souscrit 2264
capital versé 1754
capitaux bloqués 1276
capitaux fixes 1208
capitaux gelés 1276
capitaux spéculatifs 1333
carat 544
carnet d'échéances 375
carnet de chèques 613
casse d'épargne postale 1839
caution 261, 264, 416, 424, 578
caution de bonne fin 1823
caution de soumissionnaire 366
cautionnement 261
cautionner 262
cave des coffres-forts 2257
cédant 211
céder 201, 937
certificat 585, 2416

crédit agricole 1168
crédit ajourné 909
crédit à la caisse 559
crédit à long terme 1563
crédit au consommateur 719
crédit-bail 1501
crédit bancaire 290
crédit budgétaire 457
crédit confirmé 703
crédit de banque 290
crédit de l'Etat 1913
crédit d'exploitation 2445
crédit différé 909
crédit d'impôt 2296
crédit documentaire 1003
crédit documentaire irrévocable
 1461
crédit en blanc 395
créditer 784
créditer en trop 1735
créditeur 796
créditeur avec droit à saisie
 1130
créditeur de deux charges 1018
créditeur double 1018
créditeur non privilégié 1291
créditeur sans garantie 2389
créditeur secondaire 1486
créditeur unique 2185
crédit financier 1183
crédit-fournisseur 2271
crédit non confirmé 2364
crédit par acceptation 10
crédit pour l'exportation 1145
crédit pour l'importation 1352
crédit provisoire 451
crédit réciproque 2278
crédit restreint 2062
crédit révocable 2089
crédit saisonnier 2123
crédit sans réserve 631
crédit syndical 2281
crise 805
crise de liquidité 1547
cross rate 808
culture commerciale 560
culture de rapport 560
curateur tutélaire 831
cycle économique 479

date 846
date d'échéance 1141
date de clôture 650
date d'entrée en vigueur 1054
dater 847
débit 602, 868
débit différé 910
débiter 599, 869
débiter en trop 1736

débiteur 875
débiteur hypothécaire 1636
débiteur solidaire 1476
déboursement 971
déboursements 1724
débourser 970
décharge 48, 50, 974, 2015
décharger 46, 2014
déclaration 255, 883
déclaration de revenus 1367
déclaration sous serment 2279
déclarer 223, 254, 885
déclarer nul 146
décommander 772
décompter 891
découvert 1738
découvert de trésorerie 561
découvert technique 2298
décréditer 986
décret 1071
décréter 1070
dédommagement 1380
dédommager 1377
dédouanage 636
dédouanement 636
dédouaner 634
déduction 892
déduction, sans ~ 1655
déduire 891
défaut 901
défaut de paiement 904
déficit 915, 1289, 2169
déficit budgétaire 459
déficit commercial 2325
déficit de paiement 1808
déficit de resources 2045
déficit de trésorerie 561
déficit d'exercice 1711
déficit global 1732
déflateur 921
déflation 920
déflationniste 990
dégâts 843
délai 924, 1625, 2396
déléguer 925
délivrance 928
délivrer 927
demande 154, 498, 626, 932
demande comprimée 1816
demande d'adhésion 156
demande de bilan 285
demande de prêt 1551
demande de retrait (d'un
 compte de prêt) 157
demande globale 98
demander 158
demande refoulée 1816
demander le remboursement
 d'un prêt 499

demeure 924
démonétiser 938
démontrer 1907
deniers publics 1914
département d'encaissement
 667
dépense d'investissement 511,
 515
dépenser 2210
dépenses 1137, 1724
dépenses de fonctionnement
 1712
dépenses d'équipement 533
dépenses d'exploitation 1712
dépenses par le déficit
 budgétaire 918
déplacement de fonds à court
 terme 2165
déport 258
déposant 941
déposer 275, 942
dépositaire légal d'un document
 1100
dépôt 943
dépôt à terme 1212, 2314
dépôt à vue 611, 934, 2177
dépôt bancaire 291
dépôt conditionnel 946
dépôt d'avarie 249
dépôt de garantie 2136
dépôt d'épargne 2118
dépôt en banque 291
dépôt en garantie 1315
dépôt involontaire 1454
dépôt irrégulier 1459
dépôt préalable 83
dépôts à intérêt 944
dépôt spécial 2200
dépréciation 954
dépréciation de la monnaie 956
déprécier 952
déprécier, se ~ 952
dépression 957, 1035
dernier héritier 2050
dernier solde 2354
déséconomies 987
désépargne 992
déséquilibre des paiements
 internationaux 1340
déshérence 1097
désignation 163
désigné 161
désigner 160, 1666
désinvestissement 991
destinataire 70, 1957
destinataire (d'une remise) 2018
détenteur d'actions 2245
détenteur du droit de retour
 successoral 2088

détériorer 844
détournement de fonds 1065
détourner 1064
dette 872, 1376, 1529
dette active 60
dette annulée 506
dette comptable 429
dette consolidée 1285
dette de rang inférieure 1487
dette extérieure non amortie 1730
dette fixe 1211
dette flottante 1227
dette portant intérêt 60
dette privilégiée 1848, 2144
dette recouvrable 2196
dette résultant d'un jugement 1485
dettes 1527
dettes de la société 1776
dettes démontrables 1906
dettes en monnaie 818
dettes en souffrance 1728
dettes non productives d'intérêt 1781
dette soldée 1540
deuxième hypothèque 2129
dévaluation 959
dévaluer 958
devise forte 1319
devises 814, 1108, 1243
devises bloquées 408
devises dépréciées 953
devises étrangères 1243
devis quantitatif 382
devoir 1750
dévolution de biens à l'État 1097
différé d'amortissement 1303
différence 1578
différence entre deux types d'intérêts 2215
différence entre la valeur nette et la charge hypothécaire d'une propriété 1091
différences de caisse 576
différer 906
difficultés financières 1184
dilution du capital 2242
diminuer 1, 828, 889
diminution 2, 829, 890
directeur de banque 292, 304
directeur-inspecteur d'une banque 690
discréditer 986
dispacheur 246
disponibilité 241
disponibilités 1538, 1545
disponibilités monétaires 1621

disponible 242
dispositif du fonds régulateur 464
dispositions relatives au fonds régulateur 463
dissolution 993
dissoudre 994
distribuer 118
distribution 449, 995
distribution d'actions gratuites 427
dividende 996
dividende, avec ~ 810
dividende cumulatif 813
dividende de liquidation 1541
dividende de priorité 1850
dividende en actions 2243
dividende en nature 1893
dividende extraordinaire 426
dividende fictif 2155
dividende non cumulatif 1671
dividende provisoire 1431
dividende, sans ~ 1127
dividende supplémentaire 2275
dividende supplémentaire en espèces 556
diviser 2158
document 372, 893, 1001, 1404, 1757
documentation 845
document cadastral d'un immeuble 6
document commercial 2326
document de dépôt 1595
document déposé en garantie 1098
document de propriété 2099
document employé pour le paiement d'actions acquises sur marché étranger 2085
document incomplet 1360
document quasi-négociable 1923
documents du marché 369
documents émis par une banque d'une ville dans laquelle se trouve une banque de la Réserve Fédérale 1170
dommage 843
donation 1014
données 845
donner 361
donner pouvoir 1069
dossier d'appel d'offres 369
doter 1081
douane 836
double de chèque 1040
douer 1081
droit 1042, 2317

droit bancaire de rétention 301
droit de consommation 1126
droit de douane 838
droit (de douane) ad valorem 79
droit d'entrée dans un consortium bancaire 2282
droit de préemption 1844
droit de prescription 1859
droit de propriété 1899
droit de rétention 1531
droit de retour successoral 2086
droit de souscription attaché 812
droit de succession 1102
droit de timbre 2222
droit de transit 2338
droit hypothécaire de rachat 1093
droit prioritaire de rétention 1871
droits consulaires 717
droits de bassin 1000
droits de brevet 1784
droits d'entrée 1353
droits de tirage spéciaux 2201
droits d'exportation 1146
droits d'importation 1353
DTS 2201
"dumping" 1038
durcissement des conditions de prêt 1320

écart 1289
écart entre les taux d'intérêt 1427
échange 337, 1107
échange d'actions 2211
échanger 338
échéance 848, 1032, 2307
échéance d'une lettre 2306
échéance fixe 1217
échéances à moins d'un an 824
échoir 1140, 1165
économie 2113
économie de consommation 723
économie de marché 1588
économie dirigée 742, 1572
économie du marché libre 1271
économie fermée 647
économie nationale 1009
économie ouverte 1703
économie planifiée 583
économies d'échelle 1053
économiser 2111
effacer 926
effet 372
effet à recevoir 386
effet à vue 2176
effet bancable 980

revenu fixe 1213
revenu imposable 2292
revenu monétaire 568, 1615
revenu national 1646
revenu net 1657
revenu par habitant 1818
revenu par tête 1818
revenu(s) 1361
revenus domaniaux 1894
revenus financiers 1185
revenus hors-exploitation 1675
revenus retenus 2068
réversible 2087
réversion 2086
révoquer 772, 2090
risque 86
risque assurable 1408
risque de change 1119
rotation des capitaux 542

saisie 220, 2140
saisine 2138
saisir 217, 2139
salaire 126, 2107, 2419
salle des coffres 2408
sans frais 1272
sans valeur 2412
sceau 2122
scellé 2122
schilling 2166
seconde hypothèque 2129
semestriel 363
sentence arbitrale 256
séquestration 2140
séquestre 1062
service de la dette 879
service d'escomptes 982
service des crédits 789
service fiduciaire 1175
seuil d'admissibilité 841
seuil de rentabilité 450
seule de change 2193
signature 2182
signature autorisée 240
signature en blanc 401
signer 2181
signer un acte 1129
situation des paiements 1809
situation sans issue 856
société 215, 683, 695, 754, 1774
société à investissements
   restreints 2094
société anonyme 1482
société à responsabilité limitée
   1536
société d'assurances 1412
société de crédit mutuel 802
société de financement 1180

société d'épargne et de crédit
   2115
société de placements de
   capitaux 1450
société d'investissement 1446
société d'investissement à
   capital fixe 648
société d'investissement à
   capital variable 1704
société d'investissement ayant
   le droit d'administration 1574
société en faillite 322
société fiduciaire 2347
société financière de
   développement 962
société holding 1330
société par actions 1482
société privée 646
solde 266
solde créditeur 786
solde débiteur 1738
solde de compte 268
solde de paiement 269
solde de trésorerie 554
solde disponible 2372
solde dormant 1017
solde journalier 2231
solde négatif 1648
solde non utilisé 2372
solder 1539
soldes bancaires 282
solide 2197
solvabilité 804, 2055
solvable 2057, 2195
somme 67, 135
somme des chèques pas encore
   crédités 1220
sortie de capitaux 1723
souffrance, en ~ 3
soumissionnaire 367
sous-capitaliser 2366
souscripteur 1570
souscripteur d'une émission
   d'actions 2371
souscrire 2263
souscrire à des actions 2286
sous-estimer 2369
sous-évaluer 2369
sous-investissement 2367
sous-location 2260
sous-louer 2261
soutien de famille 448
spéculateur 2209
spéculateur à la baisse 345
spéculateur à la hausse 466
spéculateur insolvable 1493
spéculation 2207
spéculation à la baisse 353
spéculation hasardée 86

spéculer 2204
spéculer à la baisse 344, 2205
spéculer (à la bourse) 1468
spéculer à la hausse 488, 2206
spirale prix-salaires 2417
stabilité 2216
stabilité des changes 1121
stagflation 2219
statut 2233
statuts d'une société 188
stipulation 2238
stock monétaire 1610
stocks d'or de l'Etat 1696
structure de l'investissement
   1785
structure financière 537
subornation 1304
subside 125, 2267
subvention 1359, 2267
subventionner 2266
succursale 445
succursale de banque 284
superdividende 2275
supplémentaire 1156
surcapitaliser 1733
surcharge 1734
surdépréciation 1737
surévaluer 1749
surplus 2274
surplus d'exploitation 1715
surplus du consommateur 722
surplus non distribué 2359
sursalaire 425
surtaxe à l'importation 1356
suspens, en ~ 3
syndic 281, 2349
syndicat 2280
syndicat de banques 1310
syndic en faillite 327
système bancaire 299
système d'alerte 1044
système de banques associées
   596
système de double comptabilité
   1030
système monétaire 658

talon 2287
talon de chèque 617
talon de dividende 998
tarif 2288
taux 1936
taux central 584
taux comptable 29
taux comptable d'une monnaie
   432
taux d'achat 489
taux d'actualisation critique 807
taux de change 1937

Italiano

contabile 26, 430
contabilità 28, 431
contabilità basata sul criterio di
   registro di cassa 555
contabilità delle esistenze 2240
contabilità di gestione di cassa
   555
contabilità in partita doppia
   1019
contante 549
contanti 1939
contanti, in ~ 551
contanti, per ~ 551
contare 763
conti da incassare 33, 1953
conti da pagare 32
conti da riscuotere 33
conti nazionali 1644
contingente di importazione
   1355
conti sociali 2189
conto 24, 370
conto anticipi 1357
conto aperto 1700
conto attivo 57
conto bancario 280
conto bloccato 219, 406, 1275
conto codificato 653
conto commerciale 674
conto congelato 1275
conto congiunto 1471
conto corrente 820
conto corrente sociale 1475
conto creditore 797
conto d'affari 477
conto dei pagamenti 972
conto dei prestiti 1550
conto delle differenze 966
conto delle entrate 1362
conto del tesoro 1124
conto (di) acquisti a credito 600
conto di base 342
conto di capitale 508
conto (di) cassa 552
conto di controllo 740
conto di esercisio 1710
conto di garanzia bloccato 1099
conto di introiti 2083
conto di liquidazione 2152
conto di negozi 477
conto di operazioni 1710
conto di risparmio 2114
conto di speculazioni al ribasso
   346
conto di spese 30
conto entrate lorde 2327
conto impersonale 1347
conto inattivo 852, 1016
conto in garanzia 209

conto nostro 1683
conto nuovo 92
conto profitti e perdite 1884
conto provvisorio 2277
conto pubblico 1912
conto saldato 31
conto scoperto 1741
conto separato (per il
   pagamento di assegni,
   cambiali, ecc.) 2137
conto sequestrato 219
conto soggetto a processo
   giudiziario 2147
contrarre 732
contrattare 732
contratto 731
contratto bilaterale 1958
contratto collettivo 1473
contratto di donazione 897
contratto di mezzadria 1600
contratto d'indennizzo 1382
contratto di noleggio 606
contratto di prestito alla grossa
   441
contratto di prestito marittimo
   441
contratto ipotecario 1633
contratto per prezzo globale
   1567
contratto sociale 898
contribuenti 738
contributo 737
contribuzione 737
controfirmare 773
controfirmatario 671
controllare 610, 1400
controllo 739
controllo degli scambi 1113
convenio di credito di sviluppo
   961
convenire 182
convenzione 102, 183, 331, 778
conversione 744
conversione alla pari 745
convertibilità 747
convertire 746
convocare 191
convocazione 497
cooperativa d'investimenti 1450
copertura 780
copertura a termine 1256
copertura degli interessi 1422
copertura (delle operazioni a
   termine) 1323
coprire 779
corona 809
corporazione 754
corso 1936
corso d'apertura 1707

corso delle valute 1937
corso tel quel 2302
costare 758
costi 601
costi di base 340
costo 757
costo addizionale 93
costo, assicurazione e nolo 620
costo complementare 93
costo della mano d'opera 1492
costo della vita 761
costo di inattività di capitale
   545
costo di investimento 511
costo in divise 1114, 1244
costo non ricorrente del
   capitale 2269
creazione di liquidità 1432
crediti sull'estero 1240
credito 553, 783
credito agricolo 1168
credito ai compratori 485
credito al consumatore 719
credito allo scoperto 395, 1702
credito a lungo termine 1563
credito anticipato 451
credito bancario 290
credito confermato 703
credito confermato ed
   irrevocabile 2254
credito d'avviamento 2444
credito del consorzio 2281
credito di accettazione 10
credito di cassa 559
credito di esportazione 1145
credito differito 909
credito di fornitori 2271
credito d'importazione 1352
credito di sfruttamento 2445
credito documentario 1003
credito documentario
   irrevocabile 1461
credito finanziario 1182, 1183
credito in bianco 395
credito incondizionato 631
credito in corso di risoluzione
   1833
credito limitato 2062
credito non confermato 2364
credito provvisorio 451
credito pubblico 1913
creditore 796
credito reciproco 2278
creditore con garanzia 417
creditore con pegno 1790
creditore del fallito 317
creditore esecutore 1130
creditore garantito 417, 2133
creditore in partecipazione 1474

creditore ipotecario 1634
creditore non garantito 2389
creditore ordinario 1291
creditore per doppio
  addebitamento 1018
creditore per giudizio 1484
creditore privilegiato 1847
creditore secondario 1486
creditore unico 2185
credito revocabile 2089
credito rinovabile auto-
  maticamente 2091
credito stagionale 2123
credito tributario 2296
crise 805
crise di liquidità 1547
crisi 805
custodia 830, 832, 2106

danneggiamento 843
danneggiare 844
danno 843
data 846
data d'entrata in vigore 1054
data di chiusura 650
datare 847
dati 845
dattore di lavoro 1067
dazio 1042
dazio ad valorem 79
dazio d'importazione 1353
dazio doganale 838
debiti 1527
debiti attivi 1728
debiti che si possono provare
  1906
debiti della società 1776
debiti passivi 1781
debito 868, 872, 1376, 1529
debito attivo 60
debito cancellato 506
debito consolidato 1285
debito contabile 429
debito differito 910
debito esterno pendente 1730
debito fisso 1211
debito fluttuante 1227
debito non riscuotibile 260
debito per giudizio 1485
debito principale 2144
debito privilegiato 1848, 2144
debitore 875
debitore in partecipazione 1476
debitore ipotecario 1636
debito saldato 1540
debito secondario 1487
debito solvibile 2196
declinazione 887, 1029
decretare 1070

decreto 1071
dedurre 891
deduzione 892
defalzionare 919
deficit 915, 1289, 2169
deficit commerciale 2325
deficit del dollaro 1007
deficit di bilancio 459
deficit di cassa 561
deficit di esercizio 1711
deficit di pagamento 1808
deficit ed eccedenze di cassa
  576
deficit globale 1732
deflatore 921
deflazionario 990
deflazione 920
defraudare 922
delegare 925
demonetare 938
denaro 619, 1613
denaro a basso interesse 609
denaro a breve 501
denaro ad alto interesse 863
denaro deprezzato 953
denaro improduttivo 336
denaro inattivo 1337
denaro non convertibile 1370
denuncia per deterioramento
  1346
deponente 941
deporto 258
depositare 275, 942
depositario legale di documenti
  1100
depositi ad interesse 944
deposito 943
deposito anticipato 83
deposito a risparmio 2118
deposito a scadenza fissa 1212
deposito a termine fisso 2314
deposito a vista 611, 934, 2177
deposito bancario 291
deposito condizionato 946
deposito di garanzia 1315, 2136
deposito di sicurezza 2257
deposito involontario 1454
deposito irregolare 1459
deposito notturno 1663
deposito per avaria 249
deposito speciale 2200
depressione 957
deprezzamento 954
deprezzare 952
deprezzarsi 952
designare 1666
destinare 110, 173
destinatario 70, 1957

destinatario (di una rimessa)
  2018
destino 175
detentore del diritto di
  successione 2088
detentore d'una procura 1911
detrarre 891
dichiarante 941
dichiarare 223, 254, 885
dichiarare un dividendo 886
dichiarazione 255, 883
dichiarazione delle entrate 1367
dichiarazione di fallimento 71
dichiarazione di interruzione
  dei pagamenti 62
dichiarazione di premi 884
dichiarazione sotto giuramento
  2279
differenza 1578
differenza fra due tipi di
  interessi 2215
differenza fra il valore netto ed
  il gravame ipotecario di una
  proprietà 1091
differire 906
difficoltà finanziarie 1184
dilazione 924, 2053, 2396
diluizione di capitale 2242
diminuire 1, 889
diminuzione 2, 890
dimostrare 1907
direttore 73
direttore dell'ufficio valute 691
direttore di banca 292
direttore di banca con funzioni
  ispettive 690
dirigere 1571
diritti 1042
diritti consolari 717
diritti di brevetto 1784
diritti di darsena 1000
diritti di esportazione 1146
diritti d'importazione 1353
diritti doganali 79
diritti speciali di operazione
  2201
diritto 2317
diritto a dividendo, senza ~
  1127
diritto da pagare 2100
diritto d'entrata in un consorzio
  bancario 2282
diritto di bollo 2222
diritto di precedenza
  nell'acquisto 1844
diritto di prescrizione 1859
diritto di proprietà 1899
diritto di ritenzione 1531
diritto di riversione 2086

facilitazioni per far fronte ad
un eventuale scoperto 1739
facoltare 1069
fallimento 316, 1164
fallimento, in ~ 312
fallimento involontario 1455
fallire 354, 1163
fallito 312, 324
fallito riabilitato 586
fallito risolto da un concordato
586
falsificare 769, 1167
falsificatore 770
falsificazione 768, 1166
far(e) fallimento 354
fare fallire 313
fare operazioni di banca 276
fare una transazione 860
fas 1265
fattore di produzione non
monetario 1669
fattore endogeno 1075
fattore esogeno 1135
fattura 370, 1453
fattura consolare 718
favore 19
favorire 17
fiduciario 1173, 2349
fiduciario custode 831
fiduciario in fallimento 327
filiale 89, 445
filiale bancaria 284
filiale di banca 284
finanza 1177
finanze 1177
finanziamento combinato 404
finanziamento complementare
1232
finanziamento congiunto 1477
finanziamento con tasso
d'interesse fisso 1216
finanziamento mediante deficit
di bilancio 917
finanziamento parallelo 1763
finanziamento previo 1851
finanziamento retroattivo 2074
finanziamento supplementare
2270
finanziare 1178
finanziario 1181
finanziere 1195
fini di lucro, con ~ 1886
fiorino 1230
firma 2182
firma autorizzata 240
firma in bianco 401
firmare 2181
fissato di borsa 735

flessibilità dei tipi di cambio
1117
flusso circolare 622
flusso di capitale 517
flusso di fondi 563
flusso equilibratore di capitali
1086
fluttuazione dei prezzi 1867
fob 1273
foglio di bilancio 273
fondi 1286
fondi bloccati 409
fondi consolidati 715
fondi d'assicurazione 1413
fondi di garanzia 1316
fondi di riserva 2044
fondi disponibili 2198
fondi fiduciari 2350
fondi in consegna legale 1101
fondi liquidi 1939
fondi liquidi inattivi 1338
fondi provenienti da un credito
1878
fondi pubblici 1914
fondi senza destinazione 2357
fondo consolidato 711
fondo d'ammortamento 2186
fondo di garanzia bancaria 2218
fondo di perequazione 1085
fondo di previdenza 1908
fondo di regolazione 461
fondo di riserva per spese
impreviste 725
fondo di stabilizzazione 2217
fondo fiduciario irrevocabile
1463
Fondo Monetario Inter-
nazionale 1437
fondo rinovabile 2092
formalità 1254
formazione di capitale 518
forza maggiore 1236
franchigia 1261
franco 1264
franco a bordo 1273
franco (di) spese 1272
franco lungobordo 1265
frode 1262
fruttare interessi 351
fuga di capitali 516, 1723
funzionario 1694
funzione del verificatore di
conti 233
fusione di monete di oro o
argento per la fabbricazione
di gioielli 1290

garante 264, 424, 579, 1314
garante in fallimento 326

garantire 262, 1312, 2415, 2425
garantire un prestito 2132
garantito da una obbligazione
418
garanzia 780, 1311, 2135, 2273,
2424, 2428
garanzia bancaria 297
garanzia di indennizzo 423
garanzia di pagamento 1803
garanzia generale 1292
garanzia per il buon fine 1823
garanzia permanente 730
garanzia personale 1830
garanzia senza documenti 1830
garanzia supplementare 660
generale 397
gerente di banca 304
gestione economica 1051
giacente 3
giornale di cassa 557
giorni di favore 1233
giorni di grazia 851
giorno di scadenza 853, 1141
giorno lavorativo 480
girante 1080
girare 1076
girata 1079
girata assoluta 4
girata condizionale 697
girata condizionata 1918
girata di favore 22
girata in bianco 396
girata in pieno 1281
girata intera 2202
girata irregolare 1460
giratario 1078
girata ristretta 2065
giro dei capitali 542
giudizio ipotecario 1238
globale 97
gratificazione 425
gravame 195, 1074
gravame bancario di protezione
301
gravame fluttuante 1226
gravame privilegiato 1203
gravame tributario 1526
gravare 193, 2290
gravare da imposte 474
gravato di ipoteche 473
gruppo di depositi riuniti per
controllo 343
gruppo di entrate 1364
guadagnare 1046
guadagni distribuiti 2067
guadagni soggette a imposte
2293
guadagni trattenuti 2067
guadagno 357, 1048, 1882

lettera di credito commerciale 677
lettera di credito documentaria 1004
lettera di credito incondizionata 633
lettera di credito irrevocabile 1462
lettera di credito per viaggiatori 2340
lettera di credito stampata al margine di una cambiale 1582
lettera di credito sussidiaria 138
lettera di debito 378
lettera di deposito 1517
lettera di garanzia 1518
lettera di ipoteca 1519
lettera di moratoria 1521
lettera d'indennità 1520
lettera di porto 380
lettera di vettura 380, 2432
lettera fiduciaria 2351
lettera per esigere pagamento 1039
lettera sollecitatoria 1039
liberare 2014
liberare il tipo di cambio 1229
liberazione 2015
liberazione del tipo di cambio 1221
libero 1264
libretto bancario 1779
libretto (di) assegni 613
libretto di depositi 949
libro degli investimenti 1447
libro dei conti bloccati 221
libro delle accettazioni 12
libro delle cambiali scontate 984
libro di cassa 557, 567
libro di conti 27
libro giornale 849
libro mastro 1502
libro mastro dei conti correnti 821
libro mastro delle filiali 446
libro mastro di banca 300
libro mastro di controllo 614
libro mastro generale 1293
licenza 1530, 1824
licenza di esportazione 1149
licitazione pubblica 685
limitare 2061
limite di credito 1514
limite massimo 580
limite massimo dei prestiti 1514
limite massimo di risconto 1971

limite variabile 1059
linea di credito 790
linea secondaria di riserve 2126
liquidare 994, 1539, 1811, 1944, 2150, 2437
liquidare conti 635
liquidatore 1544
liquidazione 643, 993, 1543, 2151
liquidazione completa 1283
liquidità 1545
liquidità internazionale 1436
lira 1841
listino di Borsa 2162
livellamento 1523
livello di entrate 1364
livello massimo 580
locazione 2028
lucrativo 1566
lunga scadenza, a ~ 1561
lungo termine, a ~ 1561

magazzino doganale 420
maggiorazione 1734
mallevadore 579, 1314
mancanza di complimento delle obbligazioni 903
mancanza di pagamento 904
mancata accettazione 988
mancato pagamento 988
mandante 1575
mandare in fallimento 313
mandare un conto allo scoperto 1740
mandatario 225, 1577, 1910
mandato 1576, 1880, 2422
mandato di pagamento 1023
mandato postale 1620
marca 447
margine 1578
margine tra i tassi di interesse 1427
massa fallimentare 325
massa monetaria 1610
massa monetaria (in circolazione) 1621
maturare 35
media ponderata 2434
mediazione 453
mercantile 1597
mercato 1586
mercato al ribasso 352
mercato aperto 1589
mercato dei cambi 1245
mercato dei capitali 531
mercato delle divise 1245
mercato delle Euro-divise 1103
mercato favorevole ai compratori 486
mercato fiacco 1034

mercato finanziario 1186
mercato in rialzo 471
mercato libero 1270, 1764
mercato monetario 1617
mercato nero 391
mercato parallelo di divise 1764
merce 1599
merci in deposito doganale 419
metodo di aggiornamento del flusso di fondi 983
mettere all'asta 227
mettere al sicuro 2131
mettere il sequestro sopra 1063
mettere in conto 599
mezzi disponibili 1538
mobili 608
modulo 1253
modulo di credito (con bilancio aggiunto) 791
modulo di deposito 951
modulo di dichiarazioni dei depositi 951
modulo in bianco 400
modulo per domande 155
mondo finanziario 1193
moneta 655
moneta base 1488
moneta convertibile 748
moneta corrente 825
moneta debole 2191
moneta di corso legale 1511
moneta di riferimento 1488
moneta divisionale 2319
moneta d'oro 1296
moneta estera 1243
moneta falsa 339, 771
moneta forte 1319
moneta in circolazione 825
moneta legale 1511
moneta metallica 2203
moneta nazionale 1008
monetario 1607
moneta scelta 1060
moneta sfigurata 900
moneta spicciola 598
monetazione 657
monometallismo 1622
monopolio 1624
monopolizzare 1623
monte di pietà 1787
mora 901, 1625
moratoria 1626
movimenti di capitale 532
movimenti stagionali 2124
multa 1196, 1250
multare 1197
mutuatario 437
mutuatario secondario 2259
mutuo 1549

negoziabile 1650
negoziare 332, 860, 1652, 2322
negoziatore 1654
negoziazioni 1653
negozio 2321
netto 1655
noleggiare 604
noleggio 90, 603
nomina 163
nomina, chi ~ 162
nominale 1664
nominare 160, 1666
nominato 161
non accettare 989
non accreditato 2365
non assicurato 2378
non pagare 989
non pagato 2387
non percepibile 1670
non riscotibile 2363
non tassabile 1679
non trasferibile 1680
non valido 1440
nota di addebito 871
nota di consegna 930
nota di credito 795
nota di debito 378
nota di debito non negoziabile
    e priva di interessi 1674
nota di deposito 1595
nota di favore 23
nota di pegno 2426
nota di peso 384
notaio 1684
notaro 1684
notifica 171, 1685, 1686
notificare 170, 1687
nullo 1440, 2412
nullo e di nessun valore 1688
numero di monete che entrano
    in una determinata quantità
    di oro o argento 1605
nuova emissione 2010
nuova emissione, con ~ 812

obbligare 388
obbligazione 58, 415, 865
obbligazione al nominativo 1987
obbligazione al portatore 348
obbligazione attinente al
    servizio del debito 881
obbligazione contingenziale 727
obbligazione conversion 749
obbligazione convertibile 749
obbligazione del Tesoro 2345
obbligazione di prima ipoteca
    1205
obbligazione in moneta estera
    816

obbligazione in mora 902
obbligazione ipotecaria 1632
obbligazione non ammor-
    tizzabile 1457
obbligazione non assicurata
    1642
obbligazione perpetua 1826
obbligazione rinviata 908
obbligazione trasferibile per
    somme parziali 867
obbligazioni 1090
obbligazioni a vista 2179
obbligazioni ben collocate 967
obbligazioni il cui interesse si
    paga in monete d'oro 1295
obbligazioni in circolazione
    1726
obbligazioni pagabili in sterline
    2237
offerente 367
offerta 365, 1692, 2305
offerta (ad un'asta) 368
offerta di capitale 538
offerta eccedentaria 1748
offerta e domanda 2272
offerta monetaria 1621
offrire 364, 1691
oggetti di valore 2402
omologare un testamento 1876
onorario 1171
onorario anticipato (a un
    avvocato) 2069
operare 1709
operazione 1716
operazione di clearing 638
operazione di compensazione
    638
operazioni allo scoperto 1258
operazioni a premio 1718
operazioni a termine 1258
operazioni finanziarie 1187
opzione di compera di azioni
    2248
opzione di comperare o
    vendere nella borsa 2252
opzione doppia 1916
ordinazione 1719
ordinazione condizionale 698
ordine 1719
ordine condizionale 698
ordine del giorno 95
ordine di consegna 931
ordine di pagamento di
    dividendi 999
ordine di pagamento di
    interessi 1430
ordine di trasferimento 2336
ordine per pagamento in
    contanti 570

organismo incaricato di
    amministrare il fondo
    regolatore 462
organizzare 1722
organizzazione senza fini di
    lucro 1677
oro ed argento in verghe 468
oro fino 1198, 2224
ottenere benefici esorbitanti
    1885
ottenere fondi 1934
ottenere un prestito 2132

pacco d'azioni 1765
paese che può ottenere
    finanziamenti combinati 403
paese creditore 798
paese deficitario 916
paesi a entrate elevate 1328
paga 2419
pagabile 1792
pagabile all'ordine 1795
pagabile a presentazione 1793,
    1794
pagabile a vista 1793
pagabile dietro domanda 1033
pagamenti arretrati 1802
pagamenti fra banche a mezzo
    compensazione delle
    differenze 1120
pagamenti multilaterali 1638
pagamento 49, 971, 1543, 1801
pagamento anticipato 1804, 1856
pagamento a pronta cassa 571
pagamento arretrato 1743
pagamento contro consegna 569
pagamento di contropartita
    1593
pagamento in eccesso 1747
pagamento integrale 1282
pagamento parziale 1888
pagamento parziale in
    riconoscimento di un debito
    2320
pagamento per contanti 571
pagamento preferenziale 1849
pagamento totale 1282, 1805
pagare 47, 970, 978, 1539, 1791,
    1811
pagare interamente 1812
pagare (una cambiale) 1332
pagare un debito 2071
pagato 1753, 1807
pagatore 1798
pagherò 1890
panico nella Borsa 2120
pareggio 265
pareggio di titoli 271
pari, alla ~ 1761

rendere invalido 1441
rendimento 1883
rendimento crescente 1371
rendimento dell'investimento 2079
rendimento descrescente 968
rendimento scalare 2081
rendita 1883
rendita annuale 144
rendita individuale 1818
rendita monetaria 1615
rendita nazionale 1646
rendita non proveniente dalle operazioni 1675
rendita vitalizia 1532, 1534
rendite su proprietà pubbliche 1894
rentista 2032
rescindere 2035
rescindibile 2036
rescissione 2037
residuo 2051
respingere 2012
respiro 2053
responsabile 2058
responsabilità 1528, 2056
responsabilità finanziaria 1191
responsabilità per danni causati alla proprietà presa in affitto 1345
responsabilità solidale 1472
restituzione 1980, 2060
resto 2051
restringere 2061
restringimento del credito 1192
restrizione 2063
restrizione dei pagamenti 1810
restrizione dei trasferimenti di fondi 2064
restrizione del credito 2312
restrizioni di cambio 1118
retribuire 2072
retroattività 2075
retroattivo 2073
retrocessione (di una proprietà dopo il pagamento della ipoteca) 1961
reversibile 2087
revisore (dei conti) 232
revisore di banca 281
revocare 772, 2090
riabilitare 1997
riabilitazione 1998
riabilitazione del fallito 976
riaffittare 2013
rialzista 466
rialzo 434
riassicurare 2006
riassicurazione 2005

ribassare 1
ribassista 345
ribasso 2, 128, 887, 892
ricapitalizzare 1950
ricapitalizzazione 1949
ricevitore 670, 1954
ricevuta 974, 1951
ricevuta a saldo 1952
ricevuta legale 2234
richiamare 496, 625
richiedente 153
richiesta 154, 626, 932
richiesta di deposito anticipato (sulle importazioni) 84
richiesta di prelievo (da un conto di prestito) 157
ricompensa 1874, 2093
riconoscimento formale di un debito 654
ricorsi 2052
ricorso 55
ricostruzione 1960
ricuperabile 1965
ricuperare 1964
ricupero del investimento 2078
ricupero di un prestito 1556
ridurre 1, 828, 889
ridurre il valore nei libri 2447
riduzione 829, 890
riemissione di una lettera di cambio 2011
rifinanziamento 2098
rifinanziamento di buoni scaduti 1974
rifinanziamento di debito 877
rifiutare 1982
rifiuto 1981
rigettare 2012
rilancio 1975
rilasciare una scrittura 1129
rilassamento 1035
rimandare 906
rimborsabile 1967, 1977
rimborsare 1966, 1976, 2000
rimborso 1969, 1980, 2001
rimborso anticipato 85
rimborso in quote uguali 1524
rimessa 122, 2017
rimessa bancaria 329
rimessa in bianco 402
rimettere 119, 2002, 2016
rimunerare 2020
rimunerazione 684, 2021
rimunerazione dei fattori 1162
rinegoziabile 2022
rinegoziare 2023
rinnovare 2024
rinnovo 2025
rinuncia 1925, 2027

rinunciare 2014, 2026
riorganizzazione di debito 876
riparare 2002
ripartire 118, 164, 2158
ripartire al prorata 1902
ripartizione 121, 165, 449
riporre 2002
riportare 546
ripresa 1975
riprestito 1699
risarcimento 2004
risarcimento danni 1380
riscaglionamento del servizio di un debito 2034
riscatabile 1967
riscatare 1966
rischio 86
rischio assicurabile 1408
rischio cambiario 1119
risconto 1970
riscontro di cassa 2300
riscossione 665
riscotibile 663
riscuotere 662, 1072
riserva 2048
riserva bancaria 311
riserva di capitale 535
riserva di cassa fluttuante 1225
riserva di divise 1115
riserva in contanti 575
riserva in eccedenza 1106
riserva legale 1510
riserva obbligatoria 2047
riserva per deprezzamento 955
riserva per imprevisti 728
riservare 2040
riservato al pagamento di determinati conti 1045
riserve 2048
riserve disponibili 1274
riserve in oro 1298
riserve insufficienti 1358
riserve internazionali 1438
riserve liquide marginali 1580
riserve monetarie 1609
riserve per fini speciali 2276
riserve primarie 1868
riserve statutarie 2235
risorsa 2052
risorse 2052
risparmiare 2111
risparmiatore 2112
risparmio 2113
risparmio forzato 692
risparmio interno 1010
risparmio nazionale 1010
risparmio negativo 992
rispondere 149
rispondere di 150

Español

abonar 1791
accidente de trabajo 1690
accidente industrial 1385
acción 52, 55, 2157
acción bancaria 328
acción de preferencia 1846
acción de primera emisión 1721
acciones 1090, 2250
acciones con derecho de voto 2414
acciones con intereses garantidos 1313
acciones de administración 1573
acciones de compañias de navegación 2168
acciones de fundador 1259
acciones de garantía 1919
acciones de preferencia con participación en el beneficio 1770
acciones de prioridad 2146
acciones desvalorizadas 2431
acciones diferidas 911
acciones en premio 428
acciones enteramente pagadas 1756
acciones extraordinarias 428
acciones habilitantes 1919
acciones industriales 1387
acciones no distribuidas 2356
acciones no emitidas 2379
acciones no gravables 1668
acciones no inscritas 2385
acciones no subscritas 2392
accionista 2245
acción nominativa 1988
acción ordinaria 1721
acción sin valor nominal 1681
aceptación 9
aceptación absoluta 629
aceptación a posteriori 91
aceptación bancaria 279
aceptación comercial 2323
aceptación condicional 1917
aceptación en blanco 393
aceptante 14
aceptante (de una letra) fallido 314
aceptar 8
aceptar (una letra) 1332
acreditar 34, 784
acreditar en exceso 1735
acreedor 796
acreedor asegurado 2133
acreedor con caución 417
acreedor de bancarrota 317
acreedor de dos gravámenes 1018

acreedor ejecutante 1130
acreedor en segunda instancia 1486
acreedor hipotecario 1634
acreedor ordinario 1291
acreedor por juicio 1484
acreedor prendario 1790
acreedor privilegiado 1847
acreedor sin garantía 2389
acreedor solidario 1291
acreedor único 2185
acreencia 1182
acta de garantía 781
acta probativa de un testamento 1875
actas 1606
activo 56, 198, 199
activo circulante 1223
activo corriente 822
activo fijo 1208
activo flotante 1223
activo líquido 1538
activo realizable 822, 1924
activos a la vista 2175
activos en el exterior 1240
activos intangibles 1419
activo social 1775
activos sobre el exterior 1240
acto 893
acto de intervención 63
actuar 51
actuario 64
acuerdo 102
acuerdo contingente 2227
acuerdo de cesión 212
acuerdo sobre un producto básico 681
acuerdos sobre fondos de regulación 463
acuerdo stand-by 2227
acumulación 39
acumular 35
acumularse 35
acuñación 657
acuñador 659
acuñar 656
acusación por deterioro 1346
acusar recibo de 42
acuse de recibo 41
adelantar 80
adelanto 81, 2069
adelantos y atrasos 1498
adeudar 1750
adeudo 1375
adición 67
adicionar 65
adjudicación 120
adjudicar 110, 117
adjuntar 218

adjunto 1073
administración 74
administración pública 624
administrador 73, 2349
administrador de los bienes de un demente 1955
administrar 1571
administrativo 75
admisión 77
adquirente 44
adquiridor 44
adquirir 43
adquisición 45
aduana 836
ad valorem 78
advertencia 1685
affidavit 88
afirmar 254
afluencia de capitales 1393
aforador 169
aforar 168
aforo 167
agente 96, 862
agente de cambios 1111
agente de comercio 1598
agente de(l) fallido 315
agente fiduciaro 831
agente mercantil 1161
agio 100, 1470
agiotaje 1470
agotado 940
agregado 97
agregar 218
agregarse 35
agroindustrias 103
aguinaldo 425
ahorrador 2112
ahorrar 2111
ahorrista 2112
ahorro 2113
ahorro forzoso 692
ahorro interno 1010
ahorro negativo 992
ajuste cambiario 1109
albacea 1132
alcista 466
alegar 108, 254
alivio de la deuda 878
almanaque 494
alquilar 2029
alquiler 1501, 2028
alquiler de una propiedad 2030
alquiler máximo 1929
alteración 129
alteración falaz de un balance 2436
alto empleado de banco 308
alto funcionario de banco 565
alza 82

beneficio por muerte 864
beneficios 1048
beneficios adicionales 1372
beneficios de indemnización
1381
beneficios económicos 1049
beneficios sin destino asignado
2358
bienes 1057
bienes de capital 509, 514
bienes de consumo 720
bienes de equipo 514, 521
bienes de la sociedad 1775
bienes de sucesión asignados
por un tribunal de equidad
1088
bienes inmuebles 1342, 1940
bienes muebles 608, 1637, 1828
bienes muebles de una
empresa 1218
bienes personales 1828
bienes raíces 1342, 1945
billete de banco 306, 373
billetes de banco 1305
billetes de banco cortados al
medio y enviados
separadamente por correo
1318
billetes de banco que pueden
ponerse de nuevo en
circulación 2009
blanco, en ~ 392
bloquear 405
bolsa 442
bolsa clandestina 455
bolsa de valores 2244
bolsa ilegal 455
bolsa negra 390
bonificación fiscal 2296
bono 415, 865
bono de ingresos 1363
bono del Tesoro 817, 1125, 2344
bono de prima 1854
bono de reintegro 1978
bono perpetuo 145
bonos de ahorro 2117
bonos en circulación 1726
bono sin vencimiento 145
borrar 926
brecha 1289
brecha de recursos 2045

cabeza, por ~ 1817
caducar 1165
caída 1029
caja 547
caja de ahorro 2116
caja de ahorro postal 1839
caja de caudales 2103

caja de seguridad 2104
caja fuerte 2103
caja registradora 574
cajero 566, 669, 2299
cajero de banco 286
cajero jefe 1322
cajero-pagador 1800
cajero pagador y recibidor 2383
cajero principal 1322
calcular 492, 694, 1959
cálculo 493, 693
cálculo de costos 760
calderilla 598
calendario 494
callejón sin salida 856
cámara de compensación 642
cámara del tesoro 2408
cambiar 338, 550, 597
cambio 337, 598, 1107
cambio a la vista 2180
cambio de acciones 2211
cambista 503
cancelación 147, 505
cancelar 146, 504, 772, 2437
cancelar una deuda 2071, 2438
capacidad crediticia 804
capacidad de absorción 5
capacidad de endeudamiento
438
capacidad para atender el
servicio de la deuda 882
capitación 543
capital 507, 2239
capital activo 59
capital autorizado 239
capital bloqueado 1276
capital circulante 621, 1224
capital congelado 1276
capital declarado 2229
capital de especulación 2096
capital de explotación 2443
capital desvalorizado 2430
capital de trabajo 2443
capital de un trust 755
capital emitido 1466
capital en acciones 2160
capital en acciones con
participación en el beneficio
1771
capital en acciones diferidas
912
capital en acciones ordinarias
2411
capital en acciones reservado
para el caso de conclusión de
negocios 2043
capital en giro 621, 2443
capital en inmuebles 1209
capital en préstamo 1553

capital especulativo 1333
capital fijo 1209
capital improductivo 859
capital inactivo 1336
capital inicial 1705
capital integrado 1754
capitalista 524
capitalización 525
capitalizar 526
capital libre de gravámenes
2377
capital nacional 536
capital no integrado 2361
capital nominal 1159, 1665
capital productivo 59
capital social 1480, 2160, 2239
capital suscrito 2264
capital totalmente integrado
1284
carga 1074
cargar 599
cargar en cuenta 869
caro 1138
carta de acarreo 380
carta de adjudicación 1515
carta de compromiso 1522
carta de crédito 1516
carta de crédito a la vista 2178
carta de crédito comercial 677
carta de crédito comple-
mentaria 138
carta de crédito confirmada e
irrevocable 2254
carta de crédito de viajero 2340
carta de crédito documentaria
1004
carta de crédito impresa al
margen de una letra de
cambio 1582
carta de crédito irrevocable
1462
carta de crédito simple 633
carta de depósito 1517
carta de garantía 1518
carta de gracia 1521
carta de hipoteca 1519
carta de indemnización 1520
carta de moratoria 1521
carta de pago 50
carta de porte 380, 2432
carta de solicitud de pago 1039
carta fiduciaria 2351
carta orgánica de una sociedad
1594
carta-poder para la venta de
valores 2249
cartera de préstamo 1555
casa bancaria 298
casa de banca 298

depreciación 954
depreciación de la moneda 956
depreciar 952, 958
depreciarse 952
depresión 957, 1035
derecho 1042, 2317
derecho a dividendo, sin ~ 1127
derecho (aduanero) ad valorem 79
derecho a sorteo, con ~ 811
derecho de aduana 838
derecho de ingreso en un consorcio bancario 2282
derecho de prescripción 1859
derecho de prioridad en la compra 1844
derecho de propiedad 1899
derecho de retención 1531
derecho de reversión 2086
derecho de sellos 2222
derecho de sucesión 2086
derecho de tránsito 2338
derecho hipotecario de rescate 1093
derecho mercantil 1497
derecho prioritario de retención 1871
derechos consulares 717
derechos de dársena 1000
derechos de exportación 1146
derechos de importación 1353
derechos de patente 1784
derechos especiales de giro 2201
desacreditar 986
desahorro 992
descargar 46
descargo 48, 2015
descenso 887
descontabilidad 979
descontable 277
descontar 891, 977
descontar (una letra) 1332
descubierto 1738
descubierto formal 2298
descuento 892
descuento de caja 562
descuento hecho por adelantado 2373
descuento para pago al contado 562
descuento, sin ~ 1655
deseconomías 987
desembolsar 970
desembolso 971
desembolsos 1724
desembolsos de capital 533

desequilibrio de los pagos internacionales 1340
desfalcar 1064
desfalco 1065
desglose 449
designación 163
designado 161
designar 160, 1666
desinversión 991
desmonetizar 938
despachar (en la aduana) 634
despacho 774
despacho de aduana 636
destinado para el pago de determinadas cuentas 1045
destinar 110, 173
destinatario 70, 1957
destinatario (de una remesa) 2018
destino 111, 175
desvalorización 954
desvalorizar 952
desvalorizarse 952
detención 856
detener el pago de un cheque 2251
detentor del derecho de sucesión 2088
deuda 872, 1376, 1529
deuda anulada 506
deuda atrasada 185
deuda consolidada 1285
deuda contabilizada 429
deuda efectiva 60
deuda exigible y cobrable 2196
deuda externa pendiente 1730
deuda fija 1211
deuda flotante 1227
deuda incobrable 260
deuda por juicio 1485
deuda prioritaria 2144
deuda privilegiada 1848
deudas 1527
deudas activas 1728
deuda saldada 1540
deudas de la sociedad 1776
deudas que no producen intereses 1781
deudas que pueden probarse 1906
deuda subordinada 1487
deudor 875
deudor hipotecario 1636
deudor solidario 1476
devaluación 959
devaluar 958
devengar 35
devengar interés 351
día hábil 480

día laborable 480
días de cortesía 851
días de gracia 1233
días de prórroga especial 851
diferencia 1578
diferencia entre dos tipos de interés 2215
diferencia entre el valor neto y el gravamen hipotecario de una propiedad 1091
diferir 906
dificultades financieras 1184
dilución del capital 2242
dinero 1613
dinero barato 609
dinero contante 549, 1939
dinero depreciado 953
dinero efectivo en caja 572
dinero en efectivo 1939
dinero extranjero 1243
dinero falso 771
dinero improductivo 336
dinero inactivo 1337
dinero no convertible 1370
dinero pagadero a corto plazo 501
dinero pagadero a solicitud 501
dinero que se presta a alto interés 863
dirección 68
director 73
director de banco 292
director de banco con funciones inspectivas 690
director del departamento de divisas 691
directorio 412
dirigir 69
dirigirse 69
dirigirse a 159
disminución 2, 890
disminuir 1, 828, 889
disolución 993
disolver 994
disponer 182
disponibilidad 241
disponibilidad en dinero 1545
disponibilidades 1538
disponible 242
disposición 1909
disposiciones 1996
distribución 121, 165, 449, 995
distribución de los recursos 114
distribución porcentual 1821
distribuir 118, 164
dividendo 996
dividendo acumulativo 813
dividendo, con ~ 810
dividendo de liquidación 1541

rehusar 2012
reintegro 1980
reinversión 2008
reinvertir 2007
relación capital-producto 534
relación capital-trabajo 528
relación entre el activo
  disponible y el pasivo
  corriente 40
relativo al presupuesto 458
rematador 228
rematar 227
remate 226
remesa 2017
remesar 2016
remisión 2017
remitente (de una remesa) 2019
remitir 2016
remuneración 2021
remunerar 2020
rendimiento 2076
rendimiento a escala 2081
rendimiento corriente 827
rendimiento de la inversión
  2079
rendimientos crecientes 1371
rendimientos decrecientes 968
rendir interés 351
renegociable 2022
renegociar 2023
renovación 2025
renovar 2024
renta 1361
renta anual 144
rentabilidad 1883
renta sobre propiedades
  públicas 1894
renta vitalicia 1532, 1534
rentista 143, 2032
renuncia 1925, 2027
renunciar 2014, 2026
reorganización 1960
reorganización de la deuda 876
reparación 2004
reparar 2002
repartición 1772
repartir 164, 2158
repartir acciones 2213
reparto 121, 165, 1772
reponer 2002
reposición 2003
représtamo 1699
requisito de depósito previo (a
  la importación) 84
rescatable 1967
rescatar 1966
rescindible 2036
rescindir 2035
rescisión 2037, 2308

reserva bancaria 311
reserva de capital 535
reserva en efectivo 575
reserva en exceso 1106
reserva flotante en efectivo
  1225
reserva legal 1510
reserva obligatoria 2047
reserva para depreciación 955
reserva para imprevistos 728
reservar 2040
reserva(s) 2048
reservas de divisas 1115
reservas disponibles 1274
reservas en oro 1298
reservas estatutarias 2235
reservas internacionales 1438
reservas líquidas marginales
  1580
reservas monetarias 1609
reservas primarias 1868
residuo 2051
responder 149
responder por 150
responsabilidad 1528, 2056
responsabilidad financiera 1191
responsabilidad por daños
  causados a la propiedad
  alquilada 1345
responsabilidad solidaria 1472
responsable 2058
respuesta 148
respuesta de primas 884
restitución 1980, 2060
resto 2051
restricción 829, 2063
restricción del crédito 1192
restricciones a las
  transferencias 2064
restricciones cambiarias 1118
restricciones crediticias 2312
restricciones en los pagos 1810
restringir 828, 2061
resumen de cuentas 7
retardo 924
retención de garantía 2070
retener 2066
retirar 2439
retirar de circulación 2441
retiro 2440
retrasar 923
retrasos en los pagos por
  importaciones 1350
retraspaso (de una propiedad
  luego de pagada la hipoteca)
  1961
retribución 125, 684
retribuir 2072
retroactividad 2075

retroactivo 2073
reunión de acreedores 799
reunirse 190
revalorización 1946
revalorizar 1947
revaluación 2082
revalúo 2082
revender 2039
reversible 2087
reversión 2086
reversión de bienes
  abintestatos al estado 1097
revisar 1400
revisar (cuentas) 229
revisión de cuentas 231
revisor de banco 281
revisor de cuentas 232
revocar 772, 2090
riesgo 86
riesgo asegurable 1408
riesgo cambiario 1119

salario 2107, 2419
saldar 1539, 1812, 2150
saldo 266
saldo acreedor 786
saldo-crédito no utilizado 2391
saldo de caja 554
saldo de cuenta 268, 2059
saldo de pago 269
saldo inactivo 1017
saldo negativo 1648
saldo no utilizado 2372
saldos bancarios 282
saldos bloqueados 407
salida de capital(es) 1723
salir de fiador 262
sección de créditos 789
sección de descuentos 982
secuestrar 704
secuestro 2140
segunda hipoteca 2129
seguro 1410
seguro contra accidentes 15
seguro contra estafas de
  empleados 1172
seguro contra incendios 1200
seguro contra robos 475, 2097
seguro de garantía personal
  1643
seguro de indemnización 1383
seguro de vida 1533
seguro en exceso 1745
seguro marítimo 1583
seguro sobre el crédito 792
seguro social 2190
seguro total 109
seguro vigente 2375
sello 2122, 2221

sello de caja 2301
semestral 363
servicio de la deuda 879
servicio de sobregiro 1739
servicio fiduciario 1175
servir 17
sin asegurar 2378
sindicato 2280
síndico 232, 281, 2349
síndico en bancarrota 327
síndico en quiebra 327
sin pagar 2387
sin valor 2412
sistema de alarma 1044
sistema de amortización de
  saldo decreciente 888
sistema de bancos associados
  596
sistema de compensación 641
sistema de doble
  contabilización 1030
sistema monetario 658
situación de liquidez 1546
situación de los pagos 1809
sobrecapitalizar 1733
sobrecarga 93, 1734
sobredepreciación 1737
sobregirar 1740
sobregiro 1738
sobregiro aparente 2298
sobrevaluar 1749
sociedad 215, 695, 754, 1774
sociedad anónima 1482
sociedad cuyos dirigentes
  poseen todas las acciones 646
sociedad de ahorro y crédito
  inmobiliario 2115
sociedad de créditos 802
sociedad de inversión con
  cartera de composición fija
  648
sociedad de inversión con
  cartera de composición
  variable 1704
sociedad de inversiones con
  derechos de administración
  1574
sociedad de inversiones
  restringidas 2094
sociedad financiadora 802
sociedad por acciones 1482
socio 1773
socio comanditario 2187
socio en bancarrota 323
solicitar 158
solicitud 154, 498
solicitud de ingreso 156
solicitud de préstamo 1551

solicitud de retiro de fondos (de
  una cuenta de préstamos) 157
solicitud oficial de presentación
  del análisis financiero de un
  banco 285
sólido 2197
solvencia 804, 2055
solvente 2057, 2195
sostén de familia 448
subarrendar 2261
subarriendo 2260
subasta 226
subastador 228
subastar 227
subcapitalizar 2366
subestimar 2369
subprestatario 2259
subscribir acciones 2286
subsidiar 2266
subsidio 125, 2267
subvención 2267
subvencionar 2266
subvención de intereses 1429
sucursal 445
sucursal de banco 284
sueldo 126, 2419
sujeto a impuestos 1041
suma 67, 135
suma de los cheques todavía no
  acreditados 1220
sumadora 66
suma pagadera en caso de
  muerte 864
sumar 65
superávit 2274
superávit de explotación 1715
superávit de operación 1715
superávit presupuestal 460
superávit presupuestario 460
superávit sin asignar 2359
supercapitalizar 1733
superdepreciación 1737
suplementario 1156
suscribir 2263
suscriptor 1570
suscriptor de una emisión de
  acciones 2371
suspender el pago de un
  cheque 2251
suspenso, en ~ 3

tachar 926
talón 2287
talonario de cheques 613
talón de cheque 617
talón de dividendo 998
talón de intereses 775
talón (de letra de cambio) 116
tarifa 2288

tasa 1936
tasable 166
tasación 167, 196, 1139, 2403
tasación de averías 72
tasación de daños 72
tasa de actualización de
  equilibrio 807
tasa de descuento 985
tasa de descuento bancario 310
tasa de interés 1426
tasa de interés sobre préstamos
  a corto plazo 502
tasa del mercado monetario
  1619
tasa de rendimiento económico
  1052
tasa de rendimiento financiero
  1190
tasa de rentabilidad aceptable
  841
tasa de rentabilidad interna
  1434
tasa diferencial de rentabilidad
  1373
tasador 169
tasador de averías 246, 628
tasador de daños 628
tasar 168, 194, 2405
tasar en exceso 1749
tasar en menos 2369
tasa vigente en el mercado 1864
tendencia al alza 470
tendencia alcista 2394
tendencia descendente 1021
tenedor 1329
tenedor de acciones 2245
tenedor de libros 430
tenedor de obligaciones 421, 866
tenedor de títulos 421
tenedor de una letra 377
tenedor en buena fe 414
teneduría de libros 431
tenencias oficiales de oro 1696
teoría cuantitativa del dinero
  1920
terminar 2437
Tesorería 2343
tesorero 2342
tesoro 2341
Tesoro 2343
tesoro del banco 330
testador 359
testamento 2310, 2435
testigo 224
testimoniar 223, 2442
testimonio 222
timbre 2221
timbre fiscal 2084
tipo 1936

Nederlands

wenden tot, zich ~ 159
werkdag 480
werkelijk rentepercentage 1941
werkend kapitaal 59
werk gaan, te ~ 51
werkgever 1067
werkkapitaal 621
werkkapitaalkrediet 2444
werkuitvoeringsgarantie 1823
werkzaam 56
wet 53
wetboek van koophandel 1497
wettelijke belegging 1505
wettelijke reserve 2047
wettelijk ontvangstbewijs 2234
wettelijk voorgeschreven
  rentevoet 1509
wettelijk voorgeschreven
  reserve 1510
wettig betaalmiddel 1511
wijziging 129
wille zijn, ter ~ 17
winst 357, 1882
winstaandeel 996
winstbejag, met ~ 1886
winstdelend aandelenkapitaal
  1771
winstdelende preferente
  aandelen 1770
winsten 1048
winst-en-verliesrekening 1884
winstgevend 1566
winstgevende belegging 1881
winsttotaal 465
wiskundig adviseur 64
wissel 371, 379, 1022, 2427
wisselarbitrage 180
wisselboek 375
wisselborgtocht 244
wisselbrief 379
wissel doen accepteren, een ~
  2174
wisselen 550, 597
wisselgeld 598
wisselhouder 377
wisselkoers 1107, 1937
wisselkoers vrijgeven, de ~
  1229
wisselkredietbrief 1582
wissel luidende in vreemde
  valuta 815
wisselmakelaar 374, 1111
wissel met vaste looptijd 2313
wissel op het buitenland 1241
wissel op korte termijn 2171
wissel op lange termijn 1562
wisselpariteit 1767
wisselregister 387
wisselruiterij 1490

wissel trekken, een ~ 1026
wissel uitgegeven in meerdere
  exemplaren 2149
wissel zonder beperking 632
woeker 2399
woekerrente 137

zaak 476, 861, 1716, 2329
zaak doen, een ~ 860
zaakwaarnemer 2194
zaken 476
zaken doen 1709
zakenman 481
zakenrekening 477
zeeassuradeurs 1585
zeeassurantie 1583
zeer hoge afschrijving 1737
zeeverzekeraars 1585
zeeverzekering 1583
zegel 2122, 2221
zegelrecht 2222
zekerheid gedeponeerde
  hypotheekakte, tot ~ 1089
zekerstellen 2131
zelffinanciering 2141
zender (van een remise) 2019
zending 2017
zichtdeposito 611, 934
zichtkoers 2180
zichtkredietbrief 2178
zicht, op ~ 2173
zichtwissel 933, 935, 2176
zichtwisselbrief 933
zwakke valuta 2191
zwarte beurs 390
zwarte markt 391

Deutsch

D

abbezahlen 1811
abbuchen 2447
Abgabe 1526, 2289
Abgabenfreiheit 1343
abgabepflichtig 1041
Abkommen 102, 183, 778
Abkommen über den Puffer-
stock 463
Abkommen über Grundwaren
681
ablehnen 1982, 2012
Ablehnung 1981
abliefern 927
Ablieferung 122, 928
ablösbar 1967
ablösen 1966
Ablösung 1980
Ablösungshypothek 1979
Ablösungsschuldverschreibung
1978
abmachen 182, 2150
Abnahme 890
abnehmende Grenzerträge 968
abnehmende Tilgung 888
Abnehmer 2285
abordnen 925
abrechnen 891, 978
Abrechnung 1543, 2151
Absage 1981
Abschaffung 147
abschätzbar 166   ·
abschätzen 168
Abschlag 892
abschliessen 696, 2437
Abschluss 265, 2329
Abschnitt 939
Abschöpfung 829
abschreiben 46, 2448
Abschreibung 48
absenden 1255
absolutes Akzept 629
Absorptionsvermögen 5
Abstand nehmen 2026
abtreten 201, 751
Abtretender 211
Abtretung 208, 594, 752, 936
Abtretungsurkunde 896
Abwanderung der Intellek-
tuellen 444
abwerten 958
Abwertung 959
Abwertungsbetrag 955
abzahlen 1811
abziehen 891
Abzug 128, 892
Abzug bringen, in ~ 891
Addiermaschine 66
Addition 67
Adressat 70, 1957

Adresse 68
adressieren 69
Affidavit 88
Agent 96, 1161
Agent des Bankrotteurs 315
Agio 100, 1470
Agiotage 1470
Agrarkredit 1168
Akkreditiv 677, 1516
Akkumulierung 39
Akte 893
Aktie 2157
Aktien 1090, 2250
Aktienbank 1481
Aktien beziehen 2286
Aktiengesellschaft 1482
Aktieninhaber 2245
Aktienkapital 2160
Aktienkapital bereitgestellt für
Geschäftsabschlüsse 2043
Aktienkapital mit aufge-
schobenen Zinsen 912
Aktienkapital mit Teilhaber-
schaft am Gewinn 1771
Aktienkurszettel 2162
Aktien mit garantierter
Dividendenzahlung 1313
Aktienpaket 1765
Aktienschein 2161
Aktien splitten 2213
Aktienübertragung 2335
Aktienverkaufsrecht 2248
Aktien zeichnen 2286
Aktienzertifikat 2161
Aktie ohne Nominalwert 1681
Aktionär 2245
Aktionärsversammlung 2246
aktiv 56
Aktiva 198
Aktivposten 197
Aktivseite 199
Aktuar 64
Akzept 9
Akzeptant 14
Akzeptbank 11
Akzeptenbuch 12
Akzeptenregister 13
akzeptieren 8
akzeptieren (einen Wechsel)
1332
Akzeptkredit 10
Akzeptsurkunde 1405
Alarm-System 1044
Alleinhandel 1624
Alleinvertrieb 1624
allgemeines Hauptbuch 1293
allgemeine Unkosten 1698, 1744
Allonge 116, 2287
Allrisk-Versicherung 109

alternativer Begünstigter 131
Alternativtrassat 130
Amortisation 132, 1969
Amortisationsfonds 2186
Amortisationstabelle 133
amortisierbar 1967
amortisieren 134, 1966
amtlich 1695
amtlicher Goldbestand 1696
Analyse 449
anbieten 1691
Änderung 129
aneignen, sich ~ 172
Aneignung 174
Anfangskapital 1705
Anfangskurs 1707
anführen 108
Angaben 845
Angebot 365, 1692
Angebotsdokumente 369
Angebotsgarantie 366
Angebot und Nachfrage 2272
angegebenes Kapital 2229
Angleichungssatz 807
anhäufen 1
Ankaufskurs 489
Anlage 1444
Anlageinvestitionen 1215
Anlagekonto 1447
Anlagepapier 1448
Anlagetitel 1448
Anlagevermögen 509, 1208
Anlageverzinsung 2079
anlegen 1443
Anleihe 18, 1549
Anleihe bekommen, eine ~
2132
Anleihe besichern, eine ~ 2132
Anleihebeteiligung 2256
Anleihe für Bauprogramme
1887
Anleihe für Projekte 1889
Anleihekapital 1553
Anleihekonto 1550
Anleihe ohne Deckung 2390
Anleihe ohne Verfallfrist 855
Anleiheportefeuille 1555
Anleiheschein 1554
anmelden 885
Anmeldung 883
Annahme 77
annehmbarer Preis 1948
annehmen 8
Annuität 144
annullierbar 2036
annullieren 146, 251, 504, 1441,
1689, 2035
annullierte Schuld 506
Annullierung 147, 253, 505, 905

Bankdiskont 310
Bankdiskontsatz 310
Bankeinlage 291
Bankenkonsortium 1310
Bankenliquiditätslage 302
Bankenliquiditätsverhältnis 303
Banken vorgenommener
  Zahlungsausgleich,
  zwischen ~ 1120
bank(e)rott 312
Bank(e)rott 316, 1164
Bank(e)rotterklärung 62
bank(e)rottgegangene Firma
  322
bank(e)rottgegangener Akzeptant 314
bank(e)rottgegangener Bürge
  326
bank(e)rottgegangener Teilhaber 323
bank(e)rottgegangener Trassant
  321
bank(e)rottgegangener Trassat
  320
bank(e)rottgegangener Treuhänder 327
Bank(e)rott machen 354, 1163
bankfähiger Wechsel 980
bankfähiges Projekt 278
Bankfiliale 284
Bankgarantie 297
Bankgarantiefonds 2218
Bankgebühren 61
Bankgeschäfte machen 276
Bankguthaben 282
Bankhauptbuch 300
Bankhaus 298
Bankier 294
Bankkassierer 286
Bankkonto 280
Bankkosten 287
Bankkredit 290
Banknote 306, 373
Banknoten 1305
Banknoten in der Mitte zerschnitten und getrennt per
  Post verschickt 1318
Bankprovision 289
Bankrate 310
Bankreserve 311
Bankrevision 295
Bankrevisor 281, 296
Bankrotteur 324
Banksatz 310
Bankscheck 288
Bankspesen 61, 287
Banktratte 283
Banktresor 330
Banküberweisung 329

Bankvorsteher 304
Bankwechsel 283
Bankweisung 612
Bankwerte 309
Bankwesen 299
Bankzweigstelle 284
bar 551
Baratterie 335
Barbestand 564, 572
Barbetrag aus einem Grundbesitz 1897
Bareinkommen 568
bare Reserve 575
Bargeld 549, 1939
bargeldloser Produktionsfaktor
  1669
Barmittel 564
Barrabatt 562
Barren 1395
Barreserve 2409
Barrückkaufwert 577
Barwertrechnung 983
Barzahlung 571
Barzahlungsauftrag 570
Bausparkasse 2115
Beamter 1694
beanstanden 625
Beanstandung 626
beantworten 149
Beantwortung 148
beaufsichtigen 1400
beauftragen 925
Beauftragte(r) 161, 1577
Bedarf 932
Bedenkzeit 2053
bedingte Annahme 1917
bedingte Einlage 946
bedingter Auftrag 698
bedingter Zins 726
bedingtes Akzept 1917
bedingtes Indossament 697,
  1918
Bedingung 2238
bedingungsloser Kredit 631
bedingungsloses Akzept 629
befrachten 604
Befrachtung 90, 603
befreien 2014
befristete Einlage 2314
befristetes Darlehen 2315
Befugnis 2422
begebbar 1650, 1942
begebbare Wertpapiere 1651
begeben 1652
beglaubigen 34, 223, 234, 593,
  1907, 2442
beglaubigter Scheck 592
beglaubigtes Konnossement 591
Beglaubigung 222, 235

begleichen 2150
Begleichung 2151
begrenzter Rentabilitäts-
  Prozentsatz 841
Begünstigter 356
Begutachtung durch Sachverständige 1139
behaupten 108
Beifall 176
beifügen 218
Beilage 1073
beilegen 218
Beistandkredit 2228
Beitrag 737
Beitragenden 738
Bekanntgabe 171
bekanntgeben 139, 1687
bekanntmachen 1687
Bekanntmachung 1685, 1686
bekräftigen 701
Bekräftigung 702
belasten 193, 599, 869, 2290
belasten mit einer Hypothek
  1628
belastet mit Hypotheken 473
Belastung 195, 1074
Belastungsanweisung 871
belaufen auf, sich ~ 136
Beleg 2416
belegen mit Beschlag 217, 2139
belegen mit Steuern 474
Beleihungsgrenze 1514
belohnen 2020, 2072
Belohnung 1874, 2021, 2093
benachrichtigen 170
Benachrichtigung 171, 1685
Benefizient 356
Berater 87
berechnen 492, 694, 1959
berechnen nach Verhältnis 1902
Berechnung 493, 693
Berechnung von Kapitalfluss
  573
berechtigte Unterschrift 240
Bereitschaftsabkommen 2227
Berufsunfall 1690
beschädigen 844
beschädigter Scheck 1641
Beschädigung 843
beschaffen 43
bescheinigen 234, 593
Bescheinigung 585
Beschlagnahme 220, 1062, 2140
beschlagnahmen 217, 1063, 2139
Beschlag nehmen, in ~ 217,
  704, 1063
beschränken 2061
beschränkte Nachfrage 1816
beschränkter Kredit 2062

Extraspesen 1157

Fabrikpreis 1134
Faktoreinkommen 1162
Faktur(a) 1453
Fall 887, 1029
fallende Tendenz 1021
fälliger Wechsel 385
fällig sein 1165
falsche Münze 339
fälschen 769, 1167
Fälscher 770
falscher Scheck 1251
falscher Titel 2156
falsche Überweisung 1252
Falschgeld 771
Fälschung 768, 1166
fas 1265
fehlerhaftes Konnossement
  2362
Feingehalt 1199
Feingold 1198, 2224
feste Aktiven 1208
feste Einlage 1212
feste Kapitalanlagen 1209
fester Termin 1217
feste Schuld 1211
festes Einkommen 1213
festes Kapital 1209
feste Spesen 1210
Festlegung von Kapitalien 1560
festliegende Gelder 1276
Festsetzung 2238
fest untergebrachte Obligationen 967
festverzinsliche Finanzierung
  1216
festverzinsliche Obligation 58
festverzinsliche Wertpapiere
  1214
Feuerversicherung 1200
Feuerversicherungsgesellschaft
  1201
fiduziär 1173
fiktive Dividende 2155
Filiale 89, 445
Filialenhauptbuch 446
Finanz 1177
Finanzen 1177
Finanzerträge 1185
Finanzgeschäfte 1187
finanziell 1181
finanzielle Haftung 1191
finanzielle Schwierigkeiten
  1184
finanzieren 1178
Finanzierungsgesellschaft 1180
Finanzierungsgesellschaft für
  Entwicklungszwecke 962

Finanzierungskosten 1179
Finanzierungskredit 1183
Finanzierungsplan 1189
Finanzjahr 1194
Finanzmann 1195
Finanzwelt 1193
Firma 1202
Firma in Konkurs 322
Firmenkonto 1347
flauer Markt 1034
Flaute 1035
Flexibilität der Kurse 1117
flüssige Aktiva 1538
flüssige Anlagen 1223, 1538
flüssige Grenzreserven 1580
flüssige Mittel 1538, 1939
flüssiges Kapital 2198
Flüssigkeitskoeffizient 2046
fob 1273
Fonds 1286
Fonds eines Kredits 1878
fordern 496, 625
Forderung 498, 626, 932
Forderungen 1953
Formalitäten 1254
Formular 1253
Frachtbrief 380, 2432
Frachtvertrag 606
Franchise 1261
Francraum 1260
Franczone 1260
franko 1264
frei 1264
frei an Bord 1273
freie Marktwirtschaft 1271
freier Devisenmarkt 1764
freier Grundbesitz 1267
freier Makler 1673
freier Markt 1270
freie Rücklagen 1274
freies Grundeigentum 1267
Freigabe 2015
Freigabe des Wechselkurses
  1221
frei gewährtes Darlehen 1269
frei konvertierbare Devisen
  1266
frei Schiffseite 1265
freistellen 2014
Freizeichnungsklausel 248
Fremdwährung 1243
Fremdwerte 1240
Frist 853, 1303, 2307, 2396
Fristtage 851
führender 1131
fundierte Schuld 1285
Fürsorgefonds 1908

galoppierende Inflation 1287,
  2101
Garant 1314
Garantie 1311, 2135, 2273, 2428
Garantie auf Schadloshaltung
  423
Garantiebrief 1518
Garantiefonds 1316
Garantiehinterlegung 1315
Garantiekonto 209, 1099
Garantiemittel 1316
garantieren 1312, 2425
garantierter Gläubiger 417
Garantieschein 1326
Garantieversicherung 1172
geben 361
Gebot 365, 368
gebräuchlich 834
Gebühren 1042, 1171
Gebührentabelle 2119
Gefälligkeit 19
Gefälligkeitsgiro 22
Gefälligkeitspapier 23
Gefälligkeitsschein 23
Gefälligkeitstratte 21
Gefälligkeitswechsel 20
gefällig sein 17
gefälschter Scheck 1251
gegenseitiger Kontrakt 1958
gegenseitiger Kredit 2278
Gegenwartswert 1863
gegenzeichnen 773
Gehalt 126, 2107
Gehilfe 213
gekreuzter Scheck 806
Geld 1613, 1607, 1813
Geldanleihen im Ausland 1242
Geld auf Aufruf 501
Geld beschaffen 1935
Geldeinheit 1612
Gelder 1286
Geldflüssigkeit 1545
Geld leihen 16
Geldmarkt 442, 1617
Geldmarktpapiere 1618
Geldmarktsatz 1619
Geldmenge 1621
Geldmittel 2052
Geldmittel auftreiben 1935
Geldmittel beschaffen 1934
Geldschein 306
Geldstrafe 1196
Geldstrafe verhängen, eine ~
  1197
Geldstück 655
Geldverknappung 1611
Geldverleiher 1616
Geldvolumen 1621
Geldwechsler 503

zählen 763
Zahler 1798
Zahlmeister 1798
Zahlung 49, 1543, 1801, 2021
Zahlung erhalten 1807
Zahlung mahnen, die ~ 1083
Zahlungsanweisung 305, 1023
Zahlungsaufschub 1626, 2053
Zahlungsbedingungen 2309
Zahlungsbeschränkungen 1810
Zahlungsbilanzdefizit 1808
Zahlungsbilanzlage 270
Zahlungsbürgschaft 1803
Zahlungseinstellung 904
Zahlungsempfänger 1797
zahlungsfähig 2195
zahlungsfähige Schuld 2196
Zahlungsfähigkeit 804
Zahlungslage 1809
Zahlungsrückstände 1802
Zahlungssaldo 269
zahlungsunfähig 1399
Zahlungsunfähigkeit 1398
Zahlungsunfähigkeitserklärung
62
Zahlungsverzug 904
Zedent 211
zedieren 201
zeichnen 2181, 2263
Zeichner einer Aktienausgabe
2371
zeitlich befristete Police 2316
Zeitpunkt des Inkrafttretens
1054
Zeitrente 2303
Zeitwechsel 2313
Zentralbank 582
Zentralverwaltungswirtschaft
583
Zertifikat 585
Zession 208, 594, 936
Zessionär 210, 595
zessionsfähig 205
Zessionsvertrag 212
Zeuge 224
zeugen 2442
Zeugnis 222, 585
Ziffer 1176
Zins 1420
Zinsausgleichsteuer 1423
Zinsdeckung 1422
Zinsen 1420
Zinsenauszahlungsschein 1430
Zinsen bringen 351
Zinsen tragen 351
Zinsertrag 1428
Zinseszins 688
Zinsfuss 1426
Zinsgefälle 1427

Zinssatz 1426
Zinssatz für Tagesgeld 502
Zinsschein 775, 1421
Zinsspanne 2215
Zinszuschuss 1429
Zirkulargeldfluss 622
Zoll 836, 838, 1042
Zollabfertigung 636
Zollager 420
Zollagergüter 419
Zollamt 836
Zugeständnis 689
zulassen 124
Zulassung 77, 127
zunehmende Erträge 1371
zurückbehalten 2066
zurückbehaltene Gewinne 2067
zurückbehaltenes Einkommen
2068
Zurückbehaltungsrecht 1531
zurückerstatten 1976
zurückgestellt zur Bezahlung
bestimmter Rechnungen 1045
zurückgewiesener Scheck 2077
zurückhalten 2040
zurückweisen 2012
zurückziehen 2439
zusammenrechnen 65
Zusammenrechnung 67
zusammenrufen 191
Zusammenschluss von Banken
596
zusammenzählen 65
Zusammenzählung 67
zusätzliche Anleihe 2033
zusätzliche Unkosten 93
Zuschlag 1734
Zuschuss 125
zusichern 254
Zustimmungsbescheinigung für
Ausgaben 115
zuteilen 110, 118
Zuteilung 111, 121
Zuteilung der Geldmittel 114
zuviel belasten 1736
zuviel gutschreiben 1735
zuweisbar 203
zuweisen 110, 117, 173, 200
Zuweisung 111, 120, 175, 206
Zuweisung der Geldmittel 114
Zuweisungsbrief 1515
Zwangsanleihe 1234
Zwangssparen 692
Zwangsverkauf 1235
Zwangsverkauf auf Grund
einer verfallenen Hypothek
1239

Zwangsvollstreckung betreiben
aus einer Hypothek, die ~
1237
Zwangsvollstreckung einer
Hypothek 1238
zweckgebundene Rücklagen
2276
zweifacher Gläubiger 1018
zweifelhafte Zinszahlung 2042
Zweiggeschäft 445
Zweigstelle 445
zweistufige Anleihe 2353
zweitklassige Wertpapiere 2128
Zwischendividende 1431
Zwischenmakler 2247